ARCHIBALD G. BROWN

Yours very faithfully,
Archibald G. Brown

ARCHIBALD G. BROWN

Spurgeon's Successor

Iain H. Murray

THE BANNER OF TRUTH TRUST

THE BANNER OF TRUTH TRUST
3 Murrayfield Road, Edinburgh EH12 6EL, UK
P.O. Box 621, Carlisle, PA 17013, USA

*

© Iain H. Murray 2011

ISBN: 978 1 84871 139 6

*

Typeset in 11/15 pt Sabon Oldstyle Figures at
The Banner of Truth Trust, Edinburgh
Printed in the USA by
Versa Press, Inc.,
East Peoria, IL

With thankfulness for my friends
JOHN AND MAUREEN EYERS
whose commitment to seeing
ARCHIBALD GEIKIE BROWN
remembered today
brought this book into being.

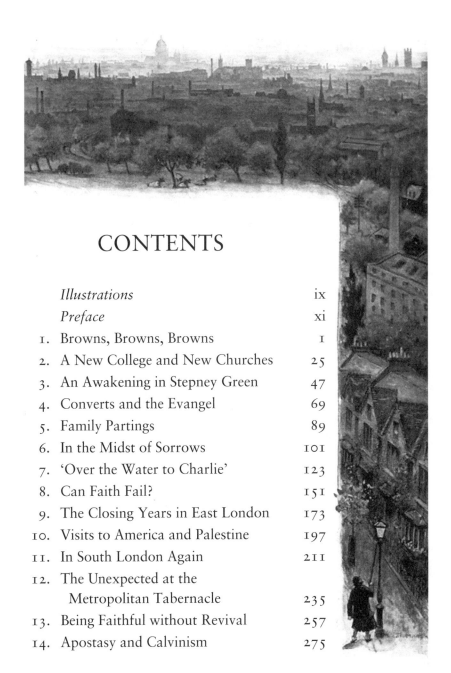

CONTENTS

vii

ILLUSTRATIONS

PREFACE

I have read of preachers who occasionally owed the texts
on which they preached to the suggestions of friends.
Something like that may also happen with the writing
of books, but it had never happened to me until this title.
Unexpectedly one day came a letter from John Eyers, a friend
of many years ago, proposing Archibald Brown as a subject
for me to take up. My first reaction was not to take the suggestion seriously for I barely knew the name and what I did
know could have been written in one or two sentences. But
with further correspondence from Mr Eyers came further
surprise. I found I was being offered much more than a suggestion. My friend, having long prized Brown's sermons, had
gathered much information on him, and my eyes grew wide
with interest when, with subsequent letters, came treasures he
had gathered. Almost instantly I shared my correspondent's
enthusiasm, and so this became the first book I have ever been
'given'. No author can be in a happier position!

Usually, unless a biography is prepared soon after the subject's death, there is little hope of gaining enough material
many years later. Archibald Brown died in 1922 and no biography followed. It was due to no small research on the part of
my friend that enough was discovered to fill these pages. He
had for a starting point, *The Life and Work of Archibald G.
Brown,* by Godfrey Holden Pike; that book has been a real
help to us and yet a limited one. For one thing, Pike concentrates on Brown's work as a philanthropist, and this because

a main part of his book was originally written on the social and spiritual needs of the East End of London, and first appeared for that purpose in *The Sword and the Trowel.* More than that, Pike's book was published thirty years before his subject's death and leaves a major part of his life unreported. Much therefore needed to be gleaned from other sources and John Eyers left no stone unturned in his labour of love.

Subsidiary but much valued help has also come from others. Dr Ann Sharpley of Oxford, whose husband, David R. Heath Brown, is related to Edward Heath Brown (1853-1934), a brother of the subject of these pages, has aided us with original manuscript information not previously made public. All the church records of the East London Tabernacle were lost when the building was bombed during the Second World War. Chatsworth Road Baptist Chapel was also bombed, but the records of Deacons' and Members' Meetings from Brown's period as the pastor survived, and copies of relevant parts of those records have been kindly copied and supplied by Miss Joyce Silk, a member of that church. Dr Peter Masters, the present minister of the Metropolitan Tabernacle, London, trusted us with the loan of rare volumes of *The Sword and the Trowel,* and also made available the Minutes of the Deacons' meetings during the time that Brown was serving that church. Careful copies of everything relevant in those Minutes were generously made for me by Mr Peter Batchelder. Mrs Jenni MacKenzie, Archivist of the Baptist Union of South Africa, has brought many things to light on Brown's life after 1910. We are also in debt to Mrs Emily Burgoyne (Library Assistant at Regent's Park College, Oxford); and Mr Christopher Lloyd (Tower Hamlets Social History Library).

At various points the help of others has also been much appreciated. These friends include Hanneke Araujo, Rod Badams, Arthur Holden and Simon Finch of Bromley Local Studies Library, and Stephen Taylor of the Evangelical Library, London.

My wife, who left her much-loved work in the East End of London to marry me in 1955 never expected we should both 'return' there so much in our thoughts. We have certainly done so in the last two years while this book was in preparation, and, as ever, Jean's aid has been indispensable.

No author could wish for a more efficient and enthusiastic publisher than I have again enjoyed. I am grateful to all the staff of the Banner of Truth Trust. I also speak for them all when I say that our thoughts are especially with our dear friend Douglas Taylor whose life and work has meant so much in the editorial department over the last fifteen years. Now in serious illness, it has been a labour of love for Douglas to contribute the Index to these pages. We thank God for him. Together we believe that the God of yesterday is the God of today and of tomorrow. 'Art thou not from everlasting, O Lord my God, mine Holy One? We shall not die' (*Hab.* 1:12).

The life and message of Archibald Brown will speak to many hearts today as it has done to our own. This book has been for me a special reminder of the providence of God. That a preacher of a century ago should reappear from obscurity is no accident. Here is the type of man for which we are to pray: 'Pray ye therefore the Lord of the harvest, that he will send forth labourers into his harvest' (*Matt.* 9:38).

IAIN H. MURRAY,
Edinburgh
August, 2011

I

BROWNS, BROWNS, BROWNS

Archie Brown as a young man.

'A man who does not feel he is called to do anything will succeed in doing nothing in particular. The force of a man's character is in great measure to be found in the strength of his conviction that he has been called of God to do what he undertakes. It is the first grand essential for service. Let a man be only persuaded that he is called of God to go and do a particular thing, and what can stay him?'

AGB on 'Be Strong and Do It' (*1 Chron.* 28:10),
November 19, 1878.

IN the eighteenth century 'Browns' were as frequent as salmon on the river Tweed. When numbers of them spilled over into England there was sometimes apprehension on the part of parents. A young John Brown, from Haddington, East Lothian, was in London in 1776, and disturbed his father by the speed of his attachment to a young lady. The father—the famous minister of Haddington—sent his second son, Ebenezer, south to dissuade the elder brother from making, as he thought, a wrong life choice. But Ebenezer was to return with the startling news, 'Father, if John does not marry her, I am going to marry her myself.' Marriage was to follow in due course.

The marriage of another Brown, also questioned beforehand, was to take place in 1814, with a happy outcome. The bridegroom was again a John Brown, and the bride Ann Geikie. In this case it was the bride's London parents who raised objections to the match, so much so that her father, Alexander Geikie, was not present when the event took place at St John's Church, Horsleydown, Southwark. At the sight of the wedding ring on his daughter's finger, he could only say, 'Well, you have made your bed and you must lie on it.' The Geikies were a distinguished family and it may be that the prospect of a son-in-law who worked at the Custom House for £100 a year was what disturbed them. It cannot have been the young man's Scots ancestry, for the Geikies also came from north of the border.

The John Brown who thus married in 1814 was the grandfather of the subject of these pages. There is no record that this line of Browns had any link with the Brown of Haddington dynasty, but one thing they certainly had in common was their Christian commitment. The husband of Ann Geikie was to be nicknamed, 'Bible Brown', 'on account of his often and eloquent public speaking on behalf of the Bible Society's meetings'. That interdenominational organisation was then in the springtime of its world-wide influence.

It would seem that initially John and Ann Brown had little of this world's goods as they lived for seven years with his parents.[1] This arrangement at 6 St John Street, Bermondsey, was not without occasional tensions. A family record notes, 'Old Mr Brown [*i.e.*, John's father] was a most particular man and most orderly. He did not at this point get on with his daughter-in-law who liked to go out to see the fashions in Regent Street, and thought she left the child too much.'[2]

The 'child', John William Brown, born in 1815, was the father of the subject of this book. There is no sign that his upbringing was neglected, and family records were to speak of his father's 'unremitting untiring work'. At some point he left the Custom House and joined Alexander's, a mercantile and banking Company, established at 40 Lombard Street in the City in 1810. Originally a clerk in the firm, by 1831

---

[1] The parents were John (1768-1836) and Sarah Brown (1760-1836). This John Brown was born in Scotland from where he had moved with his father, yet another John Brown (1735-1788). For Brown family tree, see Appendix 2.

[2] MS of Mary Louisa Brown (1846-1933), written in 1895.

4

he had risen to become a partner. The Company prospered and eventually he was to make a small fortune. From a first home on the Old Kent Road, they moved to 'a nice house', 13 Peckham Rye Terrace, where his parents would rejoin them in their latter days. His father-in-law had died in 1819, too early to see their prosperity.

John William Brown, the only son, joined his father's Company and was married from their Peckham home to Emma Heath in 1840. Why the wedding took place at the Independent York Street Chapel on Walworth Road is not on record, for both families belonged to Maze Pond Baptist Chapel; his father ('Bible Brown') had taken a leading part in the erection of the Maze Pond building, and Emma's father, Job Heath, served there as a deacon.[3] This marriage was further to multiply the Browns. A daughter, Ann, was born in 1842, followed by Arthur Geikie the following year. Arthur only lived for eight months, and it was not long after his death that Archibald Geikie Brown, the subject of these pages, was born on 18 July 1844, at 10 St Ann's Place, Claremont Villas, Brixton Hill. This was near his paternal grandparents, who had moved into Oakland Lodge, in the same district, in 1843. 'Archie' was to have three more sisters, Mary, Eleanor, Emma, and, finally, two brothers, John and Edward.

Brixton Hill, running into Streatham Hill, was the main road south out of London to Brighton, and was more countryside than town. It appears that the further-out location of John and Emma Brown's home led them to attach themselves to Union Chapel, an evangelical church which had been formed in 1832. Its Deed stated that it was 'of the Congregational

---

[3] This Maze Pond Chapel stood on the present site of Guy's Hospital, Southwark and was one of the old Baptist causes in London.

Order, admitting to full membership the disciples of our common Lord, irrespective of their sentiments on the subject of infant or adult baptism'.[4]

When Archie was seven the family moved to what was to be the best-remembered home of his boyhood. This was a fine new house, 'Brathay Lodge', on Thornton Road, in the sought after area of Clapham Park.[5] It was a gift to his parents from the paternal grandparents. The Browns had expected to change homes sometime in 1852. But in January of that year, when the building was still unfinished, the eldest daughter, Ann, was taken ill with scarlet fever, and it was hastily decided that the best way to preserve the rest of the children from the infection was for them to go to the new home at once. Mary, the second daughter, recalled the event in later years:

> We were quickly removed by our father in one of the flys[6] the same night. We were:—my brother Archie, myself, Ellie, Emma and John, a baby on nurse's knee.[7] My father carried the old dining room clock, and we arrived at our future home which was not even quite finished, and never returned to Streatham.
>
> We liked to hear our voices echoing up the large stone staircase in the new empty house. My mother remained with Elizabeth Guess (housemaid) to nurse my sister and later completed the move. The house was then beautifully furnished by our father in the best style.

[4] *The Story of Congregationalism in Surrey,* Edward E. Cleal (London: J. Clarke, 1908). Union Chapel was situated at the southern end of Brixton Hill, where its first minister was John Hunt, followed in the years 1851-64 by John Hall.

[5] The house is named on the map to be found on the web under, http://london1864.com/stanford36b.htm

[6] A one-horse covered carriage.

[7] Edward, the last of the family, was not born until May 1853.

Our nurse Mary Austin was with us 17 years and our upper housemaid, Elizabeth Guess 22 years. Our gardener MacDonald several years and later Mr George Legg several years in their employ.

Other family memories of a more general character were preserved by Edward, the youngest of the family, in a letter written on his fortieth birthday in 1893:

You children come from a worthy ancestry and I want you all to have some little memorial of those who have gone before, otherwise, if uninformed, you will be the losers of a most precious heritage, one for which you should be devoutly thankful and of which you may even feel honest pride. The Wallis', Heaths, Geikies, and Browns make up a history not unresplendent in the honourable annals of Church life and Business. Their lots were cast in that great 'Middle Class' of our land which certainly in former times was the mainstay of our Country's prosperity and of the maintenance of Truth and Righteousness in the Land. Gentleness, Simplicity, Learning and Money-making were perhaps the distinguishing features of these four quarters from whence our generation came, and above all, and I may say sanctifying these characteristics, was that of true and real God-fearing Piety in each and all of them.

These qualities were all prominent in Archie's maternal grandfather, Job Heath. The Heath family had belonged to the Maze Pond church for over 100 years. The turning point in Job's life had been back in the year 1802 when he was twenty-one, brought about by a letter from his mother. To the end of his days he kept a Friday night prayer meeting in his home. It is said that his conversion 'gave him unbounded faith in the power of intercession, especially in that of parents for children. One thing that he longed for, and which he fully expected to see, was a great revival of spiritual life in the churches; and that he might excite Christians to pray for this, he would give or lend such books as that by Jonathan Edwards on the great spiritual awakening that he witnessed in America.'[8]

Job Heath's practice of prayer was continued by his daughter Emma, Archie's mother. One of the infant's earliest memories was of a time when he was ill and had his cot brought downstairs from the bedroom to the breakfast room: 'I can remember having a troubled feverish sleep, and waking up to find there was a hand holding mine, and, when I looked, I saw my dear mother kneeling by the cot and praying for me. I remember her teaching me to say after her,

> Gentle Jesus, meek and mild,
> Look upon a little child.

Archie was getting older when curiosity moved him to discover why, after his father left for business in the morning, his mother would always go and lock herself in their bedroom. 'She lived', he would later explain, 'a life of prayer.' At the time he did not know what that meant and in his early school days imagined prayer could be a valuable device to save him work: 'I remember that I used to pray to God to teach me the propositions of Euclid. I thought that it would save a great deal of time and trouble if, instead of my learning them, the Lord would just teach me. But I did not find that he did.'

Grandfather Heath must have been especially encouraged by a meeting at Maze Pond which took place early in 1854, when Archie was nine years old. The Sunday School

---

[8] G. Holden Pike, *Life and Work of Archibald G. Brown, Preacher and Philanthropist* (London: Passmore and Alabaster, 1892), pp. 2-3. Hereafter cited as, Pike, *Brown*.

Anniversary that year was unusual in having for its speaker a nineteen-year-old Essex youth, very recently called to pastor the neighbouring New Park Street Chapel. Not all the Baptist ministers in South London were sympathetic to the bold newcomer in their midst, but the Rev. John Aldis, pastor of the Maze Pond Chapel is said to have been the first to invite C. H. Spurgeon to speak in another London church. The chairman of this Anniversary meeting was Archie's grandfather, 'Bible Brown'. It was not long after that occasion that, at a prayer meeting of Baptist pastors, one of them referred to Spurgeon (who was present) in the words: 'O Lord, bless thy young servant before thee, who has so much to learn and so much to unlearn.' John Aldis expressed his disagreement with the way that prayer was offered, and advised his brethren, 'Mind how you treat that young man, for if I am not greatly mistaken he will yet be one of the greatest preachers of this age—he has a fervour of spirit, a command of language, and an imagination such as I never knew in one so young.' [9]

We do not know if Archie Brown's father was present at the Sunday School Anniversary, or whether he was influenced by his pastor's estimate of Spurgeon, but it is clear that John W. Brown was not only to be found at Union Chapel on Brixton Hill. Archie would later recall, 'I remember well how at the breakfast table in Clapham Park, when I was only a child, I first heard my father speak about a young man that he had been to hear preach at Southwark.'

When the New Park Street congregation moved to the vast Surrey Gardens Music Hall for evening services, John

[9] See G. Holden Pike, *Life and Work of Charles Haddon Spurgeon* (repr. Edinburgh: Banner of Truth, 1991), vol. 1, p. 145n. Herafter cited as Pike, *Spurgeon*. This work was originally published in 6 volumes in the 1890s, the Banner of Truth printing keeps the pagination of the 6 volumes in 2 volumes. Aldis reached his hundredth year, dying on September 27, 1907.

W. Brown was sometimes present and so was Archie. In later years he would recall how at the age of thirteen, and in school holidays, he would 'run' to the Surrey Gardens on a Sunday evening. He was in the congregation on December 5, 1858, to hear one of the most awakening sermons Spurgeon ever preached, 'Compel them to come in'.[10] Of that sermon the young hearer was to say, 'I remember how I struggled against the influence of that sermon, and thought that I should be obliged to be converted in spite of myself.'

Although by December 1858, now aged fourteen, Archibald Brown was still occasionally hearing Spurgeon, he was no longer running to be there. The truth is that he had no heart for the spiritual influences around him and was giving his parents cause for concern. Undoubtedly he was remembered in Grandfather Heath's Friday night prayer meeting. Perhaps it was this concern for their eldest son, along with the wish to give him the best education, that led to the parents' decision to send him to a boarding school in Brighton. One gets the impression that at this sea-side resort, Archibald Brown was a popular, attractive, athletic and headstrong youngster. Instead, however, of passing on the faith he had heard and been taught at home, he did the opposite. At a later date he would tell others: 'Who can say where my sins end in their influence? I remember that, when I was converted, the greatest sorrow of my heart was the thought of the persons I had influenced for evil, and the knowledge that I had no power to undo the mischief thus accomplished.'

How much the education in Brighton helped Brown is not recorded. He once expressed the opinion that he spent more

---

[10] *New Park Street Pulpit* (London: Passmore and Alabaster), vol.5, 1859, pp. 17-24.

time in his youth 'larking than learning', but his later career shows he had a good education behind him. Certainly he was not lacking in self confidence, for by the time he was fifteen or sixteen it was his own decision that he had received enough education. When he surprised the family by arriving home one day with the news that he had left school, his father can scarcely have been pleased. After some consultation, it was decided there would be little purpose in sending the truant back. Instead father paid for him to begin an apprenticeship in the city with a firm engaged in the lucrative business of importing tea from China: 'My father wanted me to be a tea merchant in China.' This was considered a promising career.

By this date Archie's father was attached to Spurgeon's ministry, and when the Metropolitan Tabernacle was opened at the Elephant and Castle in March 1861, his youngest son, Edward, remembered how his father 'took a whole front pew in the Lower Gallery, and week by week as many of us as could ride in the carriage went up morning and evening. Those Sabbath services are forever fixed on my mind.' Archie's other brother, John, has also written of how they became the seat-holders of pew 391, 'thought by some to be the best pew in the place'. It was what happened at the end of the first service the family attended in the new building that especially stayed with young John:

> It was on a Sunday morning. The service was over. My father had been taken to the vestry to be introduced to the great preacher, with a view to his being subsequently elected an elder of the Church.[11] My mother, sisters, younger brother

[11] This is a mistake on the part of John Brown Jr. His father became a deacon by 1863 but was not an elder. *The Sword and the Trowel*, 1865, p. 129, noted that at the annual church meeting, William Olney spoke, followed by 'Deacon Brown, in an emphatic manner, accompanied by a donation of ten guineas to the College.'

and myself were about to descend the staircase from the gallery at the back, when just as we were passing the door on the landing which leads to the elders' room, it opened and out came Mr Spurgeon, followed by my father and others. There was a great crowd descending the staircase at the time, and Mr Spurgeon, who was anxious to shake hands with my mother and see the little Browns, cried out in his cheery, humorous way, 'Is Mrs Brown here, and all the little Browns?' I can see now as though it were only yesterday that rich black hair, that face so brimful of humour, those merry sparkling eyes, those cheeks so full, those hands so chubby, features characteristic of him at that time. I loved him at first sight, the only man I could say I loved as a child.[12]

The first Sunday in which Spurgeon's congregation met in their new building was March 31, 1861. The ten-year-old John Jr does not record the date of the occasion described above, nor why his eldest brother Archie was not there. If it was the March date, or one in early April, it was the eve of the great turning point in Archibald Brown's life.

At least some of the Brown family, and certainly the mother, kept their link with Union Chapel. We know that Archie, the eldest son, was still attending the Sunday School of that church at this date. It may well have been his mother's influence that kept him there. A younger contemporary of Archibald Brown has written: 'The boy's mother knew how to manage her son. She waited and love constrained him, the while he thought himself free.'[13]

Hereafter the magazine of the Metropolitan Tabernacle will be cited as, *S&T*.

[12] J. W. Brown, 'Personal Reminiscences of the Late Mr Spurgeon,' *The Inquirer*, 1892.

[13] James J. Ellis, biographical sketch in Archibald G. Brown, *God's Full-Orbed Gospel, and Other Sermons Preached at the Metropolitan Tabernacle*, (London: Allenson, n.d.) p. 1. This title was in print by 1911.

It was the Union Chapel Sunday School that played a real, if unexpected part, in the answer to his parents' and his grandparents' prayers. At sixteen the rebellious teenager was not too young to be an admirer of Ann Bigg, a Sunday School teacher at Union Chapel who was four years his senior. She was an attractive contradiction of what Brown had persuaded himself Christians usually were. 'I know before I was converted', he would later say, 'I had a dim idea that a Christian was a man something like an animated coffin; to be a Christian was to give up all that was nice and pleasant.'

On a Sunday in April 1861, Ann Bigg had a conversation with Archie which would have a life-changing consequence:

> She said to me, without knowing me at all, 'Are you a Christian?' Though I hated the question, yet I could not help honouring in my heart the one that had the moral courage to put it. The next question was, 'Will you go and hear Mr Blackwood preach on Monday?' Before I knew exactly where I was, I found that I had given my word.

Stevenson Arthur Blackwood was unusual in more than one respect. He was a layman preacher, belonging to the Church of England, at a time when such men were a rarity, and there was no question of his preaching for a living because he held an important post in the Treasury. Whether Archie had heard it said that 'Poor Blackwood has gone mad', the fact was that the twenty-eight-year-old whom he was to hear on April 15, 1861, was a very different figure from the man who, after Eton and Cambridge, was a gambling socialite, popular in the balls of London's high-society. It was not service in the Crimean War as an officer with the Coldstream Guards that changed him, but what happened on his return and especially the witness of Catherine Marsh.[14] At the age of twenty-four Blackwood became a new man in Christ. At once he began to seize every opportunity to speak of his Saviour and to overcome a stammer in the process. After he married in 1858, he and his wife moved to Wood Lodge, Streatham, where he began a Monday night meeting in their home. It was an evangelistic endeavour to reach all kinds of people; the first to experience a saving change was a policeman. The numbers attending the meetings so grew that his wife wrote: 'After a time it became necessary to make a weekly clearance on Monday evenings of our dining room, library and hall, which, together with the staircase, made room for between 200 and 250 people . . . In the summer the garden door was open, and many sat out in the twilight.' 'He was then', writes his biographer, 'in all the freshness and spring-time of his spiritual experience; and it seems to have pleased God to give an unusually abundant and speedy harvest to his labours for him.'[15]

Such was the man whom Archie Brown now met for the first time after agreeing to go with Ann Bigg:

> Just to keep a promise, I went to the Monday meeting at Wood Lodge, Streatham. I was a careless young fellow, and had little faith in the reality of Christians. Before Mr Blackwood had been speaking ten minutes I felt that I was listening to one who believed every word he spoke. Great was my surprise when, at the close of the meeting, he came straight up to me, put his hands on my shoulders, and looking me in

[14] Daughter of William Marsh, an evangelical leader in the Church of England, Catherine Marsh (1818-1912) was the author of the *Life of Captain Hedley Vicars*, and *The Life of the Rev. William Marsh* (London: Nisbet, 1865).

[15] *Some Records of the Life of Stevenson Arthur Blackwood, Compiled by a Friend and edited by his widow* (London: Hodder & Stoughton, 1901), p. 200. As the title suggests, this source is scarcely a biography in the usual sense of the term, but it is rich in evidence of an outstanding life and should be far better known.

the face with those loving eyes of his, said, 'Young man, you are a stranger here. Are you a Christian?' I confessed at once that I was not, and had no great desire to be. I think I can now hear him answering, 'How sad!' The question hooked itself into my heart. For two days I had no rest.

G. Holden Pike's account of that Monday night was anticipating what was to follow when he wrote: 'The convert returned from that memorable meeting in company with her who was destined to be his wife, and henceforth the two were agreed in all things.'[16] They were not yet agreed 'in all things' on that night for he was not yet a 'convert'. Brown had stifled an accusing conscience before, and would have done so again on this occasion had it not been for the grace of God.

Other accounts from him give us the fuller picture: 'I remember what he did for me when he saved my soul. In a moment he arrested a careless young man, who was cursing and swearing on Monday, and singing God's praises at twelve o'clock on Wednesday.' After forty hours of deep conviction he had come to rest on Christ alone: 'I was convinced of sin and found peace in Jesus under an oak tree in Palace Road.'[17] In delight he threw his hat up in the air, and would later say that the first thing he did as a Christian was to climb a tree to retrieve it! His testimony continues:

> I went at once to Wood Lodge, and told Mr Blackwood I could now say 'Yes' to the question, 'Are you a Christian?' He took me into his private room, kneeled down with me, and poured out his soul in thanksgiving. The next week he invited me to breakfast, and took me down to Tooting Common, where a railway was being made. He introduced me to the navvies, and told them I would come every morning

[16] Pike, *Brown*, p. 5.
[17] For a more precise location see AGB's letter on p. 225 below.

during their breakfast time and read the Word of God to them, which I did. He thus not only won my heart to Christ, but gently led me into his service. Living as I did then in Clapham Park, I used to wait about the lane from Tooting Common, just to have the pleasure of a few minutes' walk beside his horse as he rode up to the Treasury. He always pulled up to allow me a few minutes walk by his side, and his loving words helped me all the day.[18]

Stevenson Arthur Blackwood, although twelve years his senior, would be a friend for life. His example of speaking to people directly was undoubtedly an influence on Archie Brown.

Brown would later say that his first pulpit was a wheel-barrow, turned upside down, on which he sat to read the Bible and talk to these workmen in their break from work. Certainly he had all the zeal of a young convert. One day at this period, as he went up Streatham Hill he overtook one of his friends on his way to play cricket, and still as careless as he had so recently been. Immediately Brown faced him with the question, 'Carlile, do you know where you are going?' and brushing aside a response about cricket, Archie told him, 'You're going to hell.' Unwelcome although the words were, his friend would later say he wished he had heeded the warning at the time.

Archie Brown's father, accustomed to the impetuosity of his headstrong son, was somewhat more inclined to 'wait and see' than to encourage this seemingly sudden change in his son. Blackwood was just the counsellor he needed, and from the outset he may have seen in the youth a leader for the future. While not every professed convert is best hastened into

---

[18] *Life of Blackwood*, pp. 222-3.

public witness, in Brown's case the prompting was not amiss. His zeal as a young Christian made him ready to take every occasion he could to witness, which was no small surprise to those who had known him previously. When he offered to teach a Sunday School class at Union Chapel, the Superintendent doubted whether he was serious, for the only ability he had so far observed was that of entertaining fellow pupils. 'He had among his youthful friends been regarded as having a genius for acting "characters" and for mimicry in general; but these carpet exploits were no passport to the favour of the grave superintendent.'[19] The offer was declined. At which point Brown asked whether he could help if he brought his own class. Never previously faced with such a question, the superintendent could only reply, 'If you bring your own boys we cannot keep them out.' Not long after, Brown reappeared with twenty or more youths, gathered from all parts of the neighbourhood, and most of them older than himself. They formed a Bible class for young men.

The reservations of the cautious superintendent must have been soon removed for Archibald Brown now became a member at Union Chapel and was encouraged by his minister, John Hall, to speak at the Saturday evening prayer meeting. A 'sermonette' from him on that occasion quickly became a weekly event. Other engagements followed. His first public address came when he joined a city missionary who, he assumed, was to speak at a meeting in a needy area. Before this meeting began, Brown found that he had misunderstood its purpose. He had thought he was to read the Scriptures before the missionary preached. But the latter now indicated he only intended to read from *Pilgrim's Progress*. 'Is that

[19] Pike, *Brown*, p. 7.

all?' Brown queried. 'Don't you think that is calculated to do good?' was the reply. But Archie was not to be put off: 'It may do good; but there should be preaching—preaching Christ.' At which he was told, 'If you think so, you'd better preach.'

When Brown looked at the people who had assembled another thought came to him. In the room that would hold 150 people, there were about twenty elderly ladies. With the approval of the missionary, he sought a delay for the start of the meeting and went out 'to collect a congregation'. From the local streets, and from several public houses, he proceeded to gather 'thirty or forty', and to this strange crowd he preached his first 'sermon' on the words, 'Thou shalt call his name Jesus, for he shall save his people from their sins.'

Perhaps adult baptisms had ceased at Union Chapel. Whatever the reason, on the longest summer day in 1861, Brown, a month short of his seventeenth birthday, was baptised by Spurgeon at the Metropolitan Tabernacle. Prior to that day, two of the deacons had visited him at Brathay Lodge. Fifty years later he would recall 'how they walked up and down with me in my father's garden, asking if I had really received the grace of God, and had reason to believe that I was saved.'

His father's pleasure at this change in his eldest son was not without a measure of disquiet which he shared with Spurgeon and other officebearers. His thought, as stated by Pike, was that his 'son Archibald appeared to be an uncertain star, tolerably well fitted, if he did but know it, to move around the confined orbit of the Royal Exchange [the commercial centre of the City], but not at all likely to succeed in the anxious work of preaching the everlasting gospel'. But instead of receiving any sympathy for this seeming problem, 'father Brown was encouraged to be thankful that he had such a matter to think about'.

For an understanding of the father's concern something more needs to be added. After Archie had given up school, his father had paid a considerable amount to secure the boy's apprenticeship in a tea-broker's offices, as already mentioned. But it was already evident that Archie's interest in the tea trade was minimal. His mind was elsewhere, as the following story illustrates:

> I had been going round getting tea samples from different warehouses, and as I was coming back, with a blue bag over my shoulder full of samples, I had to cross Mincing Lane, and suddenly I seemed to hear a voice, I heard these words: 'Therefore being justified by faith, we have peace with God.' I stood still in the road amazed, as the realisation of the fact came home to me, and I remember I stood there until I was nearly run down by a hansom cab.

Pike comments on this stage of Brown's life, 'He attended to business in the City by day, and preached nearly every night until health failed, and the family doctor declared that either business or Christian work must be given up.'

It was clearly a situation that could not continue. The next year settled the issue. First, Archie was engaged to Ann—now 'Annie'—Bigg in June 1862. Very soon after this, once he had passed his eighteenth birthday on July 18, he went to Spurgeon's vestry, after a Thursday evening service at the Metropolitan Tabernacle, to ask about entering the Pastors' College. As soon as he was seated, Spurgeon's opening words disarmed any fears: 'Well, Archie, we've been looking for you. I have heard all about you from your father. Come into the

College at once.' It was an unusual assurance to give anyone applying to the College, especially to an eighteen-year-old. There was no other student of that age. Notwithstanding the welcome, Archie was given an application form, with questions personal and theological to be answered, and by way of explanation Spurgeon wrote on top of the first page, 'These questions are usually answered, I think it best to abide by the usual rules.'

There were nineteen questions on the form, headed 'Metropolitan Tabernacle Educational Institute'. Most were straightforward. To Age and Health, Brown gave one word answers. To secular calling, he put down, 'The tea trade.' How long have you known the grace of God in truth? '16 months', was the answer. Have you made a profession of your faith by Immersion? 'Yes, at the Tabernacle.' Are you a Member of a Christian Church, and if so, what Church? 'Yes, Union Chapel, Brixton.'[20] He answered nothing more on the form except two final questions on whether he would remain in the course for two years, and did he understand misconduct would disqualify him: he answered respectively with the words 'I will' and 'I do'.

Many years later, a Principal of Spurgeon's College saw Brown's application form and commented that much of it was left blank.[21] What he did not know was that, with the form, Brown had attached three fully written pages, because the form did not give him the room to say all he wanted! Somehow these attached pages became separated from the

---

[20] At what date Brown became a member at the Metropolitan Tabernacle is not recorded.

[21] Dr Percy W. Evans, in a Preface to George E. Page, *AGB. The Story of the Life and Work of Archibald Geikie Brown*, (London: East London Tabernacle, 1944,), p. 3.

form, but they have survived to give us the fuller picture. Question 11 on the form asked for the candidate's view on the invitations of the gospel and the duty of sinners to believe on the Lord Jesus. Brown wrote: 'I believe that the invitations of the gospel are open to all, even the worst of sinners. It is the duty of all sinners to believe on Jesus, because God commands them 1 John 3:23.' To the question, What is your motive for wishing to become a preacher of the gospel? He replied, 'To be the means of saving souls.'

What reason have you to conclude that you have the abilities suited to such an undertaking? 'Because God has blessed the word I have spoken to the conversion of some, and because of the general [opinion] of my friends.'

What educational advantages have you had? 'The usual advantages of those in the middle class.'

Question 14 was, Give an outline of your doctrinal sentiments. Brown's full answer, which we will give at the start of the next chapter, illustrates why he had abandoned using the small space allocated by the application form.

Question 16 was another that did not give sufficient room on the form itself: What experience have you had in preaching, and what ministers have heard you? Send testimonials as to your ability. On this he wrote: 'I have conducted a meeting every Tuesday evening for over 30 weeks. I have taken the week night services at Dulwich Chapel 4 or 5 times and the Sunday evening service at a Chapel near Sittingbourne, also I have very often given an address in vestry of a Saturday evening at which the Rev. John Hall has been present.'

To the final requirement to state name and address in full, he wrote on the form, 'Archibald Geikie Brown, Brathay Lodge, Clapham Park.' And all was attested by the names of John Hall and James Bigg.

Question 16 went to the heart of Spurgeon's purpose in establishing the College. He stated:

> We never dreamed of making men preachers, but we desired to help those whom God had already called to be such. Hence, we laid down as a basis, the condition that a man must, during about two years, have been engaged in preaching, and must have had some seals to his ministry before we could entertain his application . . . The College could not act upon mere hopes, but must have evident marks of a Divine call, so far as human judgment can discover them. This became a main point with us, for we wanted, not men whom our tutors could make scholars, but men whom the Lord had ordained to be preachers.[22]

Given Brown's age, and that he had been a Christian only since the April of the preceding year, his admission in October 1862, was scarcely normal. Percy Evans, a later Principal of the College, believed that Brown's acceptance broke 'many rules'. But he added that Spurgeon was 'no slave to his own rules', and that he 'recognised in Brown the quality he most loved in a preacher—the determination "by any means" to save some. Unconventionality in method, ardour in seeking, personal conviction, passion in preaching: these were the characteristics which opened the College door.'[23]

The years 1861-2 were to determine the whole course of Archibald Brown's future life. Year by year, thereafter, he would remember April 16 as the day when God united him to Jesus as his Saviour. It was that event that both gave him

---

[22] C. H. Spurgeon, *Autobiography, vol. 1, The Early Years* (Edinburgh: Banner of Truth, 1973), p. 386. Hereafter to distinguish this 2 vol. edition of the Autobiography from the 4 volume edition (cited below), I will refer to it by its subtitles, *The Early Years* and *The Full Harvest*.

[23] Page, *AGB*, pp. 3-4.

a new life and brought all his natural gifts together for one purpose. But it is also true that his life before that date had served to prepare him for his life-calling. An upbringing in a godly and distinguished family, and the Bible teaching he heard through childhood and youth, all entered into what he became as a young man. His answers to the College application form questions were not those of someone new to the faith he was required to profess.

The following chapters will tell the story of how God used Archibald Brown as his instrument to bring spiritual and physical blessing to thousands for over fifty years.

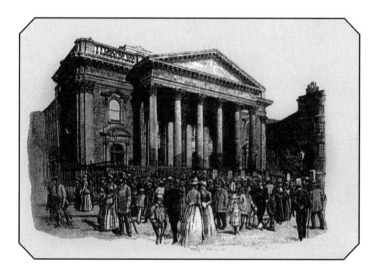

The Metropolitan Tabernacle.

2

A NEW COLLEGE
AND NEW CHURCHES

Spurgeon and the interior of the Metropolitan Tabernacle.

'I believe in God the Father, in the Deity of his Son Jesus, and in the Deity of the Holy Spirit, and in the unity of the Trinity, also in the total depravity of man and his absolute need of a Saviour in the person of Jesus, who suffered the punishment that was due to them for sin: that salvation comes alone through personal trust in him. I believe that after conversion the work of sanctification by the Holy Spirit begins in every true believer's heart, and continues increasing all his life, also that every believer is an adopted son of God, and will be kept unto the end. I also firmly believe in the doctrine of election.'

AGB, answering a question on his doctrinal sentiments in the application form for the Pastors' College, August 1862.

THE Metropolitan Tabernacle College was in its second year when Archibald Brown entered in the autumn of 1862. It had begun without a name in 1857 when Spurgeon arranged for the Rev. George Rogers, Congregational minister in the adjacent district of Camberwell, to train two young men in the gospel ministry. The name came when the infant institution moved to the Metropolitan Tabernacle on its opening in 1861; thereafter Spurgeon would no longer say 'I myself have been the committee, secretary, treasurer, and subscriber.'[1] He would remain 'the President' all his life, and Rogers the principal tutor until 1881. The Pastors' College would soon become its best-known title.

At the time Brown joined in 1862 the student body was thirty-nine in number. The Londoners who attended lived at home, as did Archie, while others from farther afield were boarded with members of the Tabernacle living in the neighbourhood. The location of the College was, of course, already familiar to Brown. Described once as 'not uplifted above the

[1] A resolution of the church noted on July 1, 1861: 'Hitherto this good work has been rather a private service for the Lord than one in which the members have had a share; but the church hereby adopts it as part of its own system of Evangelical labours.'

fog of London, but lying near the centre of the smoky metropolis', the students prized their identification with the church,
happy to make the spacious basements of the Tabernacle their
day-time residence.

While the new College was Strict Baptist in its constitution, its purpose was not primarily the advancement of
distinctive Baptist principles. Had that been the case then
Spurgeon's appointment of Rogers (a paedo-baptist) would
have been strange and, still more strange, the need for any
such agency when there were already five Baptist Colleges in
the land. The latter fact was one of the grounds on which a
number of Baptists were unenthusiastic about the new College at the Elephant and Castle. The truth is that Spurgeon's
guiding principles were almost as new to the times as was
the venture itself. Theological colleges, it was believed, exist
to make ministers and preachers. Spurgeon believed no such
thing. 'We do not make preachers, that is the work of the
Holy Spirit alone.'[2] The intention was to help and train men
who had already proved they had a God-given calling to
preach. In 1891 Spurgeon could say of the 845 men who had
attended the Pastors' College: 'These were preachers before
they applied to the institution; indeed, they had each one
been preaching for two years at the least . . . We take men
who would have been preachers whether or no.'[3] With respect
to the time element, Archibald Brown was clearly an exception, but we can be sure Spurgeon knew about the teenager's
evangelistic efforts quite apart from the evidence stated in the
application form for the College.

Spurgeon believed that the churches had no greater need,
at the human level, than the provision of earnest, Spirit-

[2] *S&T*, 1888, p. 315.
[3] *S&T*, 1891, pp. 259, 261.

anointed preachers. He was convinced that the idea that colleges could do anything to meet that need was dangerously false. The most they can do was to supply spiritual knowledge—a possession by no means to be despised—but the very best teaching given to men not sent by Christ would never make them preachers. With all the emphasis on intellect and scholarship in the nineteenth century, this principle was passing out of sight. Yet it was not novel. The Methodists, for instance, understood something about preaching. It was under a Methodist preacher that Spurgeon himself came to peace with God. When the Methodists first introduced a college for ministerial training, it was not for candidates for the ministry, but for men whose spiritual usefulness in the churches was already authenticated.[4]

A second guiding principle in Spurgeon's motivation was that men in the ministry need to be grounded not in the latest religious thinking but in the well-tried doctrinal heritage of historic, evangelical Christianity. That thinking, and the confessions and catechisms which gave it the clearest expression, was passing out of favour in Victorian England. To see that trend reversed was one of the great objects of Spurgeon's ministry, and it goes far to explaining why he spoke of the College as 'my life's work, to which I believe God has called me'. For the same reason he chose Rogers, 'a man of Puritanic stamp', who in 1866 wrote the first full statement of the 'principal features' of the College. It included the words:

---

[4] When adherence to this principle began to waver, George Smith, the Methodist historian, wrote: 'We heartily rejoice that Methodism has an efficient and well-conducted Theological Institution; but we have fears whether, on this account Superintendents have not sometimes recommended candidates for the ministry, whom they would never have ventured to propose had there been no Institution. The Institution was never meant to be the means of introducing men into the ministry who could not be respectable preachers without it.' *History of Wesleyan Methodism* (London: Longmans, 1866), vol. 3, p. 510.

Theology should be the principal subject for instruction in a Theological College . . . Calvinistic theology is dogmatically taught. We mean not dogmatic in the offensive sense of that term; but as the undoubted teaching of the Word of God.

Rogers' words should not be understood as though learning was to be confined only to one school of authors. Brown found this out on one of his early visits to the College Library. Of that occasion he says,

I took down 'C.H.M' on Exodus. All these theological books were new to me, and I am afraid I took down this one because it looked small. As the Lord would have it, I opened on his exposition of the 12th chapter of Exodus. I remember as if it were yesterday, how in that chapter, in great type, he says, 'THE BLOOD MUST STAND OUT IN SOLITARY GRANDEUR.' As a young fellow, trembling in that Library, I said, 'Lord, if Thou wilt allow me to speak or preach, I vow that the Blood shall stand out in solitary grandeur in all my sermons.'

C. H. MacIntosh was among that fellowship of Christians known as the Brethren, and they were not, in Spurgeon's mind, without aberrations in their teaching, but on the Person and Death of Christ they were to be admired.

While Brown developed a long-standing attachment to George Rogers, his principal tutor, it was around Fridays that his memories would turn most frequently in later years. That was the day Spurgeon gave largely to the students and listening to the 'dear old Governor on a Friday afternoon' became the high-point in Brown's week. He notes that for this occasion the class moved upstairs to 'the newly completed ladies' room at the Tabernacle', although giving no reason for the change in location. The choice for the higher location may

The Friday afternoon lecture room.

have been connected with Spurgeon's aphorism, 'The next most important thing to grace is oxygen.' Whether that was so or not, his men would have been no less electrified by the Friday afternoon lectures had they been delivered in a cellar.

Those who gathered on those Friday afternoons can have had no idea that what they were hearing would be available to thousands for centuries to come as *Lectures to my Students*. There would ultimately be four books of these lectures;[5] the fourth, *Commenting and Commentaries*, containing two lectures together with a 'Catalogue' produced after a review of 'three to four thousand volumes'. As a guide to the divines who 'have left us great stores of holy thought which we do

[5] *Lectures to My Students, First Series* (Passmore and Alabaster, 1875); *Second Series* (1877); *Third Series, The Art of Illustration* (1894). By the time of its 1893 reprinting, *Commenting and Commentaries* had sold 14,000 copies. All four books are bound together, complete and unabridged, in a new typeset edition as *Lectures to My Students* (Edinburgh: Banner of Truth, 2008).

well to use', the book is unique. It presents the best authors on the text of Scripture, along with occasional warnings on other titles, such as, 'Good for house-maids for lighting fires.' While any listing of 'best authors' obviously needs augmenting today, the book remains one of Spurgeon's most valuable for Christian ministers.

What the published lectures do not reveal is how accessible Spurgeon was to his men. He might lean over a student's exercise book in the course of a lecture and add a note in his own hand. He was available to speak to all individually afterwards. George Rogers could write, 'He is the personal and familiar friend of each one.' An illustration of his personal knowledge of the students, as well as of his humour, is illustrated by counsel he gave a class on one occasion, as term ended prior to Christmas. While regretting that he had no presents to give them,

> I told them what I would have selected if I had been rich. I remember one brother to whom I said that I would give him a corkscrew, because he had a good deal in him, but he could not get it out. 'As to you, my brother', I said to another student, 'I should give you a sausage-stuffer, for you need to have something put into you.' There was one friend to whom I should have liked to present a canister of Chapman and Hall's gunpowder. He was to have two pounds of it, and someone was to set it alight at the second head of his discourse.[6]

While laughter was by no means unknown in the College, the abiding mood was serious. One of the reasons Spurgeon preferred to have the students living in different homes rather than in one building was his belief that 'the residence of a

[6] *The Full Harvest*, p. 107.

number of young men in one house encourages and necessarily generates levity'. 'Live near to God, and love the souls of men', was the exhortation they most commonly heard, and he could tell them, 'Levity of conduct in my brethren brings heaviness of heart to me.'

Spurgeon was a friend to all his students, yet there was an inner group whose future usefulness he especially recognised and to whom he gave additional time. In what would be called his *Autobiography,* Mrs Spurgeon wrote: 'Among the hundreds of men whom the beloved President helped to prepare for the Christian ministry, there were none who stood higher in his estimation than the two of whom he always spoke of as, "Frank White and Archibald Brown".[7] Frank H. White has written:

> What happy days were those we spent in College, and with what eagerness did we, after the intense strain of the study and work of the week, look forward to those delightful Friday afternoons with the President! Being fewer in number, the intercourse was closer than was possible in after days. How favoured we were in the ordinary course of things. But what of those special opportunities, such as a six-days driving tour, which was once my happy lot? The letter of invitation is before me now:
>
> 'Dear Mr White,
>
> I am expecting you at my house, at 8 a.m. next Monday, to go for a week's drive . . . Breakfast at Nightingale Lane at 8; bound to me till Saturday evening; may reach home by 6 on that evening.'

---

[7] *Autobiography,* eds. S. Spurgeon and J. W. Harrald, vol. 3 (London: Passmore and Alabaster, 1899), pp. 131-2. A considerable amount of the text of the four volumes came from the hand of the editors.

Think whether a poor, worn-out, hard-worked student—such as Archibald Brown, or myself—would be glad to receive such a command, or not.

* * * * *

It was not College policy that the evangelistic work in which students were engaged before their entrance should be wholly laid aside for books. Spurgeon impressed on his own men what he would later tell others at Cheshunt College: 'You are preparing for the ministry, but do not wait till you have entered it—you may never live to do that. Win your highest honour, secure your best diploma now. Begin with speed, with fire, with learning, and live to save men now.'

What the implications of this thinking would mean for Archie Brown he was to learn very soon after his admission. The College was already engaged in planting new churches or supplying old ones. One of the new works had started at Bromley, with open-air preaching and a small Sunday gathering in the old market house. For reasons unstated, the student who began the witness at Bromley did not continue for more than twelve months, and in November 1862 Spurgeon told Brown that he wanted him to take it up. The eighteen-year-old thus made his first visit to the Kent market town, ten miles south-east of London, at nine o'clock one weekday evening, perhaps to talk with the nucleus of the work.

On November 30, a group gathered in the old market house to hear the student for the first time. They were not yet formed as a church and it was scarcely a lively group that the newcomer found. As well as taking the service, he had to open the doors, dust the chairs, and find himself a glass of water. His remuneration was the not over-generous sum of 2 shillings and 6 pence. *The Sword and the Trowel* would later report this story of Brown's first Sundays in Bromley:

> On the Monday following his second visit, in reply to an enquiry as to 'how he got on', he answered that his sermon had some effect, for the congregation of 18 persons on the first occasion had come down to 12: he had evidently 'moved' half a dozen. The next Monday he reported further progress in the same direction, for he had but 6 hearers on the third occasion, and he remarked that it only required another Sunday to finish the work.[8]

The humour of the story is characteristic of Brown, but in reality he was far from light-hearted about the discouraging situation. Part of Spurgeon's Friday duties, after the class was over, was to hear men's accounts of where they had preached, and this gave Archie the opportunity to state the poor prospects he was facing. The response was memorable, 'Hold on with your teeth, and if you cannot hold on with your teeth, hold on with your eye-lashes—but hold on somehow!'

Brown did 'hold on'. *The Sword and the Trowel* account, already quoted, continued:

> Full of youthful pleasantry, our dear brother was also full of zeal for God's glory, and prayer and faith soon caused the tide to turn; the meeting place was filled, and the White Hart Assembly Room had to be taken to accommodate the numbers anxious to hear the young preacher. It was soon necessary to admit the regular attenders by ticket.

These words appear in unsigned material in *The Sword and the Trowel,* but the evidence points to their being written

---

[8] *S&T*, 1878, p. 242. For location of sermons thus quoted see Appendix 1.

by Spurgeon. For one thing, the fact is omitted that a turning point in attendance occurred when Spurgeon himself came down to help Brown with a weekday service. If the student was unknown in Bromley, that was not the case with the pastor of the Metropolitan Tabernacle. This service was held in the White Hart Assembly Room, probably the first to be held there and, given there was only space for some two hundred, admission was by ticket only. Well before the hour of service the place was packed.

The White Hart Inn, Bromley.

'The Lord came into our midst', was Brown's summary of what took place in the following months. In 1863 a church was formed with twenty members, 'many the seals of his ministry'. 'Mr Brown gave himself to the enterprise with all his heart', wrote Spurgeon, 'and consequently he succeeded.'

The following year, on Monday, July 4, 1864, Spurgeon came again to lay the foundation stone for their own church building, this time bringing 1,000 people with him on a special train. As the population of Bromley was then only about 5,500, one is not surprised to read: 'Their progress through the High Street caused quite a stir. Bromley residents also gathered at the site in large numbers, where a "mammoth" tent had been erected for a tea gathering after the ceremony.'[9]

The programme for the occasion had been planned with the Hon. Arthur Kinnaird (later Baron Kinnaird) presiding. But the previous month (June 5) Spurgeon had preached at the Metropolitan Tabernacle against baptismal regeneration, and had included strictures on the evangelical clergy of the Church of England. It happened that the evangelical party in the Established Church was the party to which Kinnaird belonged, and he withdrew his agreement to preside at the Bromley gathering. So Spurgeon took the chair in his absence.

Spurgeon's baptismal regeneration sermon had caused widespread controversy, and the *Bromley Record* gave the new pastor some caustic criticism for siding with him. The paper also had other matters for which it criticised the occasion. Their reporter had taken down Brown as saying that the town 'had had sleep enough . . . He expressed the hope that the Baptist Chapel might be the cause of bringing the Word of God to Bromley.' These were hardly ingratiating words in a largely church-going community, where the Church of England was strong, and where, for long, the bishops of Rochester had their residence! Another complaint had to do with the congregation's impractical arrangements for the foundation-stone laying occasion. The 1,000 visitors from London had been promised a tea as part of the cost of their

---

[9] Charles T. Cook, *Bromley Baptist Church: the first hundred years 1863-1963.*

railway tickets, but when, after the service, they made their way as directed to a great tent, erected in a local park, it was only to find it already largely occupied by 'the natives of those parts'. 'Although plenty had been provided, those who could not fight their way into it, or get somebody to fight for them, could get none.'

Clearly, Brown and the infant church had no experience of the organisation required for such occasions.

Bromley Baptist Chapel.

As 1864 drew to a close Brown became involved in another local controversy. About the end of November a large poster had appeared advertising 'A Public Lecture, to be given by a local independent minister, on the subject, "The Two Church Principles—the Compulsory and the Voluntary—their respective merits"', with Archibald Brown as chairman. The title made it clear enough that the meeting would not favour the

Established Church and such were the complaints voiced in a town with decided Church of England sympathies that the speaker agreed to postpone the meeting.

Brown, however, did not agree to the postponement, suspecting that in reality it was a cancellation. Before 1864 was over he therefore publicised another meeting, and with reference to the subject that had been abandoned, announced: 'Courage and Cowardice, a Public Lecture on the above subject will be delivered by Archibald G. Brown, at White Hart Assembly Room, Bromley, on Wednesday, December 7th, at 8.30 pm. Admission free and no collection.' There was clearly no lack of interest in this meeting and from the *Bromley Record* (January 1, 1865) I give this summary:

> After a hymn had been sung and a prayer offered by Mr Brown, he began the lecture by briefly stating the cause of his appearing on the platform. He then gave various historic examples of courage and feats of daring, holding them up for the admiration of his audience. The courage of Martin Luther and John Knox, the Scottish Reformer, came in for a large share of commendation. The lecturer then commended the courage of those 'heretics' who in bygone days had been burned at the stake, declaring that he could almost wish that time would come again if only for the sake of the testing it would bring.
>
> Having established the axiom that courage is a virtue of the highest order, the lecturer contrasted it with the conduct of those who had been the cause of stopping the proposed lecture, which conduct he denounced as cowardice, and described that as one of the most despicable qualities of which a man could be possessed.

The *Bromley Record* told its readers that the speaker's earnestness was 'worthy of a better cause . . . Taking the lecture to be a fair specimen of Mr Brown's ability as a public speaker, there can be no question that he will attain notoriety.' The paper recommended him to give attention to the Scripture that says, 'Blessed are the peace-makers.'

Spurgeon, not surprisingly, had a different assessment of the lecture when it was published. He wrote in *The Sword and the Trowel* that the postponement of the meeting first announced, 'might have been good policy, but Mr Brown had no sympathy with it. The word *policy* was not in his religious creed. His parentage, his genius, his training, were of a different order. Instead of succumbing with the timid, his courage rose with the occasion. He determined to supply the place of the prohibited lecture with one of his own. That lecture is now before us, and we have no hesitation is saying it is well worthy of Mr Brown and of the occasion. It displays firmness without bitterness, self-respect without self-commendation, and liberty of speech without denying the same liberty to others.'[10]

* * * * *

It was a sign of the expectations that Spurgeon had for Brown's future that, when *The Sword and the Trowel* began, the twenty-year-old, who had left the Pastors' College in 1864, was called on for an article. It appeared in the first issue of the monthly (January 1865), under the title, 'Personal Service, by A. G. Brown, of Bromley, Late Student at the Pastor's College.'[11] In part the men of the College were responsible for this new departure, as Spurgeon (who remained editor all his lifetime) explained in the first issue: 'Our matter, for the most part, belongs not to 1865 alone, but to all time, and is of the

---

[10] *S&T*, 1865, p. 78.
[11] By the later 1860s the apostrophe in the Pastor's College was wisely moved to read, the Pastors' College.

kind which never grows stale . . . The many ministers who were students in our College will be our helpers in maintaining a variety and freshness of matter.' George Rogers was to be a leading contributor to the first volume. There was to be a second article from Brown in the May issue, 'Boldness in Distinctive Points'. It was probably given as an address at the first conference of the Association of Pastors' College students that same year. For him a main point was the one that had entered into the reason for the existence of the College:

> If in our experience we have found (I believe most, if not all present have) that God has blessed the preached gospel most when presented in a Calvinistic form, are we not bound, whether we draw on ourselves the dislike of a large part of the community or not, publicly and boldly to bring it forward, and try by all means to spread its influences?

One reason Brown had for urging bold teaching was the injury likely to come to the future if this was not done.

The only personal manuscripts of Brown's that have survived from his student years are thirty-six pages of sermon notes. They contain the outlines of twenty-three sermons he had prepared. They may be the 'sermonettes' he delivered on Saturday nights at Union Chapel, for they are too short to have been Sunday sermons at Bromley, or they may have been College assignments. They were certainly prepared to be delivered to a congregation. It was the definite policy of the College to teach men to preach without reading a manuscript, and therefore to construct a sermon with definite and easily remembered 'heads'. For Brown this method was not yet developed in these outlines.

All in all, these sermon outlines show a considerable maturity of scriptural knowledge for a writer about the age of eighteen. Characteristics that were to make his later ministry attractive were already present. For one thing, if he could present the truth as a picture, as well as a proposition in words, he would do so. Thus his outline of Jacob's dream of a ladder set up on earth with its top reaching heaven (*Gen.* 28:12), taken with John 1:51, gave him the two heads: '1. Christ is the ladder Jacob saw. 2. Christ is the ladder we may mount.' After giving doctrinal content to the words, he proceeded:

> Faith comes to the ladder and puts her foot on the first round, she takes hold and puts the other foot on, she is then off the earth. Do take heed of false ladders, Morality, Ritual, and others. There is no ladder from Hell to Heaven. There is one and only one from earth to Heaven. It comes to where thou liest. Oh! venture on it. God is waiting for you at the top. Oh! grasp, and let this place be your Bethel, your House of God.

There are also in the outlines a number of emphases that would mark his whole future ministry. Preaching on 'Salvation is given that we might serve God', from Exodus 8:1, he wrote:

> God's church has drifted far from this truth. We now hear of 'Christian workers' in connection with the church. We might almost as well talk of 'working working-men'. God did not bring the Israelites from Egypt, from the brick-kilns, that they might sit down in idleness . . . Redemption then service. God never saved a man to let him have an easy life.

In the course of his notes on the text, 'And a mixed multitude went up also with them' (*Exod.* 12:38), he wrote:

> Some here are probably thinking what a trivial thing our text is to narrate. This 'trivial thing', however, was the cause of the failure of the Israelites in the wilderness . . . Has there ever been a time when there were not traitors in the

professing church. There is a great mixture in the church. There is a great mixture in the pulpit. The greater part of the vice prevalent now is due to our recreant pulpits. Satan puts many direct emissaries in the church.

'Cling to the great collateral truths of Divine sovereignty and human responsibility', Spurgeon urged the students. Both are present in Brown's outlines and he early grasped what a later generation of evangelicals were to miss, that God's sovereignty is shown in revival. On Psalm 85:6, he said: 'God only can give revival. God's church was born in a revival. It has lived in revivals. David knew where to go for revival.' Such times, he went on, bring happiness in God, 'revive us again: that thy people may rejoice in thee'. 'May all our happiness be "in thee".'

* * * * *

I have said a good deal in this chapter on Spurgeon's College, as inevitably it would come to be called. The years there, and the friendship with the leader who was only ten years older than himself, were to be formative for the whole of Archibald Brown's future. Nearly thirty years later he would say, 'I never like to miss an opportunity of saying how I thank God with all my heart, and ever shall, that I was at the Pastors' College.' There are also lessons from the formation of the Pastors' College of permanent relevance for the preparation of an evangelical ministry. In its divergence from the current priorities on training for the ministry it drew criticism. 'Where will you place the men that you propose to train?' had been one of the objections. And who would want preachers trained in a vision of things that belonged to a former age? By 1866, when the Pastors' College had a third of the students in all the Baptist Colleges in the country, the facts gave the answer. Instead of overloading the existing church scene, a work of outreach was in progress that could only surprise the critics. Already ten new churches had been formed by students, with many of their people having recently been brought to Christ. Of Baptist chapels in the greater London area, another seventeen were now led by Pastors' College men. In seven places churches were formed without yet having their own building, and in ten situations preaching was being continued with a view to the formation of churches. Elsewhere in the United Kingdom some seventy former students were serving churches.[12]

On the issues, what kind of preachers are needed to answer the main need of the age, and whether education is more important than piety, prayerfulness, and zeal, the evidence from the Metropolitan Tabernacle did not fit the received wisdom.

> The literary attainments of our ministers, it has been said, must advance with the literature of the age. They must be prepared to stand in the foremost ranks of the scholars and critics of their day; and must have earned some literary degree, if they would secure the public confidence in their teaching. A strong current, not of public opinion, but of effort on the part of tutors and directors of our colleges, has of late years been accumulating in this direction. What has the result been? Have the students who have passed through the new method of training been better preachers, more earnest, more eloquent, more adapted to the tastes and circumstances

[12] This was only the beginning. By 1878 in 'New Chapels or Churches', forty-nine are documented in the Greater London area (*S&T*, 1878, pp. 240-62). By the year 1908, 1,111 men had been educated at the College, of which number 689 were serving as pastors, missionaries, and evangelists, while 180 were deceased. *S&T*, 1908, p. 312.

of their hearers, than those who preceded them? Have they taken more commanding positions, and been more effective in their ministrations? Have they more clearly and consistently interpreted and enforced the truths of God's Word? We unhesitatingly answer, No![13]

But it was not to the form of training that Spurgeon gave most weight. 'I devoutly bless God', he wrote, 'that he has sent to the College some of the holiest, soundest, and most self-denying preachers I know.' As we shall further see, the Pastors' College had been raised up in a time of remarkable revival; and God raised up men suited for the times of spiritual reaping which were at hand.

One of the College students recorded that the need for humility and self-discipline had been the lessons most impressed on him. Brown would not have been blessed as he was had he not also been learning those lessons. I do not find him, or his friends, in the habit of quoting numbers, and instances of success. He knew the real work was not their own. In Brown's eyes the results were as supernatural as they were in the time of Elisha. Quoting the direction given by Elisha to the wife of one of the sons of the prophets concerning the multiplication of the oil she needed (2 *Kings* 4:4-6), he commented: 'She had to borrow a great many pots. Then she had to shut the door. Why? Because she wasn't proudly to boast of it. It was not to be a public exhibition. We want more modesty. We must not make a parade of God's dealings.'

In calling Archibald Brown to his work, God gave him wisdom above his years. He was only twenty-three when he was first asked to address the London Baptist Association,

---

[13] Spurgeon in *S&T*, 1866, p. 42.

founded in 1865 at the instigation of Spurgeon with a committee of eleven men. In this address, 'Revivals of Religion, the Minister's Position and Duty towards them', he said:

> I cannot here abstain from saying (and I believe many of the brethren echo the same sentiment), how much I disapprove of anyone styling himself, or permitting himself to be called a 'Revivalist', the very term seems to claim for man the high prerogative which belongs alone to him who sits upon the throne of heaven; and to cast a slight upon the glorious work of the Spirit upon which we are so absolutely dependent.[14]

One long-remembered experience at Bromley had helped to impress on him the truth that success does not come at times the preacher can appoint. It followed an occasion when he felt specially helped as he prepared to preach on the words of Christ to the deceased son of the widow of Nain, 'Young man, I say unto thee, arise' (Luke 7:14). He was no less conscious of the power of the truth when he delivered the message and was certain that results would follow:

> I was so certain that there would be a number of conversions that I announced that on Monday evening I would be waiting in the chapel to converse with penitents. I was there, and I waited hour after hour, but not a soul came. At last I could bear it no longer, and I went out to the back of the chapel and, flinging myself on the long, rank grass, I writhed in anguish of soul. I went home at 9 o'clock, worn out and feeling that I had been 'let down'.

Commenting on this in later years, he said to other men: 'If you are cast down, remember it may be God's way of preparing you.'

---

[14] *S&T*, 1868, p. 248.

AN AWAKENING IN STEPNEY GREEN

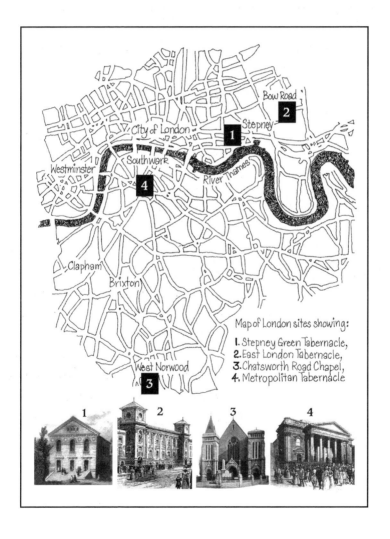

Map of London sites showing:

1. Stepney Green Tabernacle,
2. East London Tabernacle,
3. Chatsworth Road Chapel,
4. Metropolitan Tabernacle

'I think of thirty years ago, when I stood on Stepney Green for the first time in my life and looked across at that chapel that was pointed out to me as Stepney Green Tabernacle, then in want of a pastor. And I think of those who gathered round me in those early days and said, "Well, pastor, you preach, and we will pray." They constituted a noble band.'

AGB at East London Tabernacle, June 7, 1896.

STEPNEY GREEN Tabernacle, in the East End of London, was a new cause established by one of Spurgeon's students. After initial growth, it opened its own building in 1864, and called another Pastors' College student the following year. When this man remained only twelve months, the deacons came back to Spurgeon for another recommendation. In reply he told them of a man he would 'walk four miles to hear'. It was high praise from someone whose aversion to walking was well known! So it was that the deacons came to hear Archibald Brown when he was taking a midweek service at the Metropolitan Tabernacle. They decided on first sight that he was too young for their need, and then forgot their objection by the time he had finished speaking. After preaching twice at Stepney, Brown was given a unanimous call, which he accepted on meeting with the deacons at the church secretary's home on November 30, 1866.

With seventy-six members, the church at Stepney was well established by this date. Both by success and by difficulties Brown had been prepared for the larger role now before him. He also had an invaluable friend and helper whom he did not have when he started at Bromley. On October 12, 1865, at the age of twenty-one, he had married Annie Bigg, the girl to whom he attributed his conversion. Only one letter marking that wedding day has survived, and it was from the other party who had shared in his conversion.

> London, October 11, 1865
>
> Dear Friend and Brother,—I have just managed to get the accompanying little salt-cellars, which I hope will reach you this evening. Their value is insignificant, but they will I hope remind you of me, and of the sincere interest I shall always feel in you. They may also help to remind you that the speech of all those who love Christ should be always with grace, seasoned with salt. May God bless you abundantly tomorrow and always!—Your fond friend,
>
> S. A. Blackwood

A lesser Christian than Annie might have baulked at removing from Bromley to an environment which only that year had been scourged by cholera, and where the health of the previous pastor had failed in so short a period. Stepney, on the north side of the Thames, was two-and-a-half miles east of St Paul's, and included the greater part of the East End of London. In the sixteenth century its rural manor houses on the main route out to Essex were sought after by the rich; much was changed by the time of the congestion and unemployment of the 1860s. Many from the country towns and villages of Essex had flowed into the East End looking for work, and bringing their distinctive accent with them. With the population augmented from other quarters, as well as other lands, open spaces were giving way to alleys and tenement buildings; and numbers of the one-time homes of the well-to-do were in the process of being divided up for the rooms to be rented by the poor. In the Limehouse district, more than a quarter of the population lived two families to a

Houses on Stepney Green.

room in tenements, while in Shadwell, on the southern edge of
Stepney, a visitor in 1872 reported it to be a place where, 'low
houses, poor streets of brick, under red-tiled roofs, cross each
other in every direction, and lead down with a dismal look to
the river. Beggars, thieves, harlots, the latter especially, crowd
Shadwell Street.'[1] 'In years past', Brown would later say, 'I
have been into places which, thank God, you know nothing
at all about. I have climbed up staircases on which no ray
of light ever shone; and if only there had been light maybe I
should have been almost sick to death as I ascended the stairs.
The darkness hid the foulness.'[2]

[1] H. Taine, quoted by Kathleen Heasman, *Evangelicals in Action: An Appraisal of
their Social Work* (London: Geoffrey Bles, 1962), p. 3.
[2] On Hebrews 4:12, March 24, 1907.

While conditions were by no means all of this character, a degeneration of the East End was in progress in the 1860s, which would only slowly be recognised by those who never visited the area. The Stepney Baptist College had read the trend correctly when it moved across London from Stepney Green in 1856 to Regent's Park, changing its name accordingly. But while some Christians were moving out, Archie and Ann Brown were not alone in moving in. In 1864, Hudson Taylor, had moved into a little house, 10 Coburn Street, Bow, and made it the first headquarters of what was to become the China Inland Mission. Among the visitors to that house was Thomas Barnardo of Dublin, who would remain in the East End for life. Another who came to Taylor's home was the evangelist Henry Grattan Guinness; the two men had met before and became life-long friends. The thought of Grattan Guinness was turning to the training of missionaries for foreign fields, and it is said to have been Taylor's new mission which attracted him to the East End for his Missionary Institute. Guinness moved into 29 Stepney Green with his family in 1872. His wife, Fanny, described her first impressions on alighting with him 'from a horse-drawn tram in the raucous din of the Mile End Road', and being 'both fascinated and repelled by the sights'. When friends wrote to her, enquiring, 'Is it not a very disagreeable location?' she would reply:

> True, its noise is trying, its dirt and dust disagreeable, and its atmosphere anything but invigorating. We sometimes gasp for a fresh breeze, and sigh for other sights than a never-ending succession of omnibuses and market carts, and for other sounds than the shriek of the railway-whistle and the tinkle of the tram bell. But when we recall the lot of our missionary

friends in the narrow lanes and streets of undrained Chinese cities . . . we feel that we have good reason to be content.[3]

Not all reports of the East End stressed the negative. Some spoke in praise of the character of many in the area, as Brown himself would later do. G. Laurence Gomme wrote:

> It is a remarkable fact that the east end of London, so little known to the west end, possesses traits of character, peculiar customs and manners, and idiosyncrasies which stamp it at once as an independent part of London, and not the refuse ground where the poor do congregate. The east end of London, indeed, is a study well worth anyone's attention, and its solid capacity for work and patience is not the least among the valuable assets which London possesses in her population.[4]

Such was the area and the population where Archie and Annie Brown set up home at 53 Bancroft Road, off Mile End Road. He preached for the first time as pastor of Stepney Green Tabernacle on Sunday, January 6, 1867, from the text, 'And I, brethren, when I came to you, came not with excellency of speech or wisdom, declaring unto you the testimony of God' (*1 Cor.* 2:1).

The building seated 800 but Brown could later speak of the numbers when he came as 'a handful'.[5] A public meeting to mark his formal installation as the new minister was held on Tuesday, February 26, 1867. The preacher himself seemed not

[3] Michele Guinness, *The Guinness Legend* (London: Hodder & Stoughton, 1991), pp. 96-7.

[4] G. L Gomme, *London In the Reign of Queen Victoria, 1837-1897* (London: Blackie, 1898), p. 128.

[5] The *Baptist Union Handbook* gives the membership figure for Stepney Green in 1867 as 294. This, we assume, was the figure at the end of the year, while the 76 members, already noted, referred to the start of that year. The original church records from this period have not survived.

greatly interested in that event, which is not surprising because earlier that month something far more memorable had already happened. It seems to have been a tradition that annually a Sunday evening sermon was preached especially for young men and the date fixed for 1867 was February 10. Brown would later remind his people of what happened that evening:

> There are not a few present who can remember this Sabbath evening six years ago—that time when, if ever this church held a prayer meeting, it held it then—that wondrous time that we went down to the school room, when, as it seemed to us, a very tempest of prayers rose up to God,—that time when we all seemed bowed together before the throne, when all our desires joined in one; and a great—I might say an agonized cry—rose up from the throng, 'Lord, in the sanctuary above, save souls this night.' We shall never forget being literally swept up into the sanctuary that evening, not merely physically, but as it seemed to us, carried right on to the platform by an irresistible power of prayer. And what was the result? We have not yet forgotten how God marched through our midst—how there were almost as many conversions as there were pews in the place.[6]

One striking fact about the night of February 10, 1867, was that the text from which he preached was the one which, not long before, he had taken without any observable effect at Bromley, 'Young man, I say unto thee, arise.' Yet this night 'God brought in seventy souls at one sweep of mercy.' The preacher had no doubt about how that was to be understood. New life is neither from the preacher nor from the words spoken. 'It is not the means used, but the Lord's blessing on them. The teacher may teach Jesus and him only, and that with tears; but unless the Divine Master

---

[6] Psalm 25:7, February 9, 1873.

place his hands upon the blind, no miracle of grace will be effected.'

From the start of his ministry at Stepney in January 1867, Brown began to keep a sermon record book, noting date, text, subject and, frequently, a brief comment such as the following:

'Blessed time.' 'Capital subject'. 'Most glorious theme.' 'A most instructive subject.' 'A time I shall never forget.' 'Much helped.' 'Never Happier.' 'Felt God was at work.' 'Felt in heaven while preaching.' 'One of the most solemn services we ever had.' 'A good doctrinal theme, much needed now.' 'Happy as a bird.' On the Sunday following the last entry, he wrote, 'Fine theme but not happy.'

The Spirit of God was working in their midst in reviving power, and what began in the early months of 1867 was to continue through successive years. The changes that occurred at Stepney Green Tabernacle have characterised churches in every revival. As at Pentecost, Brown told his people,

> The blessing spread far and wide. If it commenced with the disciples it did not end with them. From the upper room it soon flew along the streets of Jerusalem like an electric current. The crowds gather—they surge around the building—curiosity is aroused and all cry, 'What meaneth this?' Peter preaches. The power goes abroad. Three thousand find out what a revival means. O, Sirs, there is no telling where the influence of a revival in a church may spread. It finds its way where nothing else will. It creeps into homes shut against the tract distributor. It glides into darkest places of vice. It penetrates the whole neighbourhood. A revived church will be certain to draw the multitude together. Let but a revival come and the dreary waste of empty pews to

be seen in many a sanctuary will be gone. This is the secret of getting at the masses. Our churches do not want cleverer or better ministers but revived ones. A revived church has magnetic power. The people must come to it.[7]

When Brown preached these words, there were many present who could affirm he was describing what they had seen themselves in Stepney. In May 1869 he noted in a letter to 'our hearers':

> The numbers desirous of hearing the Word are far more than we can by any means accommodate. Every Sunday evening some four hundred more than the place was built to hold are crowded in, whilst large numbers are necessarily denied admittance. This has continued for over two years. The Lord has been pleased to give what we deem a far more evident token of his blessing, *viz.:*—many additions to the church from out of the world.[8]

Such were the crowds now attending that one night the preacher's wife herself could not get in. On at least one occasion the crush led to an accident, when a woman fell on the staircase leading to the gallery and her head was split open. Brown went to see her in hospital the next day. With her face half hidden in bandages, she smiled at him and said, in a true Cockney accent, 'Oh, Mr Brown, ain't it a mercy I broke my head while going into the house of God. I might have broke it when going into a theatre!'

An eye-witness account of what was happening at Stepney Green Tabernacle comes from a reporter of the *Christian World* who was present for a service on December 20, 1868:

---

[7] Acts 2:12, May 19, 1872.

[8] Appendix to sermon on 2 Thessalonians 1:3, May 9, 1869. Even by December 1867 the *S&T* reported that Stepney Green Tabernacle was 'crowded to excess'.

So early as six p.m., a crowd of respectfully-attired people begins to cluster around the doors of the chapel, but unless they have the requisite seat tickets there is no admission for them until five minutes before the commencement of Divine service. This is rendered necessary by the significant fact that all the Tabernacle sittings, several hundred in number, have been taken by the regular members of the congregation, leaving very little space available for those who are not fortunate enough to possess the much-sought tickets. Proceeding up the broad and lofty flight of stone steps leading to the entrance doors, we enter the chapel and find ourselves in the interior of a long and spacious building of somewhat graceful aspect. It is of great length, and furnished with large galleries, the frontage of which consists of light, open ironwork . . . Each inch of available space has been utilised, a small gallery, holding about twenty persons, and ascended by a kind of ladder, having been constructed over the head of each of the two staircases. Numerous star burners are suspended from the flat ceiling. At the farther end of the building is a semi-circular recess, in which are fitted two roomy platforms, the upper being occupied by the preacher. The lower platform is generally crowded. On each side is a door leading to a vestry-room, the baptistery being situated midway between the two.

Precisely at six p.m. the ticket holders commence making their appearance. Amongst the earliest arrivals are a body of fine, stalwart-looking young men, who march in procession up the aisle, taking their places on the lower platform. These consist of the captain and crew of a collier brig, plying between London and Hartlepool, who generally manage to time their voyages so as to be present at the Sunday services here. By quarter past six the chapel is nearly half full. Ten minutes later there are few unoccupied seats. Now the non-ticket holders are admitted. In they pour through the various doors, forming a thick, continuous stream. Forms are placed wherever possible, along the aisles, between the pews, here, there, and everywhere—and when these, and every inch of standing room also, are taken possession of, the doors are reluctantly closed on the crowd outside. It is the same in the galleries. Every Sunday evening hundreds find themselves completely unable to gain admission. The congregation seems to embrace various ranks and conditions of society; but the artisan element evidently predominates most strongly. The bronzed, weather-worn features of sea-faring men are also to be found scattered here and there amid the great sea of faces patiently and earnestly gazing in the direction of the preacher.

The Rev., or rather Mr Archibald G. Brown—for, like Mr Spurgeon, he has dropped the prefix 'Reverend'—is a young and thoughtful looking man, with earnest features and devoid of mannerisms. He seems to be about twenty-eight or thirty years of age, but, in reality he is only twenty-four. But, although so young, there is nothing juvenile about him. He is grave beyond his years, and the tone of his discourses speaks his studious disposition. His labours in Stepney have proved singularly successful. He rapidly gained a powerful hold on the minds and affections of his hearers, which has progressed in ever-increasing ratio up to the present time. During the two years of his pastorate in Stepney no less than 266 persons have been admitted as members of the church over which he so energetically presides.

Mr Brown commenced with a short but touching prayer, after which 'Awake, my soul, in joyful lays', was sung, the preacher himself delivering the words and leading the singing. Then came an expository reading, plain, practical, and perfectly intelligible, of the second chapter of the First Epistle of Peter. A hymn followed, succeeded by a most impressive and powerful prayer, in which, with strange and thrilling earnestness, in melting tones of entreaty, the preacher expressed his heartfelt hope that in this, the last month of the dying year, some might be born again, and become participators in the joys of Christian life.

A convulsive throb of sympathy seemed to pervade the breasts of his hearers, and as he slowly rose from his kneeling attitude and thoughtfully gazed on the various features of his congregation, he must have met with more than one earnest countenance, the moistened eyes of which told how deeply and how effectually the words of entreaty had penetrated into the owner's heart.

Charles Wesley's beautiful and expressive hymn, 'Come, Holy Ghost, our hearts inspire', preceded the sermon, which was delivered with much force and eloquence, but without the slightest tendency towards exaggeration.

At the end of a forty-five minute sermon on 'Light and Darkness', the service concluded with Bonar's hymn, 'I heard the voice of Jesus say', a short prayer, and 'the immense congregation slowly and quietly began to disperse.'[9]

A characteristic of revival is that hunger for the presence of God is seen as much in attention to prayer as in hearing the Word of God. In a sermon already quoted from 1872, Brown reminded the people that 'the ten days' prayer meeting' that preceded Pentecost continued afterwards, and he pleaded with his people,

> Let not your prayerfulness decline. The Pentecostal blessing we are now enjoying may be traced to our gatherings for prayer. It is not alone the preaching, it is nothing of the man, it is your praying that has won the day. For five years you have flocked to the prayer meetings, as the world does to its pleasures. Let everything else go rather than the meetings for

[9] *Christian World*, January 1, 1869, p. 9.

pleading with God. May this spirit of prayer—this pioneer of revival, be ours now and ever as a church.

Church prayer meetings at Stepney Tabernacle were held every Sunday and every Monday evening. A member of Brown's church in the early days of his ministry speaks of yet another gathering for prayer, and says 'the great gathering for prayer was on Saturday evening'. This meeting was commenced by the pastor despite advice to the contrary from the deacons. They doubted it would be supported, for, at this date, Saturday was a working day until lunch time, and the evening was 'the great shopping evening' of the week. Undeterred, Brown had responded, 'Let them bring their shopping bags and baskets with them.' So a place was set aside for their safe keeping during the meeting. 'They came in crowds', the same member reports, and he goes on to give this note of how the meetings were led:

> His view of the way to conduct a prayer meeting was always to start punctually, and close punctually; and always to have a time of previous waiting upon God before he came down to the meeting. He would not allow long prayers, and if anyone was allowed to speak he must not take more than ten minutes.[10]

Many who attended these prayer meetings had spiritual concerns, and individuals might make known beforehand their particular need. In a sermon on February 14, 1869, Brown mentioned one example of this: 'Three weeks ago as fine a sailor as ever put foot on deck came to our Saturday prayer meeting, he sent in a special request for prayer that he might be enabled to live in Christ and show his colours

---

[10] Page, *AGB*, pp. 13-14. The *Christian World* reporter present in December 1868, believed that the numbers present at the Monday evening prayer meeting averaged 300, while there were 200-250 at the recently commenced Saturday night meeting.

during a long voyage he was about to take.' But instead of the long voyage, the ship *Calcutta* on which he served as mate, was involved in a disastrous collision. He 'was thrown down in the crash and half-killed, a huge wave then swept him overboard, and he sank to rise no more till the resurrection morning. Now in all affection would we commend his widow and little ones to him who is the "God of the fatherless".'

These prayer meetings were long to be remembered. Some thirty years later, about 1910, when Brown was no longer serving in East London, he came back to preach one Sunday, and recorded the following:

> I was preaching in East London last Sunday morning, and I walked from London Bridge, and as I got a little way past the Mile End Gate, I saw a workman leaning against the wall. He touched his cap and said, 'Good morning, Mr Brown; glad to see you in this neighbourhood again. Going to the old Tabernacle?' I said, 'Yes', and he then went on, 'May I walk with you?' Going along he said, 'Are not things changed Sir? I have been thinking of thirty years ago. Do you remember how there was a prayer meeting every Sunday morning, and we used to walk there sometimes up to our knees in snow; yet there used to be two or three hundred there; now you cannot get people out of bed at 10.30 on Sunday morning.'
>
> As he spoke of those old days how well I remembered them! At 7 o'clock on Sunday morning there were hundreds met for prayer. Rain, hail or snow made no difference. They were all in dead earnest.[11]

In preaching on December 6, 1868, he said:

> I cannot but look back through the two years so nearly gone with wonder and thankfulness that defy language. God has been pleased to give us as a church such prosperity as is given

---

[11] 'More Stories of Archibald Brown', June 3, 1926, *East London Advertiser*.

to few, he has permitted us to reap with one hand while we have sown with the other. The converts are not numbered by tens only but by hundreds. In no spirit of pride do we say this; for what have we that we have not received? It is his work and his only, and at his feet we delight to cast all the glory. But while rejoicing in manifest success, we cannot but remember that there are hosts of God's servants, far holier and far more able, who have been called to toil and labour on with but little encouragement. They are preparing the soil for others, and perhaps long after they have gone to their reward, someone else will 'enter into their labours'.

* * * * *

By January 1869 Brown had reached the conclusion that their building at Stepney Green had to be replaced by one at least three times larger. Possible ground for a new site was found, and he discussed the probable cost with William Higgs, a builder and a deacon at the Metropolitan Tabernacle. Around £13,000 was the estimate: while the work would be done by Higgs' firm at cost price, it was still a huge figure at that time. When the news of the proposal was reported to other deacons at the Metropolitan Tabernacle, Brown's father expressed his misgivings. 'What do you think my son is going to do?' he asked Mr Cook, another deacon—'To build a Tabernacle to hold three thousand people!' Cook, less apprehensive, replied, 'Then Brown, if he says he'll do it, he will, and the best thing we can do is to pray for him.' 'But where's the money to come from?' the father still urged, only to hear, 'Why, I expect he'll come to you first.'

Cook's conclusion was not exactly right. On January 28, 1869, Archie Brown made his way into the City of London to beg for help. His first call was at a merchant's office in

Cornhill, the man being a member of Spurgeon's church. 'I come to you first because you have always helped me', Brown explained. The response was, 'You've come at a very unfortunate time. I've so many demands on me now that I can only give a trifle.' The man's deeds, however, outstripped his words, for he pressed £500 on the young petitioner. The next call was to the office of John Sands who gave £250. With this encouragement to support him, only now did he go to his father's office. Perhaps it wasn't an accident that the date Archie chose for this visit was his father's birthday, and he opened the conversation with the words: 'Well, Father, I've come to celebrate your birthday by collecting for the new Tabernacle. How much do you think I've received in the last forty minutes?' 'Oh, well, £20', his father replied. 'Rather £750!' said the supplicant, adding, 'I want you to put another £100 on the top, and then I shall go home satisfied with my morning's work.'[12]

Holden Pike's account of this conversation might seem to suggest that Brown senior was a hesitant, possibly reluctant, supporter. The facts are against any such supposition. The £100 the father gave that morning was only the beginning; he was to enter heart and soul into the project and would ultimately contribute at least £1,250. Pike later rectifies what might have been a wrong impression when he writes: 'It was one of the chief delights of Mr Brown's life to know that his son could, by the simple, yet forcible, preaching of the gospel, attract such a crowd.'[13]

The raising of the amount required for the new building was related in an entirely unplanned way to an event in October 1868, three months before the proposal was first

[12] Pike, *Brown*, pp. 14-15.
[13] *Ibid.*, p. 49.

discussed. In that month, after pressure on Brown to agree, a publisher printed his sermon 'A Song About Redemption'. From that date a sermon was published monthly, and these were soon engaging the interest of readers in all parts of the country. Never reluctant to appeal for what he was sure concerned the cause of Christ, the preacher took the need for a new church building to these readers, and with sermons published the next year, 1869, went out circulars 'in tens of thousands', appealing for support. By the time he wrote the last sentence, for publication with the first volume of his sermons in November 1869, he could report:

> From bed-ridden ones in Suffolk, and sorrowing ones in Liverpool, as well as from workers in the Master's cause in various parts of England, and likewise Scotland, have we received kind cheering words that have made our cup run over, whilst from America we have heard of conversions through their instrumentality . . . Since the commencement of the year we have received in cash and promises over £3,000, and 'Jehovah Jireh' is still our strength and watchword.

Plans went ahead, but evidently not without problems, including losing the site he had anticipated they could secure. On August 11, 1870, his diary noted: 'This was the day we lost the ground in Bow Road by a few hours: save me from committees.' It cannot have been long after that a suitable site was at last found, building commenced, and in September 1871, a first meeting was held there. It was reported in *Baptist Union*, a New York paper:

> On Thursday evening, September 21st, we attended a very novel meeting at the new East London Tabernacle, which is being built for the Open Communion Baptist Church under the pastoral care of the Rev. Archibald G. Brown.

The building is being erected on the East Side of the Burdett Road, which runs from Mile End Road to East India Dock Road, and is close to the former thoroughfare. We say, 'is being erected', for it is by no means finished; and we were not a little puzzled when we reached the entrance to understand how it was that a meeting should be held in such a place. Our questions were fully answered before we left, and we saw that the unusualness of the meeting was but natural as the product of no ordinary mind. The Rev. A. G. Brown is evidently not to be tied down by precedents, but is quite capable of cutting open for himself a new, if not better, way. Hundreds of scaffold poles and planks had to be removed from the interior, and the floor cleared for the occasion. A temporary platform was erected, and forms and chairs had been arranged for the attendance. Still everything was in the rough above, below, around. Naked bricks with rough mortar, gallery beams and pillars, an indescribable roof—all presented an appearance anything but tasteful. To remedy this as much as possible no small amount of work was done in the way of extempore decorations. A sea-captain, member of the church, happened to be ashore, and procured a bountiful supply of ships' flags and streamers of all devices. These were hung in two lines on either side from the gallery upward, and did much to hide the bricks and mortar.

This unusual meeting, attended by about 2,000, was in part intended to raise further support. A final meeting in the old Stepney Green Tabernacle took place on February 18, 1872, and later that week the new home was opened on Thursday, February 22, when Spurgeon was the preacher. In his own remarks Brown said that support for the building had come in 2,300 separate donations, including gifts from Christians in America, India, and Japan. A few had doubted the need of such a building; they had no desire to draw anyone from other churches but, he pointed out, of the 650 received into membership since 1867, 500 'came direct from the world'. He ignored the attack on his ministry published just a few days earlier in an East End paper, which warned that the new building promised 'series of services of appalling length', 'tea with hymns', and a pastor, one of 'the elect', who 'preaches brimstone with positive enjoyment'. Other evidences of hostility in the locality were not lacking. One correspondent to a local paper (February 22, 1872) was given space to offer this opinion on 'The New Tabernacle in Burdett Road':

> Sir—About eighteen months ago a certain gentleman in Mile-end spoke about the erection of some baths in Burdett Road. The other day, while passing along the above-named road, my attention was arrested by a large prison-like building. I immediately asked a passer-by if it was the new baths that were talked about a few months since. He replied, 'Oh no, Sir, it is the new chapel.' The construction of this new building looks like some square brick-built ice-house.

Nothing at all is recorded of Archie Brown's pleasure in the fabric of the new building. His great interest lay elsewhere as is illustrated from an incident from about this time, which he has recorded in his own words:

> Some little while since, preaching in the country, a good brother said he should like to show us over the chapel before preaching. He took us up in the gallery and asked us to look at it from there. Then he took us into the pulpit, that we might view it from that position. Then he asked us to note that every pew was cushioned with a cushion of the same colour; and he also drew our attention to the fact that there were such nice brass rings and rails at the end of the pew for umbrellas. I stood it as long as I could, and said to him, 'Well, brother, I have seen a few chapels in my time. Now

you have pointed out the beauties of your sanctuary, may I just ask you one or two questions which really I am more interested in? How many drunkards did you have saved here last year?' 'Oh, my dear Mr Brown, we are a most respectable people.' I said, 'Have you had many harlots gathered in here?' I thought he would have fainted. 'Do you get many outsiders, ragged customers, in here?' He said, 'My dear Mr Brown, again I can assure you we have a most respectable congregation.' I said, 'My dear brother, I say in all love, I think my Master cares far more for drunkards and harlots and outsiders being saved in this chapel than he cares about your red cushions and brass rails.' The glory of a place of worship, after all, is just this—the ingathering of the outcasts to Jesus Christ.[14]

Spurgeon's sermon at the opening of the new Tabernacle in 1872 led to the same conclusion, from the text, 'The right hand of the Lord is exalted; the right hand of the Lord doeth valiantly' (*Psa.* 118:16). In *The Sword and the Trowel,* he was to note that the new building was 'probably the second chapel in London in regard to size, and is a noble monument to the power of the gospel when faithfully proclaimed'. It was the spiritual significance of that fact which he wanted to be understood in his sermon. After allusion to criticism in the local press, he went on: 'They say the gospel has lost its power. I read the other day that some of us were echoes of dead Puritanism, that we were not abreast of the age, and were preaching a faith that was practically dead.'

With an overview of revivals of the past, Spurgeon used his text to prove why a 'gospelless gospel has great powers of dispersion', but 'has little power of attraction'; 'but the gospel

---

[14] Sermon on 'Salvation by Faith Alone', January 12, 1890, *The British Weekly Pulpit,* p. 455.

of Jesus Christ soon draws a multitude together'. The same evidence existed in the present:

> We have seen it in some of the very darkest parts of London. Here and all around, I need not quote instances, for you know them better than I do, lions are turned into lambs, ravens into doves, and the most unlikely spots in East London that were deserts, salt lands not inhabited, that looked as if they were cursed of God, have been made to rejoice and blossom like the rose when the preacher of the gospel and his Master have set their faith upon them . . . I believe those who hear my dear friend Mr Brown once will continue to hear him, and you will continue to have a full house for many a year to come, and hundreds will be converted.

Stepney Green today.

4

CONVERTS AND THE EVANGEL

Archibald Brown.

'The gospel is a fact, therefore tell it *simply;* it is a joyful fact, therefore tell it *cheerfully;* it is an entrusted fact, therefore tell it *faithfully;* it is a fact of infinite moment, therefore tell it *earnestly;* it is a fact about a Person, therefore preach *Christ.*'

AGB

IT was not the normal practice of Archibald Brown to draw attention to people who had been converted, or to publish their testimonies. Had the story of those who came to new life in Christ at Stepney been told, it would have made a wonderful book. But we remember it was only the conversion of Saul of Tarsus that was given us in any detail in the New Testament. Little known, the vast multitudes of the redeemed pass through history, waiting the day when they will rise in the likeness of the Son of God. We need not be surprised at the lack of conversion records kept by the churches, for the glory of the church lies not in the person of the converts. In times of greatest blessing the attention is on the Builder of the church himself. In that connection Brown would sometimes draw attention to the words: 'The glory of the Lord filled the house. And the priests could not enter into the house of the Lord, because the glory of the Lord had filled the Lord's house' (2 *Chron.* 7:2, 3).

Yet it will take the reader closer to these days to know at least something of what Brown saw of the grace of God in the lives of individuals. For our source of information we are almost entirely dependent on the few references which occur in his sermons.

One of the first conversions at Stepney Tabernacle was that of William Nimkey, which took place before Brown's arrival. In speaking of him, Brown tells us: 'He was drawn to Christ by quiet and gradual means. The same Spirit has a diversity of operations, and perhaps no two sinners are converted in precisely the same manner. With a large number the work is too gradual to be detected, and they can only say with the man of old, "One thing I know, whereas I was blind, now I see."' So it was with Nimkey. When asked by what means and when he had found the Saviour, he had replied with the text, 'The wind bloweth where it listeth, thou hearest the sound thereof, but canst not tell whence it cometh or whither it goeth.'

Nimkey served Christ and the church in Stepney for about ten years before he became seriously ill, his disease being diagnosed as 'congestion of the lungs'. When there was no improvement in his condition, the doctors advised him to try the sea air at Hastings. This was planned for June 1869, and a Monday morning was fixed when Brown promised to take him. On the preceding day, however, one of the sick man's blood vessels ruptured. When he recovered enough to speak, he told his wife, 'This is my passport to heaven.' 'Seeing him on the Monday morning', Brown said, 'I could hardly refrain from weeping on observing in the room the carpet bags already packed for our intended journey. Reading my thoughts he quietly remarked, "Man proposes, but God disposes. It is Heaven, not Hastings, it is Heaven, not Hastings I am going to."'

William Nimkey died the following November. Near the end, his pastor said to him: '"Well, brother Nimkey and how are you now?" Thinking I made reference to his body, he replied, "Very low, very low indeed." "But how about the

soul, brother?" Lifting his hand slowly up and with a countenance that brightened as he spoke, he said, "That still soars,
that still soars." Among his dying requests was "Never extol
me when I am gone, for I am only a poor sinner saved by
sovereign grace."" [1]

Other conversions, though just as definite, were widely
different. Brown would frequently receive letters from readers
of his sermons directing him to addresses where there were
individuals in need. One such letter sent him on a visit to a
little back street:

> I went and found there a woman about eight-and-twenty. She
> was sitting on a hard chair, resting her elbows on the chair to
> support her, and there were a couple of children on the floor,
> one four and the other six. The moment I looked at her I saw
> she was dying. I entered into conversation with her, first of
> all feeling my way. I said, 'Dear friend, are you here by your-
> self? Have you nobody to help you?' 'No, sir.' 'Where is your
> husband?' I could not help the tender way in which she made
> the best of a bad case. 'No, sir', she said; 'he goes out werry
> early in the morning, and he don't get back till werry late at
> night.' I said, 'Have not you anyone to help you during the
> day time?' 'Oh, well, no, sir', she said, pointing to the little
> girl of six, 'She does her werry best for me, sir.' 'Well', I said,
> 'you shall have a young lady call round tomorrow. You shall
> be carefully tended for some little while.' Then, bringing the
> conversation round, I said, 'My dear friend, do you know
> that you are dying?' She started. 'Dying, sir? Do you think
> I am dying?' I said, 'My poor girl, it would not be kindness
> of me to hold back the truth. I think you are. I will do all I
> can for you, and I think it is only right to let you know. I do
> not think your days on earth are very many. Do you know

[1] Philippians 2:25, November 20, 1870.

73

anything about Jesus Christ?' The tears came in her eyes and she said, 'I heard of him when I was in Sunday School some years ago.' I said, 'Have you not heard anything of him lately?' 'Ain't bin to no place of worship to speak of for the last eight years, sir.' I said, 'Would you like to be saved?' She said, 'Do you think he would be willing to save one like me?' I put the gospel as I have tried to put it to you. I wanted to make her see that it was receiving. I could not, until, feeling in my pocket, I found a penny, and, holding it out to the little one of six, I said, 'Here, darling, you can have this'; and the little one took the penny, and said, 'Thank you, sir.' I saw the mother look wistfully. I said, 'Look! Do you understand? That is a sermon for you. That child believed that the offer was genuine, and she showed her faith by just taking the penny. All that is necessary for you is to take Christ—take his salvation.' 'Yes, sir, but do you think he will take me?' I said, 'There is no doubt whatever about that. I can guarantee that he will take you. Do you take him.'

Ten days after—it was a most rapid consumption—she lay upon the bed, quite unconscious. The children came in and out of the room, but she heard not their voices. Thank God she was not alone! There were two Christian young ladies sitting by her side, watching her. The husband had not come in. And as they sat there hour by hour she was dead to everything outside. At half past ten at night, having been speechless and insensible for five hours, and still unconscious of all around, she said—I give it in her own words—'Lord Jesus, yer will receive me, won't yer?'[2]

Not all who came to Christ were as immediately responsive. Bill Sykes had been a costermonger—a fruit seller—when one of Brown's missionaries found him in bed in his little

---

[2] 'Salvation by Faith Alone,' Sermon on Luke 7:50 at Metropolitan Tabernacle, January 12, 1890.

room on Gale Street one April morning, and only a month away from death. He showed no concern about that likelihood. To the question what could be read to him from the Bible, he replied, 'I don't care—anything you like.' After hearing a passage on the new birth his only remark was, 'That's very funny.' Baffled over what to say on account of the man's ignorance, the missionary nevertheless continued to call day by day. On April 17 he told the missionary of the delight he had had in spending his time and spare cash at the race course; but the same day, the missionary noted, 'He seemed to show some little interest. This turned to a real anxiety until on April 21, Bill said, 'Do pray with me. I want to be saved.' These calls continued daily until three days later, the missionary called twice, the second time at 10 p.m., after which he wrote:

> Found him sitting up in bed. He was more anxious about his soul than at any time yet. I explained to him again how Christ took our place, bore our sins, and suffered our death. 'I see it now', said he; 'He suffered for me then.' I said, 'Yes.' From that moment I have no hesitation in saying that Bill Sykes entered into peace. The passage most blessed to him was Isaiah 43:25: 'I, even I, am he that blotteth out thy transgressions for mine own sake, and will not remember thy sins.' Christ taking Sykes' sins, and Sykes receiving Christ's righteousness, was all to him. I know not whose cup was most full of joy tonight—his or mine.
>
> April 25.—Found Sykes much worse in body but exceeding happy in soul. 'I will not remember thy sins' were the first words on his lips.
>
> April 27.—Found him cheerful but very low. His son was present, and I commenced speaking to him about spiritual matters. Bill Sykes interrupting my conversation, said, 'Give him that little bit.' 'What bit?' 'That little bit about Christ

taking my place, and how he had my punishment for me. That's the bit.'

Brown himself visited him a few days later and recorded:

Sitting by his side, we heard his story from his own lips. The man himself was the sermon. The kindling eye, the radiant face, the calm trustfulness, the bold testimony before all. These come back to us as we write. Again we can hear him say, 'Aye, Sir, it was that little bit that did the business.' Leaving the dying coster, we walked slowly home, often with a mist before our eyes, and as we walked we vowed, God helping us, 'that little bit' should be set as the central gem in every sermon preached henceforth.[3]

* * * * *

One local girl, a Miss C., paid a first visit to the East London Tabernacle one Sunday evening. For nine years her occupation had been to sing at a playhouse and to dance in ballets. That is where she would have been found the previous evening. But the word preached so touched her heart that she could not go back to it the next evening. Pike has recorded her transformation: 'Knowing what she now did of her condition as a sinner in the Lord's sight, she was afraid to go; and although the employment represented her livelihood she has never been since. She is now almost constantly employed in making garments for poor children, and is otherwise one of the most consistent and consecrated members with the East London Tabernacle.'

[3] The story of Bill Sykes was published in *A Record of One Year's Service During 1890*. A great crowd came to Bow Cemetery on May 25, 1890, to see 'the last of poor Bill'.

As with all gospel ministries, there were cases of conversion of which the preacher heard nothing until years later. A woman wrote to him to say that three years before she had come to peace through hearing Brown preach to sailors. 'Do you remember', she asked him, 'that piece about getting out of the boat? It was not enough for Peter to put one leg out of the boat and dip it in the water, but he had to take both feet right out and just stand by faith. That opened my eyes to see God's way of salvation.'

Another instance concerned a sermon he preached from the text, 'Let him that is athirst come. And whosoever will, let him take of the water of life freely' (*Rev.* 22:17). Fifteen years later one of his hearers of that day wrote to tell him the message was the means of leading him to Christ. The letter also told Brown that the writer had prayed for him ever since, and that he was shortly to leave for missionary service overseas.

The most dramatic account of a conversion is one recorded by George E. Page:

A man was much annoyed because his wife had professed conversion, and decided that he would shoot Mr Brown. It seemed to him that the best plan would be to do this during the second prayer at a Sunday evening service; so he came with a loaded revolver, and sat in the gallery near the platform. That evening the reading was Isaiah 53, and there was the usual commenting, which went right home to the man. The result was that the would-be murderer came into the vestry after the service, told the story, and handed the revolver to Mr Brown.[4]

---

[4] Page, *AGB*, p. 13. I have seen no reference to this conversion other than the one in Page's book of 1944, but Page was close to the work, being the eldest son of one of the first converts in Stepney Green in 1867; his father marrying a girl in the congregation two years later. The son became Church Secretary at the East London Tabernacle and was responsible for *East London Tabernacle, A Brief History*, in 1956.

* * * * *

While all spiritual success is the result of the work of God, wherever there is such work there will be certain conditions to be found among his people. These conditions are present, not as steps which Christians take to obtain 'results', but as the fulfilment of the grace that God gives to his people. Whether that grace is largely given, as in years of revival, or in other periods, what is needed for the health of churches is the same wherever the place, and whatever the century. It is summed up in the promise to give the Holy Spirit (*Luke* 11:13), and the primary grace which comes with his presence is *love*. This is the key to apostolic evangelism, and we see it repeated in the East End of London.

For the sake of clarity, I will look at this in relation to both pulpit and pew. When Luke explains what happened in the first century with the words, 'So mightily grew the word of God' (*Acts* 19:20), he is clearly referring to truth proclaimed. The work of salvation proceeds through preaching (*Rom.* 10:14-15). If we pause to think of what Brown was as a preacher we get close to what was happening in his church.

He could say to his people in 1873, 'You who worship here regularly will, I know, bear me witness that my general theme is the love of God.' And it was preaching prompted by love. How can Christ's love be known to others, unless the speaker experiences that love and feels it for others? As Spurgeon once said, 'If you greatly love you are the kind of man who knows how to feel for men, and with them. Some men do not know how to handle the heart at all. There is a way of handling men and women, and the art is acquired through intense love.'[5] For an example before their generation,

---

[5] *S&T*, 1889, p. 417. Brown said: 'A man may be sound as Calvin, and as eloquent

78

Spurgeon commended Robert Murray M'Cheyne, referring to the 'marvellous aroma about everything M'Cheyne preached', and saying, reading his life leads one to exclaim, 'Truly, this man must have had an infinite love in his great heart, for from it there is an unceasing flow of the noblest inspiration.'[6] The M'Cheyne spirit, better, the Spirit of Christ, was in Brown. The words, 'Truth needs to be baptized into love if it is to possess the charm of loveliness', could have been written by either of them. They were written by Brown.

When Brown was only twenty, in his first article in *The Sword and the Trowel,* he stated what became his lifelong ambition to exemplify:

> Where there is but little personal service, it is not severe to say, there is little love; for love is an active not a dormant power in the soul. If the heart be on fire with love to the Saviour, it will burn its way into active operation; and if the well-spring of true affection be there, it will, it must flow out in some channel or another.

Many years later, preaching on 'The Saviour's Defence of Sublime Devotion', he used the example of the woman who poured 'very precious ointment' on the head of Jesus. It would be a memorial to her 'in the whole world' (*Matt.* 26:13), to show how 'a person works for Christ because he loves him'. This ought to be eminently true of preachers (*John* 21:15-17). A preacher with a heart full of love for Christ is bound to speak with tenderness and compassion. In such a man there will be a persuasiveness that comes from Christ himself:

> The apostle says, 'We persuade men.' Oh, my brethren, here lies the difficulty of the work. God asks me to do what I feel

---

as a Whitefield, and yet lack the one thing that proves him to be a child of God. "He that loveth not, knoweth not God."'

[6] *S&T*, 1867, p. 494.

I cannot do as I should. It is not enough for the preacher just to state the gospel. If I were simply to say to you, 'There is God's plan', and walk down off this platform, I should not have cleared myself before God. It is not, 'We inform men.' If I were to preach properly, I should preach, I know, with streaming eyes. If I were to preach properly, I should plead with you as a hungry man pleads for bread. It is not enough to argue, or threaten, or warn. It is not enough even to tell the whole truth out. If I am to be true to the Lord, I have to try to grip you, to lay hold of you, and not to let you go until you be won over unto the side of Christ. How am I to do it? . . . Note this sentence—'We pray you in Christ's stead, be ye reconciled to God.' 'In Christ's stead', that is, in Christ's place. If I am sent of the Lord, then, according to this Book, I am standing in Christ's stead. It is Christ pleading with you. It is not the mere pastor of the East London Tabernacle; he is no one. It is in Christ's stead, as Christ himself would do it.[7]

In Brown that concern for others was lived out from day to day. 'Sow the seed everywhere', was one of his maxims. It led him to look for opportunities among all kinds and groups of people. Hospitals—especially The London—had his regular support. He was often among the disadvantaged. The blind received his care, and on occasion they would be drawn to the Tabernacle for a dinner and a gospel message. The same was done for postmen. Sailors, of whom there were many who looked for work in the docks nearby, had his special interest. A number of his sermons were preached especially for them. Nor did this spirit leave him in the night hours. There were times when it gave him a sleepless night, crushed by how people have no concern for themselves, and know no need of the mercy of God. Those who knew the pastor of the East

[7] 'We Persuade Men', 2 Corinthians 5:11, East London Tabernacle, n.d.

London Tabernacle did not suspect him of exaggeration when he said, 'I would willingly forfeit ten years of my life if some of you, yet far off from Christ, might be brought in.'

This brings us to another aspect of his preaching. Love led him to bear frequent witness to truths which are profoundly disturbing and unwelcome to the natural man:

> He will never win many souls who keeps in the background all that is calculated to alarm them. The first step towards being saved is when the sinner feels himself lost; and it is when he feels himself within a step of Hell that he is just putting his foot on the road to heaven.

This means the gospel does not start with good news. Only conviction of what sin deserves brings light to the meaning of the sufferings of Christ on Calvary.

In Brown's early days in the East End he had a conversation with an older Christian worker which more deeply impressed on him the relationship between the holiness and justice of God and the meaning of the atonement. As they were speaking together, the subject came round to those who, while professing to believe in the cross, deny that anyone will endure the wrath of God in eternity:

> He said to me, 'Mark if with them the views of men concerning the atonement are not altered. When one goes the other will go with it.' And what is the fact? Find those who most deride the idea of an awful doom awaiting the sinner, and you will find those who rob the cross of Christ of its sacrificial element. If there was nothing much to save me from, it was almost superfluous for an incarnate God to die upon the tree.'[8]

'Preach the atonement', Brown would urge his brethren, that is, show how God can now forgive sin in a manner

---

[8] 2 Peter 2:6, February 24, 1878.

consistent with his holiness and justice, because Christ has been 'made the sin[-bearer] for us' (2 *Cor.* 5:21). It is because the believer is judged in the person of Christ that he is 'redeemed . . . with the precious blood of Christ' (*1 Pet.* 1: 18-19). Unless the justice of God in the punishment which Christ bore is recognized, the gospel is reduced to a vague message about forgiveness. The truth is far more wonderful. As Brown said of Bill Sykes: 'His trust, his hope for himself and others, was all wrapped up in "that little bit" about Christ's substitution. Of course, Bill did not use so long a word. He trusted in the fact if he did not know the term. "Christ taking my sins and having my punishment", was his way of putting it.'

There is another element in apostolic preaching that was also to be found in Archibald Brown. Love brings urgency into the presentation of the gospel; it must seek an immediate response from hearers. To impart teaching is not enough, there must be directions for action. Just as Peter commanded the cripple at the Beautiful Gate of the Temple to 'Rise up and walk', so people are to be called on in Christ's name to rise:

> It is not for us to be dealing in mere explanations with sinners. I believe Christ's church has to go out, and in her Lord's name command them to believe. 'This is his commandment, that we should believe on the name of his Son, Jesus Christ' (*1 John* 3:23). 'God now commands all men everywhere to repent' (*Acts* 17:30). When we go forth as the King's servants, commanding obedience in the name of the Lord Jesus Christ, we shall find that the rebels will begin to ground their arms. I believe that the secret of weakness with many of us in our work for Christ is that we talk about a name which we do not dare actually to employ.[9]

[9] Acts 3:16.

Brown was constantly setting out in simple and direct terms what a sinner must do. For example, concluding a sermon on the word 'Amen', he addressed the unconverted in these words:

You must acquiesce to the position God gives you—lost, guilty, under judgment. Do you take the position assigned to you? When are you going to bow the head and say, 'Amen', to it? . . . What is the next step? The sweeping away of all supposed human ability. 'Not of works.' The humble soul says, 'Amen, O God' . . . The third step is this: God says, 'Sinner, in my covenant of salvation I have put the whole of your salvation in the person of my Son Jesus Christ. Any acceptance can only be an acceptance in him. It pleases my sovereign will to entrust the whole of your salvation in the person of my Son. The simple acceptance of my Son is the one condition on which I save you.' I wonder if any man or woman will bow before that word, and say, 'Amen.' If so, you are a saved man. Drop all your false pride and dignity and bow and say, 'Amen, O Lord.'

Without question, Brown's usefulness was connected with the manner in which he pressed home the gospel appeal. His question for the unconverted was, 'Are you willing to be saved in God's way?' This did not mean he was ignoring other truths, rather that there is a right sequence to learning saving truth.[10] So while urging that question, he might interject, 'We are not going into the question of how you are made willing' (that would come later), for the moment the need was to press home the truth that Christ receives all who are willing. 'Jesus Christ says, "Whosoever will, let

---

[10] 'Let a man go to the grammar school of faith and repentance, before he goes to the university of election and predestination.' *George Whitefield's Journal's* (London: Banner of Truth, 1960), p. 491.

him." Let him do what? "Let him take of the water of life freely."[11]

Brown was at the height of usefulness while still in his twenties. That could never have been if God had not given to him a true sense of what preaching the gospel means. He was only twenty-nine when he said:

> It is a vast mistake to imagine that any bungler can do God's work. The soul is too delicate a thing to be mauled about by an unthinking man. The spirit is too sensitive to be dealt with otherwise than with the greatest care. Soul winning is a holy art, and he had need to study the soul well who thinks of trying to capture it for Christ. Merely hurling texts at the heads of hearers is not likely to result in any great blessing. Nor must all be treated alike. The thunders of the law necessary in one case would be perilous in another, and the gentle wooing successful in one would be like oil on a granite slab in another. No profession on earth needs more skill than does the right sowing of the seed of the Word. Souls are fearful things to be mistaken about.[12]

*　*　*　*　*

I turn now to how this grace of the Holy Spirit affects a congregation. Where the love of Christ is present, Brown believed, it comes down like the dew of Hermon on the people, and a first consequence is unity. The closer believers are to Christ, the closer they are to one another. From the day of Pentecost, unity is the mark of every thriving church and it was at the East London Tabernacle.

---

[11] *God's Full-Orbed Gospel*, p. 80.
[12] Isaiah 32:20, January 18, 1874.

Further, just as the believers saw in their leader that love is no passive grace, it made them a working church. One consequence of every revival is the supply of Christians ready to be 'workers'. In our own times it seems inconceivable that a large church could operate with no paid staff except the pastor and perhaps a caretaker. But at Stepney the workers needed readily came forward: seventy Sunday School teachers; a thousand who went visiting every Sunday afternoon; and others who took a special interest in the infirm and the distressed. Such a church needs little organization. Love leads to spontaneous action. Just as Mary found her own service in the ointment she poured on Christ, so love will always find a way to work. Brown referred to one means the people used, when he said in 1876, that '14,000 tracts and 16,000 sermons had been circulated in the immediate neighbourhood of Stepney Tabernacle'. In the sermon already quoted on 'Supreme Devotion', he said:

> Mary came to the conclusion that there was no reason why she should not find out for herself a way of doing good. Oh, if only God's church were filled with love, what wonders we should behold! We want a little more original action. God's church wants original preachers—original givers—those who do not always give exactly the shilling at collections. The church wants a number of original workers—those who will not merely run in the rut that is already made in the road, but strike out for themselves some new ways of honouring Christ . . . O, my Lord, let me be swayed by love, ruled by love, inspired by love, until I come like Mary, with my all in my hands, and break every alabaster box I possess that thy dear head be anointed.

Different although avenues of service may be, his emphasis was that they should all terminate in speaking of Jesus

Christ, and serving him. House visitation was not in order to bestow gifts 'as a bribe to make men religious'. Such policy he denounced: 'I believe whole neighbourhoods have been cursed simply by visitors never going to speak a word about Jesus Christ, or about the soul, without accompanying it by a gift.' The church did not need 'silver and gold' in order to see conversions. That lack was no hindrance to Peter and should not be for the witness of any Christian: 'Rest assured that if you are living in vital union with Jesus Christ you are carrying about with you a power for blessing, incomparably greater than could be bought by all the wealth of the Bank of England.'

In apostolic evangelism the church herself is the centre of influence. Paul said of the believers at Thessalonica, 'From you sounded out the word of the Lord not only in Macedonia and Achaia, but also in every place your faith to God-ward is spread abroad' (*1 Thess.* 1:8). So also from Stepney, news of the believers was heard in Bethnal Green, Whitechapel, and Shadwell. Preaching on how the work of God draws attention to itself, Brown took the text, 'As I live, saith the Lord, thou shalt surely clothe thee with them all, as with an ornament, and bind them on thee, as a bride doeth' (*Isa.* 49:18). The text speaks of the church as a bride, unadorned at the time the prophet spoke, but yet to be dressed in jewels, glittering with converts from all parts of the world. This led him to the theme that converts are the true ornament on which the eyes of men 'are sure to be rivetted'. 'I know of no spectacle out of heaven more matchless in beauty than a collection of God's saints':

> An unornamented church is a powerless one, let it be rich in money or richer still in its vaunted respectability. No church can do without her ornaments. Everything in the

long-term will fail if they be wanting. A church without her ornaments may dwell in a neighbourhood for fifty years, and yet remain unknown save to a few. Ask a policemen whereabouts Bethesda Chapel is situated, and he will say, 'I am sure I don't know, for I never heard of it.' Of course not, the church has no ornaments, and therefore attracts no attention. But let that church have a revival, and let young converts be continually added to her fellowship, and the neighbourhood will soon learn her whereabouts. Converted sinners are the best advertisements in the world for a place of worship.

The application followed: 'Each one of us may help to adorn the bride.' Let the Sunday School teachers find 'young ornaments, diamonds for Christ', among their pupils. Let all come and seek to be the means of 'picking up some jewel right out of the dirt and dust and rubbish of the world, and hanging it on the Lamb's bride'.

The church at the East London Tabernacle certainly drew attention. Even the local authorities noticed that at the Saturday night prayer meetings the aisles were dangerously crowded with the goods of shoppers, and an order was placed against the space being so used. At the first anniversary of the new building, in February 1873, it was said that about 3,000 people crowded the Tabernacle on successive Sunday evenings, 'hundreds being unable to gain admission'. In the previous year 270 new members had been received, the majority with no previous Christian interest. Pike believed 'the conversions averaged one a day since the place had been opened.'

Among his people at the East London Tabernacle, Brown became known affectionately as 'AGB' and for a number thereafter so it remained. It may be that the attraction to his initials was connected with an incident reported from his childhood. It is said that one day a nurse, with perhaps justified impatience at his endless talking, declared that AGB, stood for, 'A Great Bore'. No, replied the youngster humorously, 'A Great Blessing'. Whether this incident was known or not by his church, it was certainly true that a phrase that had meant nothing to him at the time now meant much to thousands.

5

FAMILY PARTINGS

Grave of AGB's wives, Annie and Sarah,
in the City of London and Tower Hamlets Cemetery.

On TUESDAY, MAY THE 5th,

AFTER A LONG SEASON OF INTENSE SUFFERING,

ANNIE,

THE GENTLE, LOVING, WIFE OF

ARCHIBALD G. BROWN,

FELL ASLEEP IN JESUS.

"And God shall wipe away all tears from their eyes; and there shall be no more death, neither sorrow, nor crying, *neither shall there be any more pain;* for the former things are passed away."

My rest is in heaven, my rest is not here,
Then why should I tremble when trials are near?
Be hush'd my dark spirit, the worst that can come
But shortens thy journey, and hastens thee home.

It is not for me to be seeking my bliss,
Or building my hopes in a region like this;
I look for a city that hands have not piled,
I pant for a country by sin undefiled.

Afflictions may press me, they cannot destroy,
One glimpse of His love turns them all into joy;
And the bitterest tears, if He smile but on them,
Like dew in the sunshine, grow diamond and gem.

Let doubt, then, and danger my progress oppose:
They only make heaven more sweet at the close:
Come joy or come sorrow, whate'er may befall,
An hour with my God will make up for them all.

A scrip on my back, and a staff in my hand,
I march on in haste through an enemy's land;
The road may be rough, but it cannot be long,
And I'll smooth it with hope, and cheer it with song.

Cover of Funeral Sermon for Annie.

AFTER the service at the opening of the new Tabernacle in February 1872, a reception was held presided over by Mr Brown, senior. His son said of him, 'If ever my father had his heart in anything, it was in this place. As my friend, Mr Spurgeon told me the other day: "If ever I saw your father depressed, I had but to talk of the work in the East of London, and he was right directly."' The father was present again for a Monday night prayer meeting in July 1872, and of their conversation on that occasion Archie noted, 'I never saw him in apparently better health, or in a happier frame of mind. With a smile on his face, he said, "I have been thinking, Archie, that I may as well pay you what I owe you towards your Tabernacle. You had better take the cheque while you can get it; for one can never tell what will happen."'

A few weeks later John Brown was in his city office as usual, and in the afternoon went on to see a match at the Oval, already the leading cricket ground in South London. On leaving home that Thursday morning he had told the family cheerfully, 'I shall not be back till late this evening, so none of you need stop in.' At the match, however, he was suddenly taken ill with paralysis and taken home to Brathay Lodge. Only Elizabeth Guess, the housemaid who had been with them for twenty years, was in. His wife and three of the young people of the family were at Spurgeon's Tabernacle for the mid-week service, while daughter Eleanor and son Edward were at a meeting of Arthur Blackwood's at Streatham. On Emma Brown's return at 9 p.m. she found her husband lying speechless on a sofa in the library. For six weeks, while sympathetic visitors, including Spurgeon, came to see him, no word was spoken by the sufferer and he was totally unable to convey his thoughts. Among the family's many prayers, was the united plea, 'Lord, grant that before he dies he may recover speech.' It was answered and yet not as they had expected. As Archie Brown was to tell his people:

> It was on Wednesday night, just as my beloved mother was rising from her knees after praying by his bedside, that the tongue which had been dumb for six weeks began to speak as clearly as it had ever spoken through life. He said, 'In the name of Jesus Christ.' Thinking it must be a dream more than anything else, she drew near the bedside, and then again she heard his voice as clear as possible, saying 'Precious Jesus! Blessed Saviour! With thee soon. With thee where thou art. Peace, peace, peace; and then, Rest, rest, rest.'
>
> We tried to see if he was conscious of our presence. No, he was dead to the outside world. No pressure of the hand received any answer. His spirit was already dwelling in another world. 'Hear his praises, hear his praises', said the dying one! Then came the closing words, 'With Christ! With Christ! With Christ.'

John William Brown died a little before midnight the following day. His youngest son, Edward, then twenty, wrote of it many years later: 'He departed right gloriously to be with Christ on the 15th August, 1872, aged 57 years. Our father was a most just and upright man, a good father with no thought beyond our mother and ourselves. The true work of grace broke forth in a glorious sunset. We marvelled at his rejoicing home-going, though unconscious of our presence.'[1]

This event was followed by many changes in the circumstances of the Brown family. According to the father's will, Brathay Lodge, the home for twenty-one years, had to be sold as part of the division of his estate among his children, his wife also (in the words of her daughter Mary) 'was left very comfortably off'. A note in Archie Brown's preaching record, notes that he did not preach at the mid-week service on Thursday, February 27, 1873: 'I was helping mother to move from Clapham Park.' All the family, except Archie, being still at home, another good-sized house was needed and they moved to 6 Angel Terrace, which was 351 Brixton Road. But within a few years all was changed again as three of the daughters, and sons Edward and John, married, leaving only Mary at home with her mother.

In a family record for his children, written many years later, Edward, Archie's brother, wrote: 'These marriages so altered the home that your Grandma felt she would rather have a smaller house, and so in 1877 there was the removal to the house which you all know so well, *viz.*, 20 De Crespigny Park, Denmark Hill, and which you will always associate as Grandma's House. You know how you dear grandchildren were always so lovingly welcomed by her. You never came too often and were always received with the most bountiful hospitality.'[2]

---

[1] In the *S&T*, 1872, p. 435, Spurgeon wrote: 'We have been deprived of the aid of another deacon this month — *viz.*, Mr John Brown. Thus, one by one, our dear fellow helpers are removed.'

[2] The location of the home where Mrs Brown, senior, lived until her death in 1893, was chosen with regard to the home of daughter Eleanor at 64 The Grove, Camberwell. Eleanor and Emma married two brothers, John and Alfred Wilson.

* * * * *

We could wish we knew more of Archie and Annie's family life at Stepney. That it was a happy one, that six children were born to them, that they had occasional holidays in such places as the Lake District, and once on the Continent, is, however, almost all we know. No record has survived of the account he gave to his congregation at Stepney Tabernacle of four weeks spent in Austria, Switzerland and Italy in July 1871. But a letter, and short references printed in his sermons, underline how the weeks had deepened their thankfulness for the Reformation in Britain. 'Whilst I am writing these lines to you', he wrote in the letter of Sunday, July 16, from Trento, 'you are doubtless found in some sanctuary endeared to you by a thousand beloved recollections. Not so is it with me. The churches are Roman Catholic—priests abound—and in every street crucifixes and figures of the virgin are to be seen.' They saw the majestic cathedrals of Cologne and Milan, 'the peerless churches of Venice', 'and it left them with a sickening desire for something that spoke to the heart as well as captivated the eyes. No brick, no wood, no stone, no marble, however lavish the skill spent on them, can ever constitute the beauty of the sanctuary in the eyes of the saint.'

Only when they reached Lucerne were they able to attend a Protestant service, organised by the Free Church of Scotland.

> The service was held in a Roman Catholic church—the use of which had been in some manner secured—the altars were all covered up with red baize and the place made to look as plain and as Christian as possible. The service was commenced by the minister giving out that well known psalm, 'All people that on earth do dwell, Sing to the Lord with cheerful voice.'

The precentor being absent, one of the congregation at the request of the minister started the singing. The tune was the 'Old Hundredth'. Some perhaps may smile and think I was rather effeminate when I tell them that after a few bars had been sung, my voice failed me and I felt as if I must weep. That simple song of true praise did what all the peals of the cathedral organs had failed to do. The change was so great—the worship so simple—God so manifestly present. Lucerne will long linger in my memory as the place where I learnt how beautiful the place of true worship is to the child of God.[3]

Annie Brown was not long to be found worshipping in the new East London Tabernacle. By the time the building opened in 1872 she was already ill, and as the Spring of 1874 came, with her last son and future preacher, Douglas, safely born seven weeks earlier, she died at half-past four on the morning of May 5. 'Though everyone knew that she was beloved for her works sake', Pike writes, 'none were prepared for the unparalleled popular demonstration which made memorable the day of her funeral.' A local newspaper reported, 'During nearly six hours of the busiest part of the day the dense crowds filled the capacious chapel, as well as Bow Cemetery, and overflowed into, and completely blocked the leading thoroughfares.' On May 17 her husband preached a funeral sermon from the words, 'And they shall see his face' (*Rev.* 22:4), and before concluding said this about his wife:

The one whom we mourn today was very early brought to a knowledge of the truth. I believe I am right in saying that twenty years have passed by since she made public profession of her faith by obeying her Lord's command for baptism. About the age of fifteen she was brought to Jesus by the

---

[3] 'The First Sermon on Returning Home', Psalm 84:1, August 13, 1871. Further on this subject, see Appendix 3 below.

wife of one who is sitting in one of these galleries this morning. No sooner had she found Jesus than she did what every
saved one ought to do—she went into the work at once. A
more devoted Sabbath school teacher I cannot imagine. Whoever else might be absent, she was always present. Well do
I remember, when I was a fellow-teacher with her, how she
had round about her a class of boys that no one else could
manage.

It was in 1861 that I first knew what her Christianity was
like . . . This morning, I do not only mourn a wife, I mourn
one who was the means under God, of bringing me to a
knowledge of the Lord Jesus Christ. Time rolled on, and it
was in this very month in 1862, that we plighted our love to
each other. In October, 1865, we were married. Only eight
years and a half have passed by since then, and I thank God
that I can bear testimony in his presence that a happier life
was never lived, and a happier home was never found in this
East-end of London.

Let me say a word to young sisters who are here this morning; and it may serve as an example to them. With feelings
that God only knows, I took out a packet of old letters that I
received from her before we were married, and as I read them
through, hour after hour, I was amazed to find (and I press it
upon young sisters present who may be engaged) that I had
not one solitary letter that she ever wrote to me, when we
were engaged, without the word of Jesus appearing in it. No
matter what she might commence the letter about, somehow
or another it was always certain to work round to the dear
name of him whose face she sees.

As many of you know, for the last three years and a half
she suffered with intermittent agony, which came on more
constantly as time progressed, until at last there came three
months of anguish almost without a pause. If ever one went
a rough road to glory; if ever one passed through a burning

furnace into heaven, she did. She had fellowship with the Master in one respect—she knew what tears and groans and piteous cries meant. But now she is at rest. As I marked the anguish that she suffered, I often felt, 'Lord, though it will make an unutterable blank, and though it means the breaking up of the happiest home that mortal man ever had, yet I could thank thee if thou wouldst take her into thine arms, and ease her of her frightful agonies.' She fell asleep in Jesus, as you know, at half-past four on Tuesday morning, the 5th of May. Well do I remember her last words to me as, coming to consciousness at half-past ten on Monday night—after you had been praying for her—and taking me by the hand, she said, 'Well, Archie, we have had a happy life, haven't we?' I said, 'Yes, darling, that we have!' 'Ah!' she said, 'a few years at most, and you and I will see each other again. To me it will seem only like a minute or two, but I am dreadfully afraid it will seem a long time to you. Now I can sing a verse I could never sing before.' I asked, 'What is that?' She answered—

> I have no cares, O blessed Lord,
> For all my cares are Thine.

I marvelled, as I saw not only the conflict, but the complete victory. No cares! Leaving six little ones, and the youngest but seven weeks old, and yet no cares? None! For he whom she had loved many a year had come and put all cares to flight. So there fell asleep in Jesus, the gentlest, the most loving and most self-denying character, that I believe the Lord ever called home. The alabaster box of her poor frame was shivered to pieces with many and many a blow; but the sweet savour of her name this morning fills all the house.

* * * * *

More than a year later Brown believed he was given a second 'help-meet', and mother for the children, in the person of Sarah D. Hargreaves of Liverpool. He was now 31 and she 25. In every way the match with this Christian woman was eminently suitable, but the new joy in the home was short-lived. Sarah died in childbirth, with the baby, on September 20, 1876. At a meeting of the London Baptist Association on 26 September 1876, Spurgeon announced sadly that Brown could not be present 'as he was that afternoon attending the funeral of his wife and still-born baby daughter'. Greatly upheld two years earlier, Brown was overwhelmed by this sudden sorrow. There was no question now of his preaching a funeral sermon. His mother at once took all six children into her care and Archie was desolate. Four days later, as he later wrote:

> Broken with sore grief, I went over to the Metropolitan Tabernacle. I could not preach but I thought I could worship, and how amazed I was to find that he had prepared a sermon on purpose for me. That sermon can be found among his volumes, entitled, 'Why the heavenly robes are white.'[4] As I turned round to come out at the close of the service, there was just one grip of his hand as he said, 'I have done all I can for you, my poor fellow.' I felt he had. I rode home with him that day, and had his loving fellowship as he sat with me during the afternoon.

But there could be no immediate recovery. Spurgeon placed the following paragraph in the October issue of *The Sword and the Trowel*:

---

[4] It was preached on September 24, 1876, and will be found in *Metropolitan Tabernacle Pulpit*, vol. 22, number 1,316. The first sentence reads, 'Our curiosity enquires into the condition of those who have newly entered heaven. Like fresh stars they have lit up the celestial firmament with an added splendour.'

All our brethren will be grieved to hear that our beloved brother, Mr Archibald Brown, of the East London Tabernacle, has been heavily bereaved. His second wife has been taken away, just when she seemed essential to his little ones, and to the church at Stepney. His anguish is most acute, and we invite all our brethren to pray that he may be sustained, and enabled to pursue that wonderful career of usefulness for which our Lord has raised him up.

Sarah Brown was buried beside Annie Brown, and to the recently erected gravestone the words were added:

Also SALLIE, the beloved wife of
ARCHIBALD G. BROWN
For one short year she made him the brightest of homes
THEN FELL ASLEEP IN HER SAVIOUR
SEPTEMBER 20th 1876, IN HER 29th year.

Not until the last Sunday morning in October was Brown able to appear again in his pulpit, and for months to come he had to curtail the extent of his work. But any restriction imposed on him did not last long, for engagements outside his church were soon taken up again. In 1874 he had been appointed to the committee of the London Baptist Association, Vice-President in 1876, and President in 1877 at the age of thirty-two. Far from regarding the position as an honorary title, he proposed that presidents should give leadership in itinerant preaching and the establishment of new churches. Numbers of causes called for his help. In the autumn of 1878 he gave a month to such work in Bedfordshire, Buckinghamshire, and Hertfordshire, preaching twenty-nine times in twenty-four days. A London evening newspaper, commented that Brown appeared to be 'going at it' with 'a forty-parson power'.

Earlier in 1878 he had remarried, his bride being Edith C. A. Barrett. They were to share in seventeen of his hardest-working years and three boys and a girl were added to the already numerous family circle.

* * * * *

The 1870s were a period in Brown's life when the promise, 'He prunes it that it may bring forth more fruit' was being quietly realised. The sorrows through which he passed were not without a purpose. They deepened the sympathy and compassion for what was yet before him. In the words of James Ellis, 'Among the high endowments with which Mr Brown was stocked for his East London ministry may be reckoned his heavy afflictions. Undoubtedly the severity of his trials contributed to the enrichment of his character.'

6

IN THE MIDST OF SORROWS

London homes. *Top:* Interior of a middle class house c. 1871.
Bottom: An Attic occupied by a family of ten, Bethnal Green
c. 1863. *Illustrated Times.*

'The poor of London have no better friend working among them; and although the pastor is still hardly more than a young man, his experience is that of a veteran of long service. The people therefore recognize him as such in a way that we have never seen equalled. If he stands but a few minutes in a street talking with a stray friend of the poorer sort, others will come pouring out of their houses, glad of an opportunity of telling their grievances, or of making known their wants. This phenomenon must be seen to be fully understood and credited.'

G. Holden Pike on
'Pastor Archibald G. Brown in East London',
The Sword and the Trowel, 1888.

THERE were now invitations for AGB to preach from places as far away as New York. Outside the work of his own church, however, his attention came to centre increasingly on the needs of the East End. I have already touched on the deprivation and the chaotic conditions in which large numbers of the population lived; some by their own choice and as the result of drunkenness, others struggling honestly to earn a living, yet with only the pittance to be obtained from what often amounted to slave labour. In a society graded by occupations, the skilled or 'artisan' class, were better off than the 'labourers' and the 'dockers', for whom employment was ever uncertain.

From the outset of his time in Stepney, Brown felt for the conditions around him. If one kept to the main roads, with their well-supplied shops, the district might seem reasonably comfortable. But ragged children standing forlorn and looking longingly in at shop windows told a different story. And behind those roads the scene could change dramatically, as he reminded his hearers in a sermon of 1872. Preaching on the helpless at the pool of Bethesda in Jerusalem, he said:

> You and I need not travel far from where we are to find Bethesda's congregation; go but into the courts and alleys of

this East End, and behold what a multitude of poor haggard pale ones, their hands so thin you can almost see through them, and, what is worst of all, the livelihood of the family depending upon them. Whilst you and I are worshipping here, remember that within ten minutes walk of this sanctuary, in any direction, there are poor dying wretches gasping out their last with hardly a comfort round about them.

I would that we could see more of the poor and penniless helping to fill our sanctuaries. Members of the church I beseech you to hear this word. Whoever else may be overlooked or unnoticed, mind a poor person is not, and whoever else may be left to stand during the service, let it not be such an one. Rather let it be yourself. And whenever you see a man who has unmistakeable signs of more than ordinary poverty about him, let him be the one that has the first grasp of your hand.

Help to the needy was being organised by Brown's congregation in these early years. At the close of a sermon on 'Sow Everywhere' (January 18, 1874), he said: 'A devoted company of brethren and sisters visits 2,900 families every Lord's-day afternoon. During the past year 900 visits have been made, with a view of investigating reported distress, and helping deserving cases.' It was, in part, to find money for such needs that he instituted an annual 'Thanksgiving Day', when he would sit all day in the vestry to receive aid from thankful Christians. Much of this came in penny coins from those whose own means were very limited, and none of the pleasure of the day was lost for Brown by his need to scrub his hands after handling so much grubby metal!

Brown's Thanksgiving Day was the subject of interesting comment in the correspondence columns of *The Times* (Britain's premier newspaper) on June 5, 1879. It came from a Church of England clergyman, who called himself 'An East London Incumbent', who wrote to comment on the words of a previous correspondent on 'the small attendance at churches' in the East End:

> The fact is that the spiritual provision for the East of London has, for a long time, been in the hands of Nonconformists. Chapel after chapel was erected long before the Church awoke to the necessities of the situation. The Nonconformists are masters of the field. Their chapels are well filled. There is a Baptist minister at the East of London who has a congregation of 2,000 persons to listen to him every Sunday morning. If he wishes to raise any money he sits in his Tabernacle early in the morning to receive the offerings of his flock, and such is their enthusiasm that some of them are there with their contributions before the doors are open. He will collect in this way in one day £300. I might sit, sir, in my church until I grew into my seat before my congregation would bring me even £30.

The reader will have gathered from an earlier quotation that Brown was no lover of committees, and he took personal responsibility for the funds thus collected. Given his sacrificial life, no one doubted how he would administer what was entrusted to him. A preacher would be unwise to adopt the same procedure unless his reputation was akin to Brown's among his people. They knew that he lived sacrificially with his own money. At one point the members of the Tabernacle gave him and Mrs Brown a gift of £235, with the wish that they would use it to make a trip to Palestine. Brown told them that, while he appreciated the money, it would be invested and the interest given to the poor.

An incident in 1877 illustrated the same trait. The Brown home suffered a burglary that year and lost a number of valuables. Especially regretted by AGB was the loss of a gold watch chain which was a gift from his father shortly before his death. Of this particular loss, he said, 'It was a bitter pill, but as I did not see the fun of spending a lot of money on another, I have contented myself with an iron one.' He said this after the church had surprised him with the gift of another gold chain.

Supported by aid from Thanksgiving Days, and other sources, Brown organised help for the neighbourhoods to an increasing degree. But the long and severe winter of 1879-80, which multiplied the numbers of the unemployed and the destitute, determined him to a larger effort. The many dockers in the area were especially hurt by hard times. Most of them were employed only by the day, half-day, or even by the hour. They had to wait at the docks to be given casual work, and if trade declined they were among the first to suffer. One eye witness wrote of scenes at the London docks: 'It is a sight to sadden the most callous, to see thousands of men struggling for only one day's hire, the scuffle being made the fiercer by the knowledge that hundreds out of the number there assembled must be left to idle the day out in want. To look in the faces of that hungry crowd is to see a sight that must be ever remembered.'

By 1880 Brown established his own mission and employed two full-time missionaries, the number being increased in the following years to six and then to nine, including both men and women. An intensive system of visitation was begun in the first winter, covering 8,000 houses, including 1,800 containing the sick and dying. Road by road, districts were surveyed, with all kinds and conditions of people and few Christians to be found among them. To spread accurate information Brown began in 1880 to publish an annual Record of

Service which commonly ran to more than fifty pages. In this document he wrote:

> This work has been quite a revelation to us. Being brought into almost daily contact with the poorest of neighbourhoods, we have become acquainted with a mass of misery, want, vice, and filth we had previously failed to comprehend. None can conceive it until they try practically to deal with it. The degrees of poverty and sorrow seem endless.
>
> Sheer want has in many cases stripped the houses as well as the little furniture once in them. Our missionaries have entered homes where banisters have been pulled down for firing, and then the iron stove sold for bread. Men and women who have been worsted in the battle of life, after every effort to retrieve the day; men who walk from morning to night 'seeking a job', until, wet through, they return to a supperless room, sleep in their drenched garments and then lie down for weary weeks racked with rheumatic pains; women who, with their husband in the infirmary, toil at the wash-tub or ply the needle for a wretched pittance, from dawn to midnight; widows who wage heroic battle against overwhelming trouble and pinch themselves to give their fatherless bread. Such cases as these we know by hundreds. Want is the short history of thousands. Their lives consist in 'not having'. The hands want work, the heart wants sympathy, the body wants bread, the mind wants light, the face wants a smile, the spirit wants hope, the nerves want rest, the conscience wants peace, the soul wants Christ.

Careful statistics were compiled on the extent of the destitution. In some districts it was found that out of every hundred families, seventy-five lived in only one room. Sometimes it was worse than that: 'In one room we found a husband and wife and four children; one corner of the room, however, was let out for sixpence a week to a woman and two children.'

In the locality of Bow Common, 36 persons were found living in a seven-roomed house, and 28 persons living in six rooms. In Shadwell 340 rooms contained 260 families. In such slum dwellings, nick-named 'rookeries', privacy was commonly impossible and, with all types of characters thrown together, 'human beings can approximate so nearly to the life of brute beasts without any particular sense of shame'. One publication which had sought information from Brown, reported: '"Marriage, as an institution, is not fashionable in these districts." And this is only the bare truth. Ask if the men and women living together in these rookeries are married, and your simplicity will cause a smile. Nobody knows. Nobody cares. Nobody expects that they are.' The same publication spoke of 'Entire courts filled with thieves, prostitutes and liberated convicts.'

Brown was now in the leadership of a work which would have overwhelmed the average man. It involved an understanding of complex and many sided-problems, untiring energy, management gifts, and caution as well as large sympathy. Caution, because not every situation of apparent need could be taken at face value. In one impoverished home, where help was given, a woman had just wrapped her deceased husband in a shroud on their bed. But as the missionary moved on to another house he recalled he had left his umbrella behind and went back to retrieve it. To his surprise the supposed widow now opened the door with smiling face, and her husband was to be seen walking about the room behind her!

Such cases, however, were by no means the majority, and Brown was early convinced of the danger of using generalisations to explain the conditions. Dishonesty, drunkenness and immorality were certainly to be found, but there were considerable numbers whose situation was not to be accounted for in those terms. He raised his voice to warn, 'In regard to the depressed classes, there has been too much lumping them, and prescribing for them as a mass.' On which statement Holden Pike commented:

> There is an immense class who, as Mr Brown affirms, cannot pay for more than one room, and can only raise that amount of rent with extreme difficulty. These people, in the main, are described as sober; as to industry, they labour incessantly; but their poverty-stricken condition is chiefly the result of fierce competition in an over-crowded labour-market. Under the condition of things now existing the weakest necessarily go to the wall; and, of course, the weakest in this case too often mean the widow and her children.[1]

Pike had long been interested in London's poor and Brown was now the means of deepening his concern. He has written of how, on a winter's morning one February, the pastor of the East London Tabernacle took him to visit in some of the neediest neighbourhoods of the East End. Their first stop was at a half-underground kitchen, 'tolerably clean', which was the home of a young widow, her two young children and a nurse. About a month before, her loving husband had drowned himself in a local canal. She explained, amid tears, that he had employment as a mat-maker until he suffered ill health. Then he could not regain work; demand for mats having fallen since prisons and philanthropic institutions had taken up their production. Distress over unemployment, and fear of being put into a workhouse, had brought on temporary insanity, despite all his wife's attempts to encourage him. Help was now left with her and the parting words, 'Now you want Christ, and he wants you.'

[1] *S&T*, 1885, pp. 20-1.

The next stopping point of the two men was a two-roomed home, one of them with pictures, ornaments, and furniture which suggested once happier days. Here a mother of thirty-three years lived with her five children, and her mother, aged sixty-six. Thirteen years earlier she had met her future husband on an outing to Southend. They married, anticipating happiness and some prosperity, which for eight years they did experience. Then she began to experience an unaccountable pain and sickness. This persisted and came to a head when her husband, about to leave home for a night, with loving words, gave her a cup of 'medicine' to help her. Instead she was violently sick. At last suspicion began to dawn. Finding some gritty substance at the bottom of the cup she had used, she took it to a chemist for analysis. He promptly informed the police of the deadly poison she had been given, and the husband was now in prison for attempted murder. Another woman had caught his fancy.

How many visits Brown and Pike made that February morning is not recorded. Another visitor, taken around by one of Brown's missionaries, was so affected that he was advised 'to see no more today', and told, 'the strongest man can stand no more'. 'I can never become used to it', Brown was heard to say, 'it turns me sick.'[2]

Following that experience with Brown, Pike was to write:

The question is, how is the want to be relieved? How are the poor to be helped, by being taught self-help, without causing them to lose self-respect, and become pauperized? 'It may be a mercy to fling a bone to a dog; but it is not mercy to fling

---

[2] It was literally so, at times. The *Nonconformist and Independent* (April 20, 1882) reported: 'We regret to learn that in consequence of severe nervous depression, which threatens paralysis, the Rev. Archibald Brown is compelled to take several months rest away from his pastorate.'

relief to a man', we are told; so that there must be both love and discrimination. The love of God in the heart of Christian people not only prompts them to do what is needed, but teaches them how to do it.[3]

Brown had learned from Christ that it is not enough to take 'a glimpse of some of London's poverty. He who merely looks at trouble and sorrow, as one of the phenomena of this world, may look long but learn little. It must be felt to be understood. Jesus did not come into this world merely to see sorrow, he came to endure it.'[4] This spirit was found in Brown. As a friend remembered him: 'No one had a tenderer heart; no one could offer thoughts and words of brotherly and sisterly helpfulness, uplifting, sympathy and encouragement than he; and no one could be more frank and outspoken whenever occasion demanded it.'[5]

A visit which Brown made in April 1880 was to have long-term significance for many. He had been asked to see a dying young widow who said she could not die until she saw him. She was—as he was to discover—oppressed by fear for the future of her six month old boy. Standing by her bedside, and looking at young Willie, Brown heard her plead that he would not allow him to be put in the workhouse, 'a school of sin'. It was an appeal the pastor could not resist although he did not know how it could be met. On her death he arranged for the boy to be cared for by neighbours, but this was followed by the conviction that a home was needed for many such boys. This led him to walk the streets looking for a suitable building

[3] Pike, *Brown*, pp. 90-1
[4] 'The more I go in and out amongst the haunts of poverty and sorrow, the more I pity the little lads that are born into it. I do not marvel if they turn out bad. I pity them because from their childhood they breathe an atmosphere of impurity, and oath, and everything that is vile.'
[5] 'More Stories of Archibald Brown,' *East London Advertiser*, June 24, 1922.

to purchase. He had no success but the subject was so much on his mind that he dreamt about it, and in his dream he met a friend who advised him to try Harley Street for the right property.[6] To Harley Street he went the next day and the last but one house on that street was secured as the orphanage. In due course it was to take sixteen boys who were educated for future employment. Although generous help from Christians was often forthcoming, there were occasions of need at the orphanage that Brown did not have the means at hand to meet. One such occasion occurred soon after the orphanage was opened. Brown believed in God's daily providential care, and the fact that it was not his habit to emphasise the extra-ordinary makes the following words the more impressive:

> The first of October set in very cold, and the matron said, 'The boys ought to have some greatcoats, Mr Brown.' I said, 'Go and ask the Lord to give us some.' She looked and said, 'Do you mean that?' I said, 'Yes.' So we just knelt down and said. 'Lord, please send us some greatcoats for these boys. They are thine, not ours.' Now then, scoffer, account for it if you can. That was at three o'clock. At five o'clock that after-noon a messenger came over from the orphan home, saying, 'You are wanted at once.' I went and saw a cab in front of No. 2, Harley Street, and in my unbelief I said, 'Dear me! Is anybody ill, and has the doctor been fetched?' When I went in there was such a scene. There were Scotch tweed coats all over the place. A whole cab-full had been sent. I said to the gentleman who had brought them, 'I have not ordered these. Isn't there some mistake?' He said, 'No, a gentleman came into our place two hours ago (that is the time the matron and I were praying) and said that we were to bring down as

---

[6] The streets and their names are considerably changed in Stepney today. It may be that 'Harley Street' corresponds to the present 'Harley Grove'.

many greatcoats as were necessary to rig out all your boys, and they were to be of the best Scotch tweed.'

The orphanage on Harley Street was only one of a number of relief measures that came into being under Brown's leadership in the 1880s. They included a soup kitchen for the hungry; an orphanage for girls; and a seaside home at 1 Marine Terrace, Herne Bay, Kent, which annually could take nearly 300 guests between spring and late autumn. Those able to afford it paid six shillings a week, while others paid nothing 'and are treated just the same as the rest'. 'Real good has been done to body and soul in this home', Brown reported. Finally, a whole block of buildings was purchased, named the 'Christian Buildings', and opened in 1889. Intended for widows and old couples, it provided twenty-four homes, each consisting of three rooms and a wash-house, which could be rented for two shillings per week.

Each year regular help was given to individuals, which could include (as in 1884), 1,000 pounds weight of tea, over 9,000 loaves, many hundred pounds weight of meat, and quantities of potatoes and rice.

It needs to be said that Archibald Brown was only one of a number of evangelical Christians who were, at this same period, addressing the social conditions in the East End. Another was Thomas Barnardo (1845-1905) who arrived at The London Hospital from Dublin at the time Brown moved to Stepney. The two men became close friends. Instead of becoming a missionary doctor, by the time of his death Barnardo had changed the lives of a quarter of a million destitute children. Others involved in mission work in the East End were William Booth and Frederick Charrington. The smell of burning hops from Charrington's Brewery was commonplace in Stepney. One night in a pub his father owned, Frederick Charrington saw a woman enter with two bedraggled children, and plead with her drinking husband for money to buy food. Instead the man knocked her to the floor. 'The blow which knocked this woman down', the Charrington heir would later say, 'knocked me out of the liquor traffic.' He started Tower Hamlets Mission, and gave a fortune of half a million pounds to evangelical work. Another reforming agency in the district was the work of Henry Grattan Guinness's Institute, already mentioned, which drew many young Christians for service to Christ. With the Guinness parents and family the Browns were to have close relations, for both families were to move to houses on the Bow Road in the 1870s, the Browns at number 22 and the Guinnesses close by at Harley House.

It was the work of these men and women, as well as that of others, that drew the attention of the British public to conditions in the East End of London.[7] Brown's *Record of Service,* which he now published annually, played a major part in awakening concern. The published *Record* for 1883 began with the words: 'Since the publication of our last year's *Record of Service* a mighty tidal wave of sympathy for the abject poor of London has swept over the land. That which was only known to the few has become the theme of many . . . For some years the subject has burned like a fire in our bones, and to the utmost of our ability we have sought to make it blaze to others.'

---

[7] For a wider survey see, Kathleen Heasman, *Evangelicals in Action: An Appraisal of their Social Work* (London: Bless, 1962); John Pollock, *Shaftesbury: The Poor Man's Earl* (London: Hodder & Stoughton, 1986); and, for the valuable work of an earlier social reformer in Stepney, Ian Shaw, *Andrew Reed, The Greatest is Charity* (Darlington: Evangelical Press, 2005).

Leading national newspapers took up the subject, including the *Daily Telegraph*. A reporter from that paper asked for an interview with Brown and found him,

> an active, bright-eyed, wiry, and athletic-looking man, as unlike a Nonconformist minister as anyone I have ever met. His dress showed no signs whatever of his calling. He might have been a banker, or a hard-working solicitor who had been an athlete in his day; but my friend was in reality one of the most popular Nonconformist ministers at the East-end of London, a man of immense nervous energy and vast administrative power, who has a larger practical acquaintance with the homes, the misery, the overcrowding, and the social horrors of the foulest corners of the East of London than anyone who could well be cited. This thorough-going and wholehearted pastor does not believe in doing things by halves.

Many publications and books took up the subject on which Brown had been giving evidence. The Congregational Union published, *The Bitter Cry of London: an inquiry into the condition of the abject poor* (1883). It acknowledged the debt which their investigations owed to the London City Mission, and to 'the Rev. A. G. Brown of the East London Tabernacle and his missionaries'. The years 1883-84 were also marked by conferences attended by a number of ministers, Nonconformist and Church of England, to discuss the issues, and in these Brown played a leading part. At one of these Brown spoke at length on the conditions which some still found hard to believe. Among instances of 'sheer misfortune' and 'cheap labour', he was reported as saying:

> If a woman had nine children under fourteen years of age, and her husband earned on average from fifteen to sixteen shillings a week, he did not think it required much knowledge

of arithmetic to come to the conclusion that there must be a condition of chronic want . . . At the house he visited, he found a hard-working woman who was engaged in finishing moleskin trousers. That woman worked on an average from seven in the morning till nine in the evening, and just managed to earn a shilling a day. He was prepared to prove that there were hundreds and thousands of women whose wage-earning power was a penny per hour. It was all very well to say that the poor were thriftless, but he should be glad if someone should tell him how they were going to save anything out of a shilling earned by fourteen hours hard work. One sentence dropped from her lips that burned into his very soul. She said, 'I have buried eight children, but not one with regret. It is the best thing to happen to children here, to die.'[8]

As to the effect of this state of society upon the young, he had last Saturday night—under a disguise and in company with a member of his congregation, a policemen—stayed till far into Sunday morning in one of the worst parts of London, and had seen how its denizens prepared for the Sabbath. Standing outside some of the brothels—places known to the authorities, be it remembered—he had seen those dens of infamy become like so many bee-hives, little girls of fourteen in many cases entering the houses with men of mature age.[9]

In the conference of 1883, Brown spoke more extensively on what should be the priorities for Christians. He was not in

---

[8] Brown identified the economic problem. The population at large sought cheap goods, and employers responded to the demand by paying wages pitifully low. Among remedies which he encouraged were training in trades, and more emigration.

[9] *Nonconformist and Independent*, April 3, 1884. Of the need that these facts should be known, Brown wrote elsewhere: 'There's a picture of positive misery and vice that ought to be gazed upon, and properly studied. Drawing a curtain over the canvas may save a nervous shock, but removes not one of the lives of shame. Reticence is not a remedy; covering is not cure; silence is no salve.'

favour of some of the methods being used in some quarters to gain the attention of the unchurched:

> The question was, how were the masses, respectable or disreputable, to be brought under the influence of the gospel. With regard to many of the recent answers to that question he had little sympathy and less faith. Evangelistic enterprise was just now in a mad mood and drunken with the wine of a rank sensationalism. It could not, however, last long. In his judgment, no new methods were needed, but new power resting on those they had: the sanctuary for those who would attend, with a consecrated man of God in the pulpit, who, out of a full heart, preached a full-orbed gospel, with trembling tenderness and unflinching faithfulness. Then, in addition, the hall, theatre, and mission room for those whose early prejudices kept them from the sanctuary. And then, beyond all, the house to house visitor.[10] If they were to be reached it must be by going to them. As the result of his practical experience he advocated the multiplication of consecrated, soul-loving, trained missionaries. Of missions they had almost enough, of true missionaries not half enough. 'London for Christ' was a magnificent war-shout but ere it ever approximated a song of triumph, a fearful battle must be fought not only in noble churches, chaste chapels, and spacious tabernacles, but in miserable, little filthy dens, amid nakedness, vermin and vice. To lay hold of the masses they must grapple with their separate families, and grip them one by one.[11]

---

[10] Of this necessity Brown said on another occasion: 'We do not reckon calling at doors anything; that is generally done by tract distributors all over London. We insist by hook or by crook in getting inside the house, and as far as possible leave no room unvisited. Door-to-door work only skims the surface. Our work must be room-to-room. Otherwise a large mass of misery and suffering would never be brought to light.'

[11] *Ibid.*, May 4, 1883.

Not all the ministers and clergy present were in agreement with Brown. The Rector of St George's, Southwark, urged that the style of the services needed to be adapted to 'the spirit of the times'. The Rev. Robert Nightingale wanted 'good music', and 'differed *in toto* as regard house to house visitation'.[12] The Rev. G. S. Reaney of Stepney was still more radical in his criticism of Brown's views. There was not, he said:

> a more earnest man than Mr Brown, nor a more active church than that at Burdett Road, and yet they found that the condition of things under the shadow of his own tabernacle were perfectly appalling. It led them to conclude that the problem they were trying to solve was insoluble, or else that they were altogether out of the way. It seemed to him that they had almost forgotten that that was to a very large extent a social problem. He was impressed with the fact that there was in Stepney a great deal more sorrow than sin, and that it was important to go and heal the sorrowful and comfort them.

It would seem that Mr Reaney was not sympathetic enough to read Brown's *Records of Service*. Had he done so he would have found that the pastor of the East London Tabernacle by no means ignored the social and the economic problems. Only by quoting him out of context could he be represented as teaching only one solution. 'If he knew less', Brown was accurately reported as saying, 'he would be able to answer the questions more easily, but he felt the problem to be awful on account of its depth'. He knew that the social reformer, the

---

[12] Brown did not say that all Christians were equipped for house-to-house visitation. On the contrary, 'With respect to ladies from the West-end coming to visit the East-end, he was afraid that without some training they would be duped wholesale.'

employers, the sanitary inspectors, and others, had all a part to play:

> No body of workers can afford to despise others, or arrogate to themselves the 'patent' for removing the evil . . . We place the gospel agency last, not because we count it least, but the crown on the whole. The people are wrong as well as their houses and circumstances, and nothing can put them right but Christ in the heart.

A gulf was widening at this date between the positions represented by Brown and Reaney. The latter believed that the conditions they sought to change were basically a 'social' problem, and should be addressed, not by traditional Christian preaching, but by organizing and promoting change at the political level. In Reaney's view, the best impetus the churches could give to this was to preach 'the Social Gospel'—a call to meet the human need by social action. Brown disagreed. The calling of the church is defined by Scripture, and concerns the salvation of individuals, not the reformation of society. Certainly love for fellow beings requires Christians to do whatever they can to alleviate suffering and need, and, as citizens to vote for it, but the church, as such, exists for a higher end.

It was on account of this belief that Brown's mission work was not run under the auspices of the East London Tabernacle. Individual Christians supported it, but it was not organised by the church, nor did it become part of its message.[13] The church has a gospel that changes life at the most fundamental level. To replace that gospel with 'the Social Gospel' was to

---

[13] A correspondent in the *East London Observer* (July 10, 1886), wrote: 'The Rev. Archibald G. Brown, of the East London Tabernacle, a few Sunday mornings ago, declared from the pulpit that a Christian minister ought not to preach politics (no doubt a gentle hint for Mr Reaney), but ought to preach the gospel.'

miss addressing the greatest need. For Brown a growing call for 'the Social Gospel' was evidence of declining interest in real Christianity. 'Among the working classes what is known as the Social Gospel has done as much harm as anything. I hate the expression Social Gospel. Sometimes I think it must have been invented by the devil.'[14]

It was true that society could be improved by social and political action, and such efforts had Brown's sympathy, but he knew society could never stay changed for the better apart from new men and women.

> An internal transformation, not an external, is needed to raise men. Change a man's nature, and he will alter his own environment; but if you change his surroundings it does not follow that you will effect a change in him.

He did not believe this principle was invalidated by the existence of true Christians whom he sometimes met among the very poor. He instanced a blind man whose only earnings came from playing a concertina. 'Do you know Christ?' Brown asked him. With a changed look on his face, the man replied, 'Know Christ! I could not live without him.'

While the secular papers were prepared to commend this social work, it was often considered a strange divergence from his creed. For Brown it was to the inspiration of his gospel that all his labours were due. His was not the vague hope of 'changing society'. The vision was for the individual salvation of young and old in view:

> Deeper than all their other needs is their need of Christ and his salvation. Let any man be saved from his sins, and he will be saved from dirt into the bargain. A saved soul includes a

---

[14] *British Weekly*, 1897, p. 157.

saved character, and that leads to new tastes and fresh aspirations. Let no social reformer despise Christian work. While he is busy erecting clean houses, the Christian is busy finding him clean tenants.[15]

[15] *One-Room Life, and A Record of One Year's Service During 1883* (London: Morgan & Scott), p. 15.

7

'OVER THE WATER TO CHARLIE'

Spurgeon preaching at the Crystal Palace, October 7, 1857.

'It has always been my joy and delight to remember that, by the providence of God, my life has been wonderfully inter-woven with that of your Pastor, and also with this Church. It is now some seven-and-twenty years since, as a lad, I used to look forward to my holidays as an opportunity of running up to hear Mr Spurgeon preach at the Surrey Music Hall. I remember that it was with awe and wonderment that I looked at him. Over and over again I felt that I would just give any-thing if he could only know me, and give me one shake of the hand, little dreaming that we would learn to know each other, or that I should ever be allowed to say a few words on behalf of the College at his Jubilee.'

AGB at Spurgeon's Jubilee, June 18, 1884.

IN the early 1950s, when my future wife and I were young Christians, one of our best tutors was a Mr F. J. Hobbs, a native of Gloucestershire, who had a small business as a tailor in the Kilburn district of London, and served Christ from the same premises by his ministry in second-hand books. Once when we were speaking about Charles Haddon Spurgeon, he surprised us by connecting him with the words of this chapter's title. 'Over the Water to Charlie' were part of an old Jacobite song referring to the exiled 'Bonnie Prince Charlie'. What we did not know was that in the nineteenth century the words were adopted by the conductors of horse-drawn trams on a Sunday, to direct would-be passengers destined to the Metropolitan Tabernacle across the river Thames.[1] To us the words seemed a rather disrespectful way of speaking of the great preacher. But another call, our friend told us, was also to be heard, for those who were not crossing London to the

---

[1] I was later to find confirmation of this anecdote in Spurgeon, *Autobiography*, vol. 4, p. 334: 'The conductor of an omnibus, while waiting on the City side of London Bridge, endeavoured to attract passengers by shouting out, "Over the water to Charlie!" A gentleman enquired what he meant by this unusual cry, and he explained that the 'bus was going over the Thames and past the Tabernacle, where C. H. Spurgeon was announced to preach. It happened that the stranger had never heard the Pastor, but he went on that occasion, and for the rest of his life he was a diligent reader of the printed sermons.'

south but to the east. Regrettably the words of this call we cannot remember exactly, but it was something like 'Going East to Archie.' It was with much affection for their memories that Mr Hobbs referred to both Spurgeon and Brown by their Christian names; he admired both and spoke of how he prized Brown's sermons.

When the call of tram drivers united the names of Spurgeon and Brown they were expressing a reality greater than they knew. While the two men's Tabernacles were on opposite sides of the Thames, their work and their lives were one. 'From the time I entered college up to the present moment, I have had no life apart from him.' So Brown could say in 1892.

Something of the closeness of the two will have been apparent from the preceding pages; many were the occasions when Spurgeon came to the younger man's aid, even to the point of preparing a sermon with the particular hope that it might help his friend in the depth of his bereavement in 1876. But the help went both ways. Although Brown was not able to continue writing for *The Sword and the Trowel,* he was one of the first to be called upon when a speaker was needed at the Metropolitan Tabernacle. It was not unusual for Brown to receive letters such as the following:

Nightingale Lane, Clapham, May 23[2]

Dear Friend,

Will you go out with me and others, on June 15, for a week, or two weeks, or three weeks, or a few days, or whatever you like? We feel that we should like your company, and we

---

[2] The letter has no year. It was clearly before August 1880 when Spurgeon moved house to Westwood, Beulah Hill. The best account of these carriage outings into the country will be found in William Williams, *Personal Reminiscences of Charles Haddon Spurgeon* (London: RTS, 1895).

think we might do you good. You are very dear to us; to me especially. We shall be very quiet, and jog along with the old greys.

I pray the Lord to bless and comfort you,

Yours so heartily,

C. H. Spurgeon

Metropolitan Tabernacle, Dec. 22, 1873

Dear Brother in very deed, —

Oblige me by complying with my request—that you do speak here on the evening of January 13, Baptist Association. If . . . you and I have each a good time, we will rouse the brethren. It is all left to me, and I am pressed with work. Say yes. I am giving up two day's holiday to be at this meeting, and pray the Lord it may be a success. — Yours lovingly,

C. H. Spurgeon

The letter found Brown caring for Annie, then seriously ill, and he had to decline. This brought a further note from Spurgeon:

Pray do not take trouble about me. I am so grieved that your wife is ill, and sorry I have asked for more work when you are tied. The Lord bless you and her! — Yours ever lovingly, C. H. S.

The 'Baptist Association' referred to above was the London Baptist Association. As early as 1868 Brown had given a first address to the members of the LBA, printed in *The Sword and the Trowel* of June that year. As already noted, he served as President of the LBA in 1877. Along with other district Associations around the country, this fellowship was linked to the Baptist Union. Spurgeon supported both organisations and would discuss their matters with Brown.

While both men thus served wider Baptist interests, nothing in the way of conferences took precedence for them over the Pastors' Conference, an annual gathering of former Pastors' College students. Brown was closely involved in its meetings. It cannot have been of Brown's planning that an evening public meeting during the Conference of 1877 was held at his church, for this was the period when he was still recovering health. We read: 'The President [CHS] spoke for three quarters of an hour with his accustomed force. He said they were attracted to the East like the wise men; and while the East was the better for having Mr Brown, he hoped Mr Brown would be all the better for being there.' In making the point that preachers can help one another, Spurgeon drew a parallel with a shepherd who once asked another shepherd, 'Lend us a bark of your dog'!

Spurgeon's fiftieth birthday, his 'Jubilee', came in June 1884 and, at the celebration at his church, Archibald Brown, was one of the ones called upon to speak on behalf of former College students. In introducing him, Spurgeon said:

> There are many ministers here tonight whom I should have been very glad to ask to speak, but I cannot go beyond the programme. Nothing gives me greater pleasure than now to present Mr Archibald Brown to you. God bless him for the sake of poor outcast London, and for all that tenderness of heart which he has! Though his sympathy with human misery sometimes brings him very low, it only qualifies him the more for the work to which God has called him.[3]

Spurgeon closely followed his friend's work in the East End, encouraging him and supporting him when he was the

---

[3] R. Shindler, *From the Usher's Desk to the Tabernacle Pulpit: The Life and Labours of Pastor C. H. Spurgeon, Authorized Edition* (London; Passmore and Alabaster, 1892), p. 223.

object of public criticism. The following Spurgeon letter, undated but c. 1876, refers to the beginning by Brown of a local ministers' fraternal in Stepney, and also to complaints published by Spiritualists on his preaching:

> Nightingale Lane, Clapham, January 29
> Three cheers for you, my true-hearted comrade! The story of your East London gathering of the clans fills me with delight. The Lord be with thee, thou mighty man of valour! Whether, in striking the Spiritualists, you are hitting the devil or the donkey, does not matter much; you have evidently hit hard, or they would not be so fierce. I am not able to take much credit for bringing you up, but I am about as proud of you as I dare be.
>
> I hope we shall have a good meeting on Friday week. It is oil to my bones to see you all.

* * * * *

A more serious and prolonged spate of public opposition to Brown in the press came 1888-89 after he had published a booklet entitled *The Devil's Mission of Amusement*. It was a response to a belief, now gaining popularity, that if the churches supplied secular activities and amusements they could better gain the interest of non-church goers. Brown argued that churches that made provision of that kind were contradicting the teaching of Christ and the apostles. He immediately had critics:

> I soon had a choice collection of titles to add to my humble name. I learned that I was 'a morbid pietist', 'a sour bigot', 'a victim of religious melancholia', 'a kill-joy', and 'one whose mental condition must cause deep anxiety to his relatives'.[4]

---

[4] *The Devil's Mission of Amusement, A Sequel, The Former 'Protest' Vindicated*

Brown's case was not against amusement as such; it was against churches substituting entertainment for what Scripture appoints as the work of the church. But this distinction was lost by his opponents. The *Daily Telegraph,* for example, queried 'The Sinfulness of a Country Walk' and 'Lawn Tennis a Short Cut to Perdition'. Frank Ballard elaborated this line of criticism against Brown in a 'brochure' entitled, *Is Amusement Devilish?*[5]

Brown suspected the distinction between amusement and 'the mission of amusement' was being deliberately confused:

> The real fact of the case is, I never dealt at all with amusement in itself, but only with amusement as a mission. This has been conveniently ignored . . . Is Amusement Devilish? is not a question I have ever asked . . . My contention is that amusement pressed into the service of the churches, and adopted as a religious agency, or a means of raising church finance, is a delusion of the Devil. To this I stand. That which is tolerable and allowable under some circumstances is an abomination under others.[6]

The *British Weekly* thought the issue Brown had raised important enough to need attention and it believed that the position of the East-London pastor was being misrepresented. This leading Nonconformist weekly thought there was evidence enough that churches were being drawn into providing amusement, and believed 'it would be a calamity if this course were generally initiated.'

Recent authors have agreed that Brown and the *British Weekly* read the trend correctly in the 1880s. Jeffrey Cox has written:

and Illustrated (London: Morgan & Scott, n.d.), p. 5.

[5] F. Ballard, *Is Amusement Devilish? A Protest against 'A Protest by Archibald G. Brown'* (London: Elliot Stock, 1889).

[6] *A Sequel,* pp. 6-7.

An ardent fisherman, Brown was not really opposed to all amusement, only to Baptist chapels going into competition with music halls. But the contrary view—that everything is religious which is not clearly irreligious—generally prevailed among the ministers and active laymen of the Congregationalists and Wesleyans and even among some groups of Baptists . . . Chapel entertainments became so common that in 1900 the Lambeth Board of Guardians heard complaints from an out-raged ratepayer about the exemption of mission halls from the rate: 'No one will make me believe that such a thing as an entertainment with singers in Highland costume rendering patriotic songs is for religious purposes. In another instance a concert was given in aid of a cricket club.'[7]

Spurgeon, in his review of what he called Brown's 'tract' in *The Sword and the Trowel,* wrote:

This earnest warning ought to be poured like grapeshot upon the enemy, till the Devil is driven to abandon the entrenchments of religious amusement. At present, in many cases, the prince of darkness feels as much at home in the church as in the world, and it is time that something was done to disturb his repose.

Disturbance there certainly was, for by the time the last paragraph was published (March 1889) a larger controversy—the most important of the century had broken upon the Protestant churches. In 1887 Spurgeon had challenged his Christian contemporaries with material based on the conviction, 'A chasm is opening between the men who believe the Bible and the men who are prepared for an advance upon Scripture.' He believed that the inspiration of Scripture, and the finality of Scripture as divine revelation, is foundational

---

[7] Jeffrey Cox, *The English Churches in a Secular Society, Lambeth, 1870-1930* (New York/Oxford: Oxford University Press, 1982), p. 86.

truth: 'Can there be an advance upon a revelation that is complete?' The Bible not simply contains the Word of God, it is the Word of God, and he was convinced that the toleration of preachers within the churches who taught otherwise had reached a point where a clarification of the issue was imperative: 'Between rationalism and faith there is an abyss immeasurable.'

At this date all the Nonconformist denominations professed to be 'evangelical', but the belief that one could be an 'evangelical' without holding to the 'traditional view' of Scripture was gaining wide support. This was the position, for example, of the *British Weekly,* edited by W. Robertson Nicoll (a minister of the Free Church of Scotland). In Nicoll's mind there was no connection between the promotion of amusement by churches (which he opposed) and 'liberty' in interpreting the inspiration of Scripture (which he did not oppose).[8] For Spurgeon and Brown, the two things were closely connected: it was the source of the changed ethos in the churches.

Spurgeon came to the conviction that the Baptist Union could no longer be relied upon to uphold Scripture. He had not come to that conviction hurriedly. Part of his information came from Brown, who, as a former President of the London Baptist Association, was a Council Member of the Union. Spurgeon did not attend Union meetings after 1881, but Brown continued to be present and, after the annual meetings in 1883, he wrote to Spurgeon (October 11): 'The

---

[8] For the influential part played by Nicoll, see Keith Ives, *Voice of Nonconformity: William Robertson Nicoll and the British Weekly* (Cambridge: Lutterworth, 2011). Ives writes that Nicoll's 'contribution was to calm the sense of crisis—albeit in favour of the modernisers—and to reduce the impact of Spurgeon's concerns. Such efforts could never be a true resolution; they merely masked a serious problem, which seemed to be growing steadily worse' (p. 120).

"spirit of the age" seems to have found a welcome in our midst . . . it is the Spirit of anti-Christ.' In a reply to this letter it appears that Spurgeon queried whether his friend was not overstating the seriousness of the situation, and was hopeful that the defection still only affected a small group of men in the Union. In Brown's reply to this he wrote (October 16, 1883): 'I wish I could believe that the spirit of the age has only tainted about a dozen men amongst us. If so they were able to make a wonderful noise in the way of applause at every "broad" statement.'[9]

Spurgeon had to revise his estimate, and by 1887 his mind was made up. His appeal of that year that the Baptist Union should declare its position had no response, the preservation of the unity of the denomination being more especially on the mind of leaders. Convinced that the Union would do nothing, he and his church withdrew their membership on October 28, 1887.

There were some members of the Union who had no great desire to see Spurgeon reconsider. Others hoped that some kind of evangelical statement on the part of the Union would satisfy him. Thus a statement was issued, carrying the signature of three well-known evangelicals, John Aldis, Samuel Angus, and Alexander MacLaren, declaring that disloyalty to Christ and the gospel was incompatible with membership of the Union, and that the Union's insistence on the ordinance of believer's baptism and the Lord's Supper were sufficient safeguards of evangelical orthodoxy. An editorial in

---

[9] The Brown correspondence in this paragraph is now in Spurgeon's College archives, being quoted by Lewis Drummond, *Spurgeon, Prince of Preachers* (Grand Rapids; Kregel, 1992), p. 667, and Mark Hopkins, *Nonconformity's Romantic Generation*, p. 195.

the *Nonconformist and Independent* (November 17, 1887) applauded their words and wrote:

> Their general statement of the beliefs of Baptists ought to satisfy all men who have confidence in the honesty of those with whom they have to deal, and that the adoption of rigid legal lines of definition would drive out the best, the noblest, and the most conscientious men from among them. An Archibald Brown might be retained by such an expedient, but it would probably involve the loss of a Richard Glover[10] . . . Mr Spurgeon and those who follow him seem to be intent upon accentuating the differences of Nonconformists, instead of seeking to draw nearer to each other by unity with their Lord.

This newspaper's words on 'rigid lines of definition' refer to the hope shared by Brown and others that a definite creedal basis for membership in the Union would bring about the division for which Spurgeon had called. A call for such a basis became the main issue of discussions which continued through 1888. At the Baptist Union Assembly, April 27, 1888, a resolution was near-unanimously passed that seemed to satisfy both sides, including as it did a creedal statement. What was not seen at the time by those on Spurgeon's side was that a preamble to the resolution took away any possibility that the creedal statements could be used to remove any members of the Union.[11] The same ploy was to be used again.

---

[10] Richard Glover was a leading Baptist minister in Bristol. On a book by Glover, first given as lectures to students at Regent's Park College, Spurgeon wrote in *The Sword and the Trowel,* that it contained 'a tincture of a spirit to which we are diametrically opposed. Where there is a chance at having a poke at Calvinism, or the Puritans, it is ingeniously used; and indirect slurs are cast upon the old theology, which are more dangerous than distinct attacks.' *S&T,* 1888, p. 557.

[11] I have written at more length on the Down-Grade Controversy in *The Forgotten Spurgeon.* The only inaccuracy known to me in my earlier account lies in my use of words of Henry Oakley which described the Assembly decision of April 27, 1888.

As a follow up of the same subject, and with, it was said, 'to win back, if possible, a beloved and honoured brother without the sacrifice of a principle', a special meeting of the London Baptist Association was held on September 25, 1888. It had before it a resolution from Dr F. B. Meyer, which sought to mediate between the two main parties in dispute. He believed that anyone defecting from evangelical truth should be dealt with personally in their churches, and gave four reasons against the need for a creedal statement: (1) Because the bond of union between Christians is rather a common life in Christ; (2) Because creeds have notoriously failed in excluding error from the churches; (3) Because the adoption of a creed is alien to the spirit of the Free Churches, which depend on the presence and operation of the Divine Spirit for the maintenance of their purity; (4) Because it would seem to underrate the sufficiency of Scripture, which is our only guide in all matters of faith and practice. He spoke against those who would impugn another man's orthodoxy without well-based charges, claiming, 'If we were to insist upon it that these charges should be made face to face with the man against whom they are made, a great deal of our present difficulty would be removed.'

An amendment calling for a statement of the leading truths intended by the words 'evangelical sentiments' was defeated by 113 to 86. But after much debate, another amendment, asking for a special committee to prepare a declaration on the

---

Although present at that Assembly, Oakley was writing from memory forty-six years later, and was wrong in representing all who supported the resolution as consciously voting against Spurgeon. With the help of documentation not earlier available, Mark Hopkins has now given a full account of that event, and has pointed out how, to the last minute, confusion existed over the resolution presented and passed on April 27. Spurgeon commented: 'We are sold, not betrayed, but entrapped by diplomatists.' Hopkins corrects other misapprehensions in his book, *Nonconformity's Romantic Generation.*

meaning of 'evangelical sentiment', was attached to Meyer's resolution which then passed by 117 to 59.

The *Freeman* (September 28, 1888), on whom I am dependent for these facts, was unsure how to summarise the meeting. 'What was the result? A compromise? Not exactly.' Whatever it was, the disagreement had been substantial, and Brown had spoken effectively against Meyer's 'no creed' argument. He is reported to have agreed with the resolution,

> until it came to the fourth reason against a creedal basis, 'lest it would seem to underrate the sufficiency of the Scriptures, which are our only guide in all matters of faith and practice'. That proceeded on the assumption that Holy Scripture is a fixed quantity among us. If a man believes in the plenary verbal inspiration of the whole Bible, Mr Brown asked for no other creed. But how could they regard the Bible as a fixed quantity among them in view of Dr Clifford's last published sermon, on the "Battle of the Sacred Books"?'[12] He was prepared to make a distinct charge in respect of that sermon.

If there was any response to these words they are not recorded. If it was not serious error to put Scripture alongside other divine 'revelations', as Clifford had openly done in that publication, words had lost all meaning. But Dr John Clifford was President of the Baptist Union in 1887, and could the disciplining of such a man be contemplated?

---

[12] The *Freeman*, September 28, 1888. John Clifford's sermon was preached, and published in twenty-eight pages, in the summer of 1888 (London: Marlborough). He refused to accept any 'theories' on the authority of Scripture, asserting, 'Our trust is in a living Leader; not in a book.' Among other 'sacred books' he named the Koran which 'owes its spiritual wealth to Moses and to Christ', although, regrettably, Mohammed 'emphasized the more harsh and stern elements of the earlier Hebrew conceptions of God.' Yet while Clifford was thus upholding 'the faith', he could say of Spurgeon, 'It pains me exceedingly to see this eminent "winner of souls" rousing the energies of thousands of Christians to engage in personal wrangling and strife.' Pike, *Spurgeon*, vol. 6, p. 297.

Contrary to the criticism that men on Spurgeon's side supported vague allegations, Clifford was proof enough that the division among them was over Scripture itself. For Clifford, the Bible, however praiseworthy, was only one of the 'sacred books'. Christians, he held, were not in possession of any exclusive saving revelation.

For Brown, a true creed does the opposite of impinging on the sufficiency of Scripture; it unites brethren in truths taught by that revelation, and distinguishes them from teachers who falsely appeal to it. 'But why', it was objected, 'have a creed if they are not always effective?' For the same reason that laws against theft continue even though the practice is not stamped out. 'No laws' would be a charter for thieves, and 'no creeds' is commonly a charter for errorists.

The follow-up special assembly of the LBA, required by the amendment, took place on October 16, 1888, preceded by meetings of the committee that had been appointed. Brown was one of the members of that committee. The two hundred pastors, and others, present at Maze Pond Church, heard their chairman, Dr Underhill, introduce the committee's resolution with much optimism, he,

> beamed benevolently upon the Assembly as he dealt upon the cordiality, the unanimity, and the general brotherly feeling that had characterised the committee meetings. Rev. D. Gracey and Rev. A. G. Brown, it appeared, had lain down in peace with such lions of 'advanced thought' as Dr Clifford and the Rev. T. Vincent Tymms. The report was the unanimous report of the Committee, and, therefore, Dr Underhill hoped it would be received in a liberal spirit, with the least discussion possible.

He was to be disappointed. While Brown had been on the

committee it had been necessary for him to leave before their resolution had been finalised. The wording contained the same prevarication as had been used in the Baptist Union resolution of the previous April. Evangelical beliefs were stated but with the same preamble that excluded them from being made a test of a minister's position. Accordingly Brown and David Gracey (of the Pastors' College) moved an amendment to omit the preamble. They claimed a statement of faith was necessary 'to enable us to affirm our allegiance to those views in recognition of which our association was founded, and to express our opinion that no pastor who is disloyal to them should continue associated with us'. Not surprisingly, the 'advanced thought' men were opposed to any such amendment. Clifford complained that 'there were some who were determined to have a creedal basis at all costs'. Regrettably, Clifford's party had the support of evangelicals such as F. B. Meyer, who were against authoritative creedal statements.

The *Nonconformist and Independent,* reporting this meeting, accused Brown of 'wonderful fickleness' turning against the resolution of his own committee, ignoring the fact that he had not signed the resolution. By proposing an amendment, they alleged he had gone back on what he had agreed: 'Such conduct on the part of such men', it commented, 'constitutes an inexplicable psychological problem.' The truth was rather that 'dubious ploys', as Mark Hopkins has said, belonged to the other side, and he quotes *Word and Work* which believed: 'The ruling desire was compromise. The aim of the majority was, not to find exact words to express a definite orthodox faith, but rather to discover language plastic enough to cover antagonistic beliefs.'[13]

---

[13] Hopkins, *Nonconformity's Romantic Generation*, pp. 214, 222. There appears to be no record, apart from contemporary newspapers, of this controversy in the

The amendment, supported by Brown and Gracey, was defeated by 101 to 77. 'The result will be', wrote the *Nonconformist and Independent*, 'that the party of the Rev. D. Gracey and Rev. Archibald Brown will withdraw. Mr Brown announced his own and his church's withdrawal on the spot.'

Some members of the London Baptist Association, notably Dr Angus, Principal of Regent's College, thought the division was based on misunderstanding, and he corresponded with Brown accordingly. 'It becomes extremely difficult', Angus pleaded, 'to meet the convictions of hearts equally evangelical in their faith.' A further Association meeting was held on January 8, 1889 which attempted yet another declaration of the meaning of 'evangelical sentiments'. But it was of no avail. The main issues remained as they were, and the now-larger majority had no intention of allowing any action that would regulate the membership. 'The declaration is all very well', Spurgeon commented, 'but ask if it means anything. Would it prevent anyone from coming in and abiding in?' In a statement of his resignation from the LBA, Brown said,

> I feel we have had a fair battle. There has been a fair trial of strength on both sides. We have been beaten. Let us accept the result like men, and not keep on trying to get by other means what we could not get by fair battle. I accept the verdict of the Association; I can say it with real, genuine love that, as a member of the Association, I now bid you farewell.[14]

Given the confusion in the discussions among pastors, it is no surprise that it was equally present in the Christian press.

London Baptist Association. W. Charles Johnson, *Encounter in London, The Story of the London Baptist Association 1865-1965* (London; Carey Kingsgate, 1965), barely touches on it.

[14] Pike, *Brown*, p. 109.

The *Christian World*—no friend to the old faith—was ready to admit that a change in the 'gospel' preached was necessary and, in response to Brown's case against church-provided amusements, deployed the argument that it was the failure of just such preaching as Brown's that necessitated the need for a new approach to attract the masses! The measures to gain the younger generation were needed because

> what is called the gospel has lost its hold . . . And if so, have earnest Christian workers, such as Mr Brown, ever seriously asked themselves whether the responsibility for this deplorable fact may not largely rest upon themselves? If men do not 'relish' their 'gospel', is it all the fault of the hearer, who, having tried it, turns wearily away?[15]

The *Christian* saw it very differently. It drew attention to the LBA meeting of September 1888 where one of the speakers—claiming to be 'one of the evangelical brethren in the London Baptist Association'—professed to believe 'the moral theory of the atonement' (over against Christ's substitutionary death), and in 'the larger hope' (over against the finality of condemnation for those who die without faith in the Saviour). The paper commented:

> Certainly neither of these would have been accepted twenty years ago as being within a hundred miles of evangelicalism. And in our judgment they are not admissible for a moment in any right definition of this venerable term . . . In some respects, this cleavage is to be regretted; but if there cannot be honest agreement in doctrinal views, it is surely better that all should be free to do their work untrammelled by hampering associations.

[15] Pike, *Brown*, p. 106.

The *Methodist Recorder* took the same position:

> No one who knows the East London Tabernacle and the gracious work it is doing, can fail to regret deeply that this step should have become inevitable. It is a time of sorrow, alike for the Association and for Mr Brown . . . For conscience sake he has elected to withdraw. His people are with him. And we, as Methodists, cannot but approve his action, sorrowfully as we may deplore its necessity.[16]

Spurgeon's place and motives in the Down-Grade controversy have been largely discussed. Men critical of him at the time, and since, have traced his 'pessimism' to his ill health. It is an interpretation that in no way accords with the facts. His book, *Cheque Book of the Bank of Faith,* was written at this very period and abounds in words of hope and comfort. But his health came into it, although not in the manner his critics suggest. By 1888-89, although still only in his mid-fifties, Spurgeon was battling serious physical problems. F. W. Boreham, who first heard him at this time, says 'he invariably moved about the pulpit leaning heavily on the table, the rail, or some other support.' The times when he could not be in his pulpit now increased. This led him to want to concentrate all the strength he had left on the work of his church and its agencies. He saw his responsibilities as more than enough without taking on what he believed was the futile work of trying to reform the Baptist Union or the LBA. His withdrawal, he hoped, would set him free from any further duties in that direction. Even so, the burden of the general defection was exceedingly heavy for him and with Brown he was drawn, in the latter's words, 'yet more closely together'.

---

[16] Quoted in Pike, *Brown*, p. 110. Sadly, Methodism was to follow in the same track, as I have written in 'The Holy Spirit and Scripture', *Wesley and Men Who Followed* (Edinburgh: Banner of Truth, 2003).

When it became apparent in 1887 that some of the men of his own College were being influenced by the new thought, Spurgeon terminated the annual Pastors' College Conference, and re-established it, inviting to it only those willing to endorse a creedal statement.[17] Brown spoke at the conferences in 1887, 1888, and 1889. The conference subject for one day in 1889 was on 'The Holy Spirit in relation to our Service'. Spurgeon spoke first, with such evidence of the presence of the Spirit of God, that a student reported,

> We bowed our heads and worshipped. Some of us felt when the President sat down, that we might have closed the meeting then. Still, we were glad the Conference continued. Pastor A. G. Brown was the first speaker after the President. We were very receptive at the time; but had we not been, his remarks would have stirred us. He raised a high platform for us when he said, 'We have to perform our service in the same Spirit in which our Lord worked, and our measure of power will be according to the measure of Christ's Spirit which we possess.'[18]

For the further strengthening of fellowship a new fraternal was also formed at this date; the first meeting met in the vestry at the Metropolitan Tabernacle, and thereafter in different manses. Spurgeon called this 'the Whitey-Brown brotherhood because of the active part taken by these two brethren in its initiation and development'.[19] At the outset thirty men signed a confessional statement, the list being headed by the names of Spurgeon and Brown.

---

[17] Pike, *Spurgeon*, vol. 6, p. 297-8, gives an unsatisfactory notice of this event, as he does also of the whole Down-Grade controversy. Doctrinal issues were not his realm. For Spurgeon's view of the changed conference, see *S&T*, 1888, p. 314, and *Autobiography*, vol. 4, p. 332.

[18] *S&T*, 1889, p. 285.

[19] Spurgeon's *Autobiography*, vol. 3, p. 132. The words must come from Joseph Harrald who was one of the founding members. 'Whitey'= Frank White.

Letters which passed between the two men at this time included the following from Spurgeon: 'They will not define evangelical doctrine, and that is all that is wanted. Let us go together in this thing till we die.' 'I have no care for myself. I care not for reputation, but if the truth of God can be helped, then let us go ahead. I heartily value the love of the dear members of the Church at the East London Tabernacle. We march together, and we will shout "Victory" on the other side.' In later years, Brown recalled in a sermon:

> I remember coming over from the East End to 'Westwood' during the Down-Grade controversy. I was sitting with dear C. H. Spurgeon. Post after post had brought in shoals of letters, and one after another had written to say he should not subscribe any more to the College; one after another had withdrawn help, in some cases to the tune of hundreds of pounds a year. I remember that grand man saying, 'Brown, let my reputation go to the dogs if only Christ's truth be maintained.'

In these years Brown several times took his friend's place at the Metropolitan Tabernacle on a Sunday. There is no record of how often this happened, but it included the dates December 16, 1888, and January 12, 1890. When Spurgeon was ill at Menton in February 1891, it was Brown who came to see him. The sufferer wrote home to his wife: 'I am very much better; indeed well. Archibald Brown has been with me for an hour; and the sight of him, and a little prayer with him, have set me up.' Shortly after this Spurgeon was back in his pulpit, but by September 1891 he was again an invalid. Brown took his place on Sunday, September 27, when he read a letter to the congregation from their pastor. It concluded: 'God bless you this day, through my dear brother A. G. Brown. May he be happy in your midst, and may God be glorified. Few men are like-minded with Mr Brown—a brother tried and proved. Peace be to you and your families!'[20]

The following month Spurgeon had to retreat again to Menton, his customary warmer haven in the South of France. His parting words to friends as he left Herne Hill station in South London on October 26 were, 'The fight is killing me.' He was not to return. Among his last letters was one to his old comrade on January 2, 1892:

> Beloved Brother,
> Receive the assurance of my heart-love, although you need no such assurance from me. You have long been most dear to me; but in your standing shoulder to shoulder with me in protest against deadly error we have become more than ever one. The Lord sustain, comfort, perfect you! Debtors to free and sovereign grace, we will together sing to our redeeming Lord, world without end.
>
> Yours most heartily,
C. H. Spurgeon.

News of Spurgeon's death on Sunday night January 31, 1892, reached London the next day. Brown was among the thousands waiting for news. He woke on that Monday, he says, with the text on his mind, 'And the sons of the prophets that were at Beth-el came forth to Elisha and said unto him, Knowest thou that the Lord will take away thy master from thy head today? And he said, Yea, I know it: hold ye your peace' (2 *Kings* 2:3). Speaking on that text the following Sunday morning, he said:

> I did not need anyone to tell me what had happened. A sleepless night had passed, and I arose early to procure the morning paper. Although my heart told me what the tidings

---

[20] Pike, *Spurgeon*, vol. 6, p. 325.

would be. The first newspaper boy I met handed me the paper, and when I saw the short telegram from Menton my lips, as well as my heart, involuntarily exclaimed in the language of the text, 'The Lord has taken away my master from my head this day.' I am not ashamed to acknowledge that for years dear Mr Spurgeon has been my 'master' . . . for the greater part of my life he has been an earthly inspiration. He has been to me a very Elijah, and I have loved in any way possible to minister to him. Our roots have been intertwined for well nigh thirty years. Is it any wonder that I feel almost powerless this morning to think of him as a preacher, as an orator, as an organizer, or as anything except the dearest friend I have ever known.

On Thursday, February 11, 1892, large areas of London stood still as 100,000 people marked the burial of Charles Haddon Spurgeon. It was Archibald Brown who was called on to read the Scriptures at the funeral service at the Metropolitan Tabernacle. His selection of texts, read with brief comment, was unusual and began:

'So Moses the servant of the Lord died there in the land of Moab, according to the word of the Lord' [*Deut.* 34:5-10].

The Holy Ghost evidently counted that to be Jehovah's servant is a higher honour than to be king in Jeshurun. Moses died there where his God took him; in his God's presence, in God's arms . . .

'. . . And there arose not a prophet since in Israel like unto Moses, whom the Lord knew face to face.'

There is this high honour of this man of God; the secret of his power. It was in this that Moses stood unapproached and unrivalled. The Holy Ghost has declared that the grand distinction in his character was that he knew God intimately.

'Behold, this day I am going the way of all the earth . . . Now therefore fear the Lord, and serve him in sincerity and truth' [*Josh.* 23:14; 24:14-16].

If it were possible for our departed Joshua to speak, I believe the words would be these: 'Serve my God, and your God in all sincerity.' As he, our President and Pastor, followed God, so may we follow hard after.

'Now Elisha was fallen sick of the sickness whereof he died. And Joash the king of Israel came down unto him and wept over his face' [2 *Kings* 13:14].

It is well when royalty acknowledges the worth of a faithful prophet in the land.

'And Elisha died and they buried him. And the bands of the Moabites invaded the land at the coming in of the year. And it came to pass, as they were burying a man, that, behold, they spied a band of men; and they cast the man into the sepulchre of Elisha; and when the man was let down, and touched the bones of Elisha, he revived and stood up on his feet' [2 *Kings* 13:20-21].

The influence of a prophet is not ended with his death. When good men die they yet speak, and life springs even from the sepulchre of the consecrated.

'God is our refuge and strength, a very present help in trouble. Therefore will not we fear, though the earth be removed, and though the mountains be carried into the midst of the sea. Though the waters thereof roar and be troubled, though the mountains shake with the swelling thereof' [*Psa.* 46:1-3].

Our Pastor's word to us is, 'Let the worst come to the worst, the children of God should never give way to mistrust.'

'Shall we receive good at the hand of God, and shall we not receive evil?' [*Job* 2:10].

'I was dumb: I opened not my mouth because thou didst it' [*Psa.* 39:9].

A saintly silence. Sometimes it is impossible to say anything that can do good, and one would not, for all the world, say a word that would do harm; we honour God best at these times by silence. Happy the experience which leads the soul to say, even looking at that coffin,

'It is the Lord; let him do what seemeth him good' [*1 Sam.* 3:18].

'For we know, that if our earthly house of this tabernacle were dissolved, we have a building of God, eternal in the heavens' [*2 Cor.* 5:1-9]

The brightest light that can be thrown upon a scene of sorrow, is the light which comes from the promised return of our Lord and Master. Let us read concerning his glorious advent,

'For if we believe that Jesus Christ died and rose again, even so . . .' [*1 Thess.* 4:14-17].

'And John's disciples came and took up the body, and buried it, and went and told Jesus' [*Matt.* 14:12]

This is all we can do.[21]

With these words he quietly turned to his seat, and an eyewitness said, 'A hush, like the hush of the grave, came upon the assembly. Surely the Lord Jesus was not far away.'[22] Brown had already told his people at the East London Tabernacle the

---

[21] The Scripture references, which I have added, were read in full. Also Acts 6:5, 7; 8:2. For unabbreviated record see, *From the Pulpit to the Palm-Branch, including Official Report of the Funeral Services* (London: Passmore and Alabaster, 1893), pp. 192-6. Brown may well have had these texts, or most of them, by memory, and the fact that he saw no need to indicate where they are in Scripture is a reminder that Bible knowledge was more prevalent in congregations than it is today.

[22] *S&T*, 1892 (London: Passmore and Alabaster), p. 150.

previous Sunday, 'Great grief is never great at talking.' As the service ended at 12.30, thirty-nine carriages waited to take the leading mourners to the cemetery at Norwood. In the first of these were Charles Spurgeon Jr, his wife, AGB. At the cemetery 12,000 people waited, and to Brown was given the responsibility of speaking the closing words. For Christians they have to be among the most memorable in the English language. With pauses to restrain his emotion, he said:

> Beloved President, Faithful Pastor, Prince of Preachers, Brother Beloved, Dear Spurgeon—we bid thee not 'Farewell', but only for a little while 'Good-night'. Thou shalt rise soon at the first dawn of the Resurrection-day of the redeemed. Yet is not the Good-night ours to bid, but thine; it is we who linger in the darkness; thou art in God's holy light. Our night shall soon be passed, and with it all weeping. Then, with thine, our songs shall greet the morning of a day that knows no cloud or close; for there is no night there.
>
> Hard worker in the field! Thy toil is ended. Straight has been the furrow thou hast ploughed. No looking back has marred thy course. Harvests have followed thy patient sowing, and heaven is already rich with thine ingathered sheaves, and shall still be enriched through the years yet lying in eternity.
>
> Here, for a little while, shall rest thy precious dust. Then shall thy Well-Beloved come; and at his voice thou shalt spring from thy couch of earth, fashioned like unto his body, into glory. Then spirit, soul and body shall magnify the Lord's redemption. Until then, beloved, sleep. We praise God for thee, and by the blood of the everlasting covenant, hope and expect to praise God with thee. Amen.

AGB speaking at Spurgeon's burial, Norwood Cemetery. Men were asked to wear hats on account of the weather being severely cold.

* * * * *

ADDITIONAL NOTE TO CHAPTER 7

JOHN CLIFFORD 1836-1923

The orthodoxy of Dr Clifford, Baptist pastor in London from 1858, and President of the Baptist Union in 1888-89, was challenged by Archibald Brown, as noted above (p. 136). While Brown's name is unmentioned in C. T. Bateman, *John Clifford, Free Church Leader and Preacher* (London: National Council of the Evangelical Free Churches, n.d. [c.1905]) the criticism that came from him and others is dismissed as the view of 'extremely orthodox Baptists' who 'exhibited too much anxiety to label him with a heterodox label. After all, there were only a handful of them, yet they voted against him' (p. 159). Elsewhere, the same men are described as 'a coterie of somewhat narrow theologians who expected every man to express their shibboleths and closed the doors of their tabernacle against him' (p. 334).

But Spurgeon's reputation was still too high to be dealt with in this fashion. Instead we are assured both by Bateman and W. R. Nicoll (in his introduction) that Spurgeon 'declined to rank Dr Clifford among the heretics', and thought his evangelical beliefs impeccable. The truth is that Spurgeon wrote of Clifford as putting himself among heretics: 'Well might the Union resent our complaints against its more obscure wanderers, when its President, before he closed his year of office, would thus publicly associate himself with the deniers of our Lord's divinity. Has the body of Baptists over which this gentleman presides become so easy-going and docile that it will by its silence endorse the action of its President?' In a follow up to this, Spurgeon accused supporters of Clifford with misrepresentation (See *S&T*, 1889, pp. 244, 297).

Clifford typified the change taking place in Nonconformity, with its claim to represent 'living Christianity' and not 'dry theology'. A formulating principle of the new belief, namely, the theory of evolution, did not come from the Bible at all, and blinded many to warnings of Scripture that man is not in the process of proceeding to 'greater goodness'. Further on Clifford's beliefs, see Hopkins, *Nonconformity's Romantic Generation*.

8

CAN FAITH FAIL?

East London Tabernacle, Burdett Road.

'The Church does not rest on man or on any number of men. And if the day should come—and personally I believe that some of the younger people here may see it—when a faithful man will be so scarce that you will have to hunt for him, and there shall be apostasy on the right hand and on the left, and the pillars of the Churches (not of the Church) give way on every hand, and it seems dark beyond all power of exaggeration, even in that day the Lord will say unto his people, "I bear up the pillars of it. My Church is not dependent upon man. I live eternally and my eternal life is her eternal guarantee."'

AGB on 'Who Bears the Pillars?', May 15, 1892.

JANUARY 1892 marked the 25th anniversary of Brown's ministry in East London. At a special gathering of the church on January 4, he was presented with a richly-bound album, an 'Illuminated Address', intended as 'a tangible memento of the memorable passage of his life', and the sum of £600 from 'Members of the Church, Congregation, and Friends'. 'Our earnest prayer', his church officers wrote, 'is that the Holy Spirit will through him, continue to abundantly manifest his power in leading sinners to a saving knowledge of the truth as it is in Christ Jesus, and to the building up of his saints; and that he may be long spared to his family and to the church'.

That January occasion was overshadowed by Spurgeon dying at Menton. I have already quoted Brown's words as he awoke on that Monday morning, February 1, and from the 'Memorial Sermon' he preached the following Sunday from the text, 'The Lord has taken away my master from my head today' (2 *Kings* 2:3). In that sermon he told his congregation, 'From the time I entered college up to the present moment, I have had no life apart from him.' Pike would later record: 'Mr Spurgeon and Mr Brown were ardent friends to the last; when the Chief died, the sorrowing survivor assured me that life and service could never more be to him what they had been.'[1]

Brown's 25th anniversary had also been marked by the publication of G. Holden Pike's *Life and Work of Archibald Brown, Preacher and Philanthropist*. There was one aspect of that book that cannot have pleased the preacher. Pike gave less than five pages to controversy relating to the Down-Grade, with more than two of those pages given to the mediating opinions of Dr Angus, and he said nothing at all on the debates in the London Baptist Association. This kind of silence was not unique and Brown protested against it in his 'Memorial Sermon' of February 7:

> I observe that in one of the accounts given of his [Spurgeon's] life by a religious paper, there is this sentence: 'The unhappy down-grade controversy is best passed over in silence.' To many of us—and I am certain to those of us who knew him best—he never appeared more truly grand than when he was willing to fling up everything, and sacrifice all for the truth. To leave that out of the record of his life is like leaving out the 18th chapter of the First Book of Kings in the record of the life of Elijah.

Brown's sense of loss at Spurgeon's death involved much more than deep affection for his friend. It was for him the removal of the leader in the midst of a battle which was already being lost in the wider Christian scene, with consequences that would run far into the future. Those now young, he told his congregation, would see a day 'when a faithful man will be so scarce that you will have to hunt for him, and there shall be an apostasy on the right hand and apostasy on the left.'[2]

[1] Pike, *Spurgeon*, vol. 3, p. 137.
[2] Psalm 7:3, May 15, 1892.

When Spurgeon was alive there were not lacking men of general evangelical beliefs who wavered over accepting whether the new teaching on Scripture was as critical an issue as he claimed it to be. They wondered whether he had gone too far when he said: 'The new views are not the old truth in a better dress, but deadly errors with which we can have no fellowship. I regard full-grown "modern thought" as a totally new cult, having no more relation to Christianity than the mist of the evening to the everlasting hills.'[3] With Spurgeon gone, Brown believed the failure in discernment was only calculated to increase.

The assessment of a recent writer of the weakness among 'Spurgeon's supporters' would appear to be substantially true: 'Spurgeon tended to presume that their personal loyalty and substantial theological agreement with him meant that they shared his thinking on the limits of communion, whereas they were not as ready as he was to insist that the time had come for a barrier to be erected between the evangelical and liberal ideas of Christianity.'[4] In other words, they did not grasp that a major departure from the faith was taking place within British Christianity.

For Brown, in February 1892, there had to be a sense of isolation and loneliness. In one of his last book reviews,

---

[3] Quoted by Pike, *Spurgeon*, vol. 6, p. 291. At a 'Memorial Meeting for the General Public', held at the Metropolitan Tabernacle (February 10, 1892), W. Y. Fullerton briefly alluded to criticism of Spurgeon when he said, 'There are some of you who think that Mr Spurgeon imagined that things were always going wrong.' *From the Pulpit to the Palm Branch*, p. 183. But Fullerton himself, one of 'Spurgeon's men', was not to stand by all Spurgeon's convictions. When his biography of Spurgeon was published in 1921, H. Tydeman Chilvers, then pastor of the Metropolitan Tabernacle, 'reviewed it in the *S&T* and expressed "surprise and sadness" that Fullerton wrote in such a non-committal tone about the Down Grade Controversy. Fullerton did not write "boldly in advocacy of Mr Spurgeon's attitude".' Eric W. Hayden, *A Centennial History of Spurgeon's Tabernacle* (London: Clifford Frost, 1962), p. 43.

[4] Mark Hopkins, *Nonconformity's Romantic Generation*, p. 232.

Spurgeon had commented on the gentlemen who say 'there are no Calvinists now alive with the exception of some half-dozen fools'.[5] Whatever the true number was, there could be no doubt it was declining. The antichristian power of which Brown wrote in 1883 had grown in influence on all sides. Behind the opposition to his booklet on *The Devil's Mission of Amusement,* and behind the 'advanced thinkers' responsible for the Down Grade, was hostility to biblical truth. Frank Ballard, who had continued to write against him, openly held a different 'gospel'. Christ, he believed, taught that there were men of 'an honest and good heart' who had needed no 'preaching' for their salvation; indeed, he claimed 'that all men and all things have share in Christ's redemption'. Brown, he objected, 'assumes that his understanding of the Word of God is the only one open to men.' 'Evangelical orthodoxy', Ballard insisted, 'was no synonym for gospel truth'. Those who think it is simply assume that Calvin got it right for all time.[6]

The view widely expressed in both the secular and religious press was that preachers of Brown's stamp were yesterday's men and a dying breed. The Newcastle paper, *The Northern Weekly Leader,* put out a questionnaire for ministers, asking them to respond to such questions as, 'Are people generally, in your observation, growing better or worse? Do you think that the secular press has, on the whole, a healthy influence?' Nearly 400 replies were received by the paper, and together they presented a hopeful picture. The tone of the press was thought generally to be healthy. People were 'as religiously

[5] *S&T,* 1892, p. 7. The review was of a fine book, *Ministers and Men of the Far North,* by Alexander Auld.

[6] Frank Ballard, *A Brief Reply to Mr A. G. Brown's 'Sequel' to 'The Devil's Mission of Amusement'* (London: Elliot Stock, 1890), p. 30.

disposed as ever, but less disposed than in past times to accept the forms and dogmas of the past'. People were less disposed to attend public worship but this 'may not indicate a want of religious faith'. The Rev. G. W. M'Cree thought 'the people have vastly improved', and the Rev. Dr Grey of Edinburgh believed 'the river of human life was flowing in the right direction'. Amid all the positive words the only dissident voice was that of the pastor of the East London Tabernacle. He believed the secular press was the reverse of healthy—'good and pure views being compressed into a few lines'.

> Dr Thain Davidson thinks there is a slow progress but steady improvement going on. Rev. Archibald Brown, again differs from the doctor, makes bold to declare that people are getting worse. 'There is a decided increase in immorality', he writes, 'and a growing indifference to religious worship. The mad expedients resorted to now in order to reach the masses demonstrates the latter. Religious sensationalism is vitiating the public taste, and simple worship is at discount.'

It was not personal comment that hurt Brown so much as the reflections on what he preached. An article professing to give a pen and ink portrait of him in *The Echo* (March 25, 1891) was typical. After some superficial words of praise, the writer continued:

> Apart from his noble social work, he is the East-end apostle of the most dismal gospel. If he preaches an eternal hope for a few, he preaches an everlasting despair for the many who live and die in this the shadow of his chapel. The old Calvinism of Elisha Coles—the favourite author of Spurgeon—still masters the mind, if not heart, of this able and loving East-end preacher.[7] That he should set up Distress

---

[7] The 1855 edition of Elisha Coles on *Divine Sovereignty* was out of print when Spurgeon had it reprinted by Passmore and Alabaster in 1867, noting, 'It is a class

Funds, Orphanages, Convalescent Homes, *etc.*, is the beautiful contradiction in a good life to a sour creed. But so it is.
Well, we can bear the creed, and rejoice in the divine charity.
Life is full of contradictions, and, in a small way, the pastor
of the East London Tabernacle is one of the quaintest contradictions we have met with for some time. Preaching an
obsolete creed, ignoring the researches of science, regardless
of Biblical criticism, and expounding the Bible by the fading
light of a dying theology.[8]

If this was painful, there was worse to come as antagonism
to his message found its way into Brown's own family circle.
His youngest brother, John W. Brown II, has not been mentioned in these pages since the days when, as a child, he went
with the family to the Metropolitan Tabernacle. Subsequently
Spurgeon baptized him and, as a member of the Tabernacle,
the youngest Brown became, in his own words, 'an ardent
defender of the Calvinistic creed'. But the later story was very
different. From early training in accountancy, he moved to
New College, St John's Wood, London, was ordained in 1884
and joined the Unitarian denomination in 1886.

On Spurgeon's death he went into print in the *Inquirer*,
narrating his personal experience of the preacher, and
accounting for his influence in terms of his 'personal mag-
netism'. 'Some of the most remarkable sermons which Mr
Spurgeon preached were in the ten years from 1861 to 1871.
I heard most of them. There was that one on "Adam, where
art thou?" I can never forget it, the pathos of the passage of
the Lord God going forth to seek Adam and Eve in the garden
after the transgression. We do not build our theology on that
fable now; but Mr Spurgeon did then . . . The charm of his

---

book with the men in the College at their entrance.' *S&T*, 1867, p. 332.
   [8] Quoted in Pike, *Brown*, pp. 117-18.

impersonation blinded the eyes of thousands to the ghastly and incoherent nature of his underlying creed.'

Along with this came the publication in 1891 of, *An Examination of Bill Sykes' Theology; or, Jesus Christ A Victim of Vicarious Suffering, and Not Substitutionary Punishment, by John W. Brown, Free Christian Minister.*[9]

Bill Sykes, we have met before in AGB's *Record of Service* 1890. He was the dying costermonger who wanted his son to hear 'that little bit', that Christ takes the sinner's place and bears his punishment. While Brown believed this was the message for every gospel preacher in the land, J. W. Brown set about 'controverting the religious beliefs of such a well-known representative of the popular Evangelicalism and worker among the poor in the East-end of London as my brother is'. The 'blood' theology, which believes in a 'transference of penalty from the person let off to the person who is punished', he utterly rejected.

The points which his critics regarded as 'wrangling' over opinions and theories were for Brown personal issues of life and death. He read in Scripture that eternal life depends on right belief. 'The fight of faith', known to Paul, is the experience of Christians, and that because supernatural power is deployed against those who would 'keep the faith'. Error concerning salvation is of no human origin, as Scripture warns in the words, 'Try the spirits whether they are of God' (*1 John* 4:1). No one who understands this should wonder that Spurgeon asked, 'Pray for me, that my faith fail not';[10] or that Brown, in 1892, should feel his own faith being shaken. He

---

[9] *Bill Sykes' Theology,* which ran to 32 pages, was published from the author's home in Hornsey, London.

[10] Part of a letter of April 26, 1888, which read, 'My brother thinks he has gained a great victory, but I believe we are hopelessly sold. I feel heart-broken . . . Pray for me, that my faith fail not.'

said to his people in a sermon in May 1892:

> Have you ever known what it is for your faith to receive a
> swinging blow on the one side and then directly afterwards
> another blow from the opposite quarter? Have you known
> what it is for your faith to become for a moment dazed, and
> go a-reeling? Nothing short of the power of God could have
> maintained faith during the years of trial through which hun-
> dreds of us have passed.

Brown preached first to himself what he preached to others, and a sermon entitled 'A Rough Night at Sandown' gives
us an insight into his own fight of faith. For reasons to be
mentioned later, he was often at this period at Sandown, a
sea-side resort on the southern shore of the Isle of Wight. He
had been there on sunny summer days but, on the dark and
stormy night which occasioned the sermon, the scene was
very different. As he stood on the balcony of the house where
they were staying, only a short distance before him, a full
tide — 'wild, tumbling, roaring' — shook the whole shore line:

> The waves curled and broke upon the sea-wall. Hurled back,
> they only returned to meet the next advancing wave, and then
> in a wild embrace the two together thundered on, and so over
> and over again. Far away were to be seen in the moonlight,
> line after line of advancing billows. They looked like charg-
> ers rushing on against that wall, and each one seemed to say
> to his fellow, 'I will back you up.' Endless reinforcements
> seemed to be coming towards the shore. There was but a
> roadway with a narrow parade between us and the deep, and
> it sounded almost like presumption to say, 'Well, it is time to
> go to bed now.' What? Go to rest with destruction so near.
> Talk about calmly sleeping when, within a few yards, there is
> power enough to sweep everything away. Yet we said, 'Bet-
> ter go to rest now', for, taking out our watch and looking at

the hour, we saw that it was high tide. 'It will not come any further', we remarked.

He had no sooner spoken these words than a train of thought began which lifted him above the tempest. Behind that great tide was,

> a power mightier than the storm, an unseen hand holding them, and saying, 'Thus far. No further.' The sea cannot go beyond the line of decree. Then it flashed through our mind, 'But suppose that it should forget to turn, that for the next six hours, instead of receding, it should still advance. Where wouldst thou be, and where thy abode, and where all thy loved ones?' But then we remembered, 'But this law is as certain in its action as the rising and setting of the sun.'
>
> The others went to rest, but I remained for some time gazing out upon that wild surging sea. I know not how long I stood, but, as I gazed upon it, it preached to me; and, as I looked at it, it seemed to assume different forms.

Those thoughts he gathered around his text, 'Hitherto shalt thou come but no further, and here shall thy proud waves be stayed' (*Job* 38:11).

> God has a 'here' at which the wildest waves must stop. As I looked I saw, first, hell's forces restrained. Then the scene changed, and I beheld temptations limited. And then a cough upstairs reminded our heart of sorrows measured. And then, lastly, as I looked out, I saw apostasy arrested.

What he feared was happening in the nation and in the churches was as real as the waves before his eyes, and his own fears were equally real, but, he said:

> I looked out and in that scene I saw apostasy arrested. The sight that presents itself to the eyes of the spiritually taught men today is something appalling. Look abroad which way

you will, there is a surging sea of infidelity; the wind has been blowing very strongly from Germany for some years. Oh, what mighty blasts of scepticism have come across, and what a sea is now rolling! How the waters thunder! As I looked I seemed to see billow after billow of 'higher criticism' sweeping in. Oh, how they broke upon this sea-wall, the Bible! And I noted how men that ought to have been preachers of the truth were themselves the critics, and the men who ought to have been leading their congregations into faith in God were busy making infidels. I heard the shout, 'Genesis is rocking. It will soon be down. We will clear off all the Old Testament before long' . . . But a voice said, 'Thou canst go to rest. There is no real danger whatever' . . . Oh, when he shall come, then will the Lord rebuke the apostasy of the day. Then shall men see in the returning Christ that every jot and every title of this book is God's.[11]

* * * * *

The funeral of Spurgeon was scarcely past when the opinion appeared in the press that the pastor of the East London Tabernacle would be his successor. The *British Weekly* wrote in 1896, 'Everyone remembers that when Mr Spurgeon died no name was more freely mentioned for the successorship than that of Mr Archibald Brown, who had been for years his intimate friend.' Whether any enquiry was made to AGB by the officers of the Metropolitan Tabernacle is not on record. Had they done so there is good reason (as we will show below) why he would have given a negative response. Even so, he could not detach himself from the congregation with

---

[11] Job 38:11, November 6, 1892.

which he had long been so close. It stood in need of his aid for all was not well at the Elephant and Castle.

Dr James A. Spurgeon, brother of CHS, was now the interim pastor at the Metropolitan Tabernacle and differences had emerged among the church officers with respect to the name of a successor to be put before the congregation. Dr A. T. Pierson, who had been supplying the pulpit for eight months around and following the time of Spurgeon's death, had been invited for a return visit starting at the end of October 1892. Meanwhile the twin son, Thomas Spurgeon, arrived back from New Zealand in June 1892, and been asked to preach for three months.[12] Although no name had yet been put to the membership, a difference of opinion had emerged over whether the choice should be Thomas Spurgeon or A. T. Pierson.

Another significant figure at the Tabernacle was Joseph W. Harrald, described (probably by Susannah Spurgeon, whom he now helped in editing *The Sword and the Trowel*) as 'the gentle, wise, indefatigable secretary of the late Pastor . . . He was, in many things, Mr Spurgeon's most trusted friend and ally. Mr Harrald is also a preacher of no mean power. On several occasions he has occupied Mr Spurgeon's pulpit with acceptance; and many will be glad to know that in future, he is to conduct the Lord's-day afternoon service.'

But something went wrong. *Lloyd's Weekly London Newspaper,* under the heading, 'Split at the Tabernacle', reported on October 30, 1892:

---

[12] Thomas Spurgeon, with twin Charles Jr, was born in 1856. A voyage to Australia for health reasons in 1877, led to that country, and especially New Zealand, becoming his field of Christian ministry until 1892. In the intervening years he was home on two visits. He was close to his father and, when the latter was ill, first took his place in the Metropolitan Tabernacle pulpit on Sunday November 10, 1878. See W. Y. Fullerton, *Thomas Spurgeon, A Biography* (London: Hodder & Stoughton, 1919).

The Rev. Mr Harrald, for many years private secretary to the late Mr Spurgeon, and at present secretary to Mrs Spurgeon, has resigned his connexion with the Metropolitan Tabernacle. It would appear that the relations subsisting between Mr Harrald and the Rev. Dr James Spurgeon, acting pastor, have recently been decidedly strained, and that open hostility was evinced after the recently held special meeting of the members, when an intimation was conveyed by Dr Spurgeon to Mr Harrald that his assistance would be no longer required in conducting the afternoon service on Sunday at the Tabernacle. This intimation was followed up by Mr Harrald being requested by the acting pastor to send in his resignation as Sunday afternoon preacher.

It is a remarkable fact that notwithstanding the prevalent divisions amongst the members, crowded congregations are to be seen every Sunday at the Tabernacle. On Sunday evening, when the Rev. Archibald Brown preached, the enormous building was overcrowded.

It is very probable that the dismissal of Harrald was connected with the last time he edited *The Sword and the Trowel* alongside Mrs Spurgeon.[13] The 'Notes' in the October 1892 issue of the magazine, led with these words:

The past month has been a time of great anxiety at the Tabernacle; and at the date of sending these notes to the printers (the 23rd instant), that anxiety has by no means abated. So

[13] Harrald continued to work with Mrs Spurgeon. Together they produced the four volume, *C. H. Spurgeon's Autobiography*, and he continued to see a weekly sermon of Spurgeon's through the press until his death in 1912. A worthy tribute, under the title, '"The Armour Bearer" Gone Home', was published in *S&T*, 1912, pp. 372-3. Further on Harrald, see *The Forgotten Spurgeon*, pp. 249-50. Fullerton writes of the trouble over the appointment of a successor to C. H. Spurgeon in a chapter entitled, 'The Tabernacle Tempest', and says, 'The rift in the ranks of the membership went deep, even to the severing of family relationships and the sundering of lifelong ties.' *Thomas Spurgeon*, p. 155. It is not improbable that this contributed to later difficulties at the Tabernacle.

serious is the crisis, and so grave are the issues involved, both for the Tabernacle church and its institutions, and the denomination at large, that we think it wise, for the present, to maintain absolute silence with regard to the position of affairs. When the right time comes, we will give our readers all the information we can.

Not without reason, Harrald distrusted the judgment of James Spurgeon. He would have distrusted it still more had he known, as he may have done, that the acting pastor 'had grown so attached to his American brother that he advised a co-pastorate with Dr Pierson as preacher, even without any change of views'.[14] 'Change of views' has reference to the fact that Pierson was a Presbyterian, for which reason C. H. Spurgeon had formerly written, 'There is no danger of him being thought of as my successor.'[15] But not to be hindered, James Spurgeon went further. Pierson's biographer writes: 'The matter [of believer's baptism] was frequently brought before him and he was urged by Dr James Spurgeon and others to join the Baptist ranks and to allow his name to be presented for election as pastor.'[16] Pierson wavered on the subject, and not surprisingly his second period as 'supply' at the Tabernacle was not as happy as the first. Harrald's opinion was representative of a large number, including Brown, who would later say, 'I threw what little influence I have on the side of Thomas Spurgeon.' The outcome was that in March 1893 the church called 37-year-old Thomas to occupy the pulpit for twelve months with a view to a permanent election to the

[14] D. L. Pierson, *Arthur T. Pierson, A Biography* (London: Nisbet, 1912), p. 244.
[15] Fullerton, *Thomas Spurgeon*, p. 150.
[16] Pierson, *Arthur Pierson*, p. 252. There was nothing unworthy about Pierson's actions, although he was perhaps unwise to continue with the second supply period in the circumstances. It was nearly three years later, long after Thomas Spurgeon was installed as pastor, that Pierson submitted to a re-baptism back in the United States.

165

pastorate. When that election took place before the end of the probationary period, James Spurgeon resigned. This faithful helper of his brother through many years died on a railway journey into London on March 22, 1899.

* * * * *

Archibald Brown lost two of his closest friends in the year following Spurgeon's death. The first was his mother, Emma Brown. For leaving this world she was well prepared. Until 1888, we are told, she kept 'minute and regular accounts of her expenses'. At the end of that year, as though satisfied that all was done, she wrote on the accounts the one word 'Closed'. In the words of a relative, she now looked forward 'to a future beyond this world in pure and certain hope'.

Of this period, her second son, Edward, wrote in the family record: 'My brother John [now Unitarian] is ever surrounded by my beloved Mother's prayers that one of the most upright and beloved of her children may be perfected in faith in the redemption which is in Christ Jesus.' Among her last words to Edward were, 'I leave John to you.'[17]

Archie had been at Sandown with his wife, on Wednesday, February 8, 1893, when he received word that his mother was 'sinking':

> Thursday was just a race against death. I could not bear the thought of her passing away without seeing her, and I thank God that I was allowed to join the family group gathered round her bed. On my taking her hand, she looked up, and there was such a smile of welcome. I had a few words with

[17] Of John W. Brown's later history little is known. His uncle Edward said that he was 'finally a sort of Theosophist'. He served New Street Meeting House, Aberystwyth, 1907-1909, in which place he died in 1939.

her, and I told her, 'Mother, there are thousands in East London praying for you.' There was a sweet smile of gratitude in her face. I asked her shortly after, 'Well, now, how is it with you?' and her answer was characteristic and beautiful: 'I have no rapture, but I believe; and blessed are those that have not seen, and yet have believed.'

Unable to speak at the last, Emma Brown slowly lifted up a hand and pointed heavenwards before 'she fell asleep in Jesus'. The burial was at her husband's grave in West Norwood Cemetery, close beside the plot where Spurgeon had been buried the year before. On Sunday evening February 19, her son Archie preached on Proverbs 31:28, 'Her children arise up and call her blessed.' 'She lived', he told his people, 'upon the Word of God. How she fed upon it,—how she knew it! If ever I called in unexpectedly at the home at Denmark Hill, I was sure to find the Bible either in front of her or close by her side; and as she neared the end of the journey the Word of God became more sweet to her. Not long since I said, "Mother, have you read this book?" And her answer was, "Do you know, Archie, I feel now as if I want to devote all the time I have left to the reading of God's Book."'

Speaking of what a mother means, when preaching on the widow of Nain's son at the Metropolitan Tabernacle in 1907, Brown said: 'I can never stand on this platform without instinctively looking to that left-hand gallery, and I think I see my mother's face there still. Oh! A mother will love you when everybody else gives you up, and a mother will cling to you when everyone else gets weary of you.'

* * * * *

In Holden Pike's *Life of Archibald Brown,* published in 1892, the Introduction was by Arthur Blackwood, who was knighted in 1887. 'Archibald Brown,' he wrote, is 'my beloved brother, fellow labourer, and friend.' The two men had kept in touch since that April week thirty-two years earlier. Of Sir Arthur, Archie would say, 'All I am and all God has been pleased to do through me are to be traced back to that dear man of God. Whenever I met him, he used always to ask with a loving smile, "How are all my spiritual grandchildren in East London?"'

Sir Arthur was taken ill on the Continent in October 1893, from where he was hurried back to Harwich for medical attention. But he was found to be beyond medical care, and a doctor gave him the news that he had only a few hours to live. Shortly after hearing this, when a nurse entered his room it was to see his face shining with joy as he told her, 'Oh, nurse, I have had such a beautiful bit of news—such a beautiful bit of news!' 'What is that, Sir Arthur?' she asked. 'Oh', he replied, 'I am going to be with Jesus tonight!'

Brown was in Menton when he heard the news of his friend's death from Lady Blackwood. In his reply (November 2, 1893), he wrote:

> Please accept my heart's sincerest thanks for the Memorial Card just received, and the kind letter in which it came. I do indeed feel the kindness which remembers me in such a time of grief. No words can tell what dear Sir Arthur was to me. I loved him with a holy reverence. From my first visit to Wood Lodge I was under his gracious spell. To see him was an inspiration. As a young man I used to wait about the Lane from Tooting Common, just to have the pleasure of a few minutes' walk beside his horse as he rode up to the Treasury. I can never hear his name mentioned without thanking God

for him. What your loss must be I dare not think. I can only pray the God of all comfort to sustain and solace you. Painful experience has taught me that in the hour of bereavement, they act most kindly who say little, but pray much.

This place [Menton] has a sacred charm through its association with another of God's aristocracy. I look out now on the hotel where dear Spurgeon breathed his last. How much he loved your dear husband I have good reason to know. Two faithful witnesses—two noble spirits—two Christ-filled men—two splendid warriors of the cross, they worship together in the presence of him they loved and served.[18]

A third friend, who also died in 1893, should not be passed over. David Gracey was a fellow-student with Brown at the Pastors' College, where he remained as a valued tutor before becoming the Principal in 1881. We noted him standing beside Brown in the struggle within the London Baptist Association. On January 31, 1893, in apparent good health, he preached at a memorial service at the Metropolitan Tabernacle marking the first anniversary of Spurgeon's death. After a brief illness, he died on February 9, at the age of 52. A service at the grave at Norwood, *The Sword and the Trowel* wrote, 'was closed with a very touching prayer by Pastor Archibald G. Brown, who had, two hours previously, been present at the funeral of his mother in the same cemetery'. The same magazine's final comment was the right one:

There were many heavy hearts and sad faces gathered around the open grave, but amid the prevailing gloom there was a firm conviction that 'the Lord reigneth', and that he will be glorified by that which to us appears so dark and mysterious a providence.[19]

---

[18] *Records of the Life of Blackwood*, p. 223
[19] *S&T*, 1893, p. 147. Unlike some mere admirers, Gracey understood what made Spurgeon what he was. When he spoke at the first anniversary of Spurgeon's death,

In the midst of troubled times, it remained true of the people of God, that 'These all died in faith' (*Heb.* 11:13).

* * * * *

Some words of Brown's testimony spoken in the 1890s well sum up his personal experience. He was preaching from the words, 'But the God of all grace . . . after that ye have suffered a while, make you perfect, stablish, strengthen, settle you. To him be glory and dominion for ever and ever. Amen' (*1 Pet.* 5:10-11):

> Thirty odd years ago I listened and I heard the call of God, and Oh, it called me into such sorrow for sin; but I found that the call did not end there. The call came from further away, and I went on, until I came to 'a place called Calvary', and I thought, 'Surely, the call has come from here.' But after I had looked and gazed upon Christ and entered into peace I found that the call still sounded far ahead. It had brought me to Calvary, but it came from beyond there. It came from the throne in glory. And then I found that when God called me as a sinner, he did not call me simply to repent and believe. He called me unto his eternal glory, and that is the purpose of his call . . . The call comes, but the glory does not come immediately after the call. When I found peace I wished that the Lord would take me to glory then and there. But God says, the glory is quite safe. You shall have it, but it shall come to you 'after that you have suffered a while'. Suffering is part of the call, as well as the glory. It is not a haphazard thing that comes in. It is all part of the plan. You say, 'But why can I

---

he said of his former friend: 'He always seemed to have a devout reverence for what was of God. It was this that brought him to peace in believing, it was this that made him a Baptist, a Puritan, a philanthropist, a soul-winner, and a trainer of other soul-winners. *Ibid.*, p. 137.

not go to heaven at once? Why should there be this interlude of suffering between grace and the glory?' The answer is found in the last line of our text, he himself will 'make you perfect, stablish, strengthen, settle you'. There is not here, today, a child of God who is not the richer and the holier for the little bit of suffering. If I am saved from sin and called to eternal bliss, all I can do during 'the little while' is to look up and say, 'Unto him be all the glory and dominion, age upon age, throughout all eternity. Amen and amen.'

9

THE CLOSING YEARS IN EAST LONDON

A cartoon of Brown preaching, from *Moonshine*, 1892.

'Renounce all the policy of the age. Trample on Saul's armour. Grasp the book of God. Trust the Spirit who wrote its pages. Fight with this weapon only and always. Cease to amuse, and seek to arouse. Shun the clap of a delighted audience, and listen for the sobs of a convicted one. Give up trying to please men who have only the thickness of their ribs between their souls and hell; and warn, and plead, and entreat, as those who feel the waters of eternity creeping upon them.'

AGB.

B ROWN'S work at the East London Tabernacle had gone on steadily through the years, supported by the continued love and prayer of his people. Towards the end of a sermon in 1888 there is this comparatively rare auto-biographical reference:

> Think me not egotistical in what I am about to say. I only mention it as a testimony to the praise of God. He has led me to preach the word among you in a very simple way for twenty-two years, and I have ignored all things else; and what is the result? There has never been a week without souls being saved. We have never known what it is for a month to pass without ingatherings at the Lord's table. To the glory of God's name be it mentioned that these hands have grasped the hands of over four thousand who have been brought out of the world into the church of God—by what? By the preaching of the truth of God.

An illustration of AGB's concern for evangelism comes from this same year 1888, when he took his summer holiday near Lowestoft, Suffolk. On July 18, the anniversary of his birthday, instead of celebrating his forty-fourth birthday quietly, AGB invited all the fishermen of the coastal village of Kessingland to join him for the occasion. The thought had been prompted by a visit there a few weeks earlier, when he had chatted to men on the beach, before speaking in the Sailors' Bethel mission. Five hundred invitations were given out for the birthday party, including to the widows of fishermen, and for the event the men built a temporary 'banqueting hall', from masts and canvas, in the grounds of the Bethel mission. When the day came, Brown was astonished to find that the preparations included an arch across the road, on which was written in red letters, 'Many happy returns of the day.' The reverse side carried the words, 'May he never fail in prayer.' The *Lowestoft Free Press* reported:

> The catering was managed by Mrs Brown, and right royally did she fulfil her duties. When I mention that 350 lbs of beef was placed on the tables, and everything else was managed on the same liberal scale, my readers may have a little idea of how the festal boards groaned under the weight of the good things provided. The day was gloriously fine. Tea was served at five o'clock, each guest bringing his or her own knife and fork and plate. There were very few latecomers, and didn't the folks enjoy themselves! It was astonishing to note how rapidly the plates of beef disappeared. 'Plenty more, my friends', said the host, and they took him at his word these Kessingland fishermen.
>
> A brief meeting was held afterwards . . . There he stood on the platform in the most unclerical garb of flannel trousers and blue serge jacket, with a cricket cap in his hand. He has a clear, resonant voice, which reached the furthest ends of the tent, and it is no easy matter to speak under canvas. His manly address laid hold of the fishermen. He bubbles over with enthusiasm, and his earnestness has a magnetic power over his hearers. He thanked the people for their great kindness to him, and said the month which he had spent at Kessingland, would be a life-long remembrance to him.

Additions to the congregation of the East London Tabernacle continued. In 1893 The *Freeman* (January 6), noted that
231 names had been added the previous year to the church
roll. But the labour of a quarter of a century as the sole pastor was putting an increasing strain on him. Even the physical
act of preaching to thousands involved a considerable burden
in days when there were no microphones. Although it was
only for one day, in 1872 Dr Thomas Binney had declined to
speak at the opening of the new East London Tabernacle on
the grounds that to address such numbers would be too much
for him. Westminster Chapel, where Martyn Lloyd-Jones was
to preach in the next century, was a building of somewhat
similar size to the East London Tabernacle. A loud-speaker
system was installed there before his settlement, about which
he was to say: 'I have thanked God for it ever since. This
building, you see, has killed men. It would have killed me
beyond any doubt whatsoever.'

In 1891 Pike raised the possibility that Brown, at 47 years
'still comparatively a young man', might be inclined to consider work 'less exhaustive or wearing . . . we take account
of the work he has done rather than the number of years he
has lived.'

That Brown himself recognized that limitations were now
restricting his East-London ministry is clear from his *Record
of One Year's Service* for 1890. It ran to 55 pages, and while
containing much heartening news, struck this note at the
conclusion:

> Most of our work must necessarily cease with our death, or
> removal from the neighbourhood. It is our hope, however,
> that the Orphan Home will be of a more permanent nature.
> For many years we have held the view that every church of
> any size should take under its wing some orphan children.

It is a bit of pure religion. Our Annual Record of Service is now finished. Accept it in a kindly spirit. It has been written amid a rush of work, and at odd hours, and with no little home anxiety pressing on the heart. To all our helpers, and specially to those who have helped us for our Master's sake, we return our Christian love and gratitude. We have tried to do our best, but poor is our best at its best. May worker, work, and helpers together be accepted of the Lord, WHEN HE SHALL COME. So prays your servant for Christ's sake, Archibald G. Brown.

To the main limitation under which Brown was working by the time of Spurgeon's death in 1892 we now turn. The public discussion whether he would follow Spurgeon at the Metropolitan Tabernacle, came only weeks after his church's generous presentation on his twenty-fifth anniversary and their hope that he would be 'long spared'. That 'hope' might have hindered any acceptance of a move, had he been approached, but there was another consideration which was much more decisive.

Since his marriage to Edith Barrett in 1878, the family had been blessed with further children. In 1892 Ashley G. Brown was now eleven, his sister Edith nine, and brothers, Donald and Cecil were seven and four respectively. But, yet again, the mother in the family had become permanently ill, and she now needed prolonged breaks away from home. The *Freeman* (February 27, 1891) reported: 'The health of Mrs Archibald Brown having greatly improved by her stay in the South of France and Italy, Mr Brown will return to London in time to occupy his usual place next Sunday.'

The report of improvement was premature. AGB's sermon on the morning of May 15, 1892, began with these unusual words:

I could almost wish that my friend, Mr Hill, with his swift pen, were not here this morning, for I am afraid it lies altogether outside my power to say anything of sufficient worth to be reported or become in any measure permanent. God only knows the difficulties that have been in my path in the way of preparation of any sort for this morning. As I watched my beloved wife in her terribly dangerous illness, the tension has been acute to a degree. I have seemed powerless to think of aught else than one matter . . . I am personally far from well. With a temperature of over 101 [F.] as I have now, and a pulse of 110, it is not altogether easy to take a very calm and deliberate view of things. But I have learnt long ere this that it is just when we are emptied out and powerless that God pours his richest blessing through the preacher.

Edith Brown's condition did not improve. The *Freeman*, recording 'a grand tea-Monday evening meeting' at East London Tabernacle in January 1893, wrote, 'The place was crowded, but it would have been brighter had not a sad trouble like a dark cloud rested on the pastor, the Rev. A. G. Brown. The severe and continued illness of Mrs Brown is a trial to our brother, and those who know his sensitive heart cannot but sympathize with him, as we do very deeply.' A note in *The Sword and the Trowel* (February 1893) spoke of Edith Brown's 'long and trying affliction, from which there is no hope of recovery'. It is clear from an aside in a sermon of August 28, 1893, that his wife had to spend much of that summer in Brighton, on the coast. While preaching on God being 'mercy-full, brimful of mercy', he interjected: 'Every week now I have a sad journey; but every week as I come home by the Brighton line, just before the train gets to Tulse Hill station, I can get a momentary glimpse of a road and some trees; and as the train dashes past I find myself involuntarily raising my hat, because I can get a view of some rising ground where there is an oak tree, and where thirty years ago God told me that he was merciful, and he has been merciful to me ever since.'

The mother of the family was at Menton in October and November 1893, with her husband present for part of the time. *The Sword and the Trowel* reported, 'The invalid bore the journey well, and was enjoying the exquisite weather of that charming spot.' The nature of her illness is not recorded. It probably concerned her lungs as mountain or sea air at the coast was stipulated by her doctors. By 1894 her husband was warned that she could not live in London again. Apart from the smoky air of East London, 22 Bow Road was no place for an invalid. For thirteen months, therefore, at this time, she was at Sandown on the Isle of Wight, and Archie 'travelled constantly back and forward between'. This was varied in the Spring of 1894 when Edith was in Switzerland, where he visited her in May, returning alone through Paris. After one of his home-comings he quoted to his congregation the words of one of his daughters: 'My dear daughter has had the charge and care of the home while I have been away, and she said this morning to the little ones, "Oh, I feel quite light. I have no responsibility now. It is all on father."' While the words were spoken as an illustration of spiritual truth, they also revealed the need in the home on Bow Road.

By 1894 help in the home was not as strong as it had been. The second daughter, twenty-three year old Nellie, went as a missionary with the China Inland Mission in 1891. Once asked if she had ever thought of going to China, she had replied, 'Yes; but I'm not going.' Later her testimony was, 'If one said one big Yes to Christ the little yesses would follow.'

She had been a member of the church for ten years, and it was observed, 'Her childhood was marked by much gentleness and sweetness of disposition. She strongly resembled her mother, who, five years after her birth, passed into glory.' At the large farewell meeting for Nellie, a lady present said she would be responsible for all Miss Brown's expenses but the *Christian World* reported, 'Mr A. G. Brown asked that the offer might apply to someone else, so that he might be allowed to provide all supplies for his daughter.'

Two years later, Gracie, the youngest daughter of his first marriage, also became a missionary to China. What it meant to the father is indicated by words in his sermon the following Sunday:

> Last Thursday was a day of sore trouble to some of us, and sorrow seemed to reach its climax. When the train steamed out of Liverpool-street, carrying with it my own bright, blessed daughter, it seemed for a few moments as if it had left me on the platform with an empty body. Heart and everything else seemed to have gone out with that train. I came straight home, and, on entering my study, I found that during my absence some thoughtful friend had put upon my table, just in front of where I always sit, a beautifully illuminated card. The words that greeted my eyes were these, 'He giveth quietness', and underneath was this text, 'When he giveth quietness, who then can make trouble?' Whoever it was that deposited that sweet truth upon my table showed not a little knowledge of heart experience, and of the Word of God. I read the text not once or twice only. It came to me as the very voice of God.

Not long after, Lucy, third daughter of the first marriage, was to marry Dr J. H. Bennett and, with the London Missionary Society, they also would go to China.

It is clear the East London Tabernacle had close links with the missionary advance in China. When the killing of many missionaries in that land occurred in the Boxer movement of 1901-2, while Brown's children were all safe, numbers died who were well known to the church. In a sermon, a few years after that event, AGB referred his hearers to a book, *Fire and Sword in Shansi*, and said,

> There, on the front page, you have the names of 150 men and women, all of whom cheerfully laid down their lives to carry the gospel of Christ to the Chinese. As I look down that list, what a number of them I knew! I think of Dr Lovitt and his heroic wife, whose hands I grasped at the East London Tabernacle, and my eyes become dim. How small I feel myself to be, how small most of us are, how little we know of that loyal spirit which hazards life for the work of God.

Annie, the eldest daughter, remained in the East End where her hands were equally full of Christian work. She was a resident Sister at The London Hospital in nearby Whitechapel. Founded in the 1740s, 'The London' was one of the oldest teaching hospitals, and second to none in its reputation for the Christian doctors and nurses who trained and served there. Annie's father had long been one of its governors. As a charity hospital it depended on funds raised by supporters such as Brown. William Alexander, Bishop of Derry, preached for that cause (as did AGB), telling his hearers that The London served more than a quarter of the population of London: 'In the course of the last twelve months it has relieved 90,000 out-door patients and 8,000 in-door patients.'

The loss that AGB must have felt by the scattering of his family was surely lightened by the devotion to Christ shown by his older children. Arthur Douglas, youngest son of the first marriage (and known as Douglas), was also an encouragement to him. He was now at the end of his school days and would serve for a time in the Merchant Navy before preparing for the gospel ministry.

* * * * *

The fact that his wife could no longer live in London, led Brown to the decision that their present constant separations should not continue; he must end his pastorate at the East London Tabernacle. In January 1895 news that he had put a written resignation in the hands of his church officers surfaced in the press. Under the heading, 'Pastor Brown's Retirement', the *Eastern Post* (January 26, 1895) reported:

> It will probably be formally announced in the course of the next few days. The reason it has not been announced before is because, ever since they received the document, the church officers have been in almost daily contact with their pastor, with the object of getting him to reconsider his determination. They even went so far as to offer him, on behalf of the church, a three years' holiday and rest from his labours . . . As everybody connected with the Tabernacle knows, the chief reason for his retirement is because of the very indifferent health of his wife, who has been a confirmed invalid now for some years past. The loss of Mr Brown to the Tabernacle will be an irreparable one. During his pastorate he has made the Tabernacle the most successful Christianising influence in East London, a result due in very large measure to the simplicity and pointedness of his preaching.

While Brown's resignation was still under discussion with his church officers, the whole scene changed. On Saturday night, February 2, 1895, with his preparations for Sunday completed, he received a telegram at 10 p.m. with the news that the condition of his wife at the coast had suddenly deteriorated. He would later say:

> I hurried off on the cold, dark, bitter morning of Sunday, with a heart, I am afraid, something like the morning. On reaching Hastings I found that my wife was rapidly passing away.

Yet she was not too ill to ask him to tell her the sermon he had planned to preach in Stepney that morning. The text was Isaiah 26:1, 'In that day shall this song be sung in the land of Judah', and together they went over each point he had prepared. The text comes in the chapters that make up 'the Apocalypse of the Old Testament'—a revelation of what shall be at the end of time, when, 'He shall swallow up death in victory; and the Lord God shall wipe away tears from off all faces' (*Isa.* 25:8). 'As I turned to the different passages, my wife said to me, "This is very singular. This would almost have done for my funeral sermon, would it not?"'

On the following day, which was to be Edith Brown's last, she asked him to go through the passages again, and the exclamation 'beautiful' was one of her last words. A few days later AGB found words recently written by her faltering hand:

> I am no longer eager, bold, and strong:
> > All that is past!
> I'm ready to do nothing now,
> > At last! At last!
> My half-day's work is done—
> > To give patient Lord
> My willing heart.

The next Sunday morning was February 10 and, in the midst of his great sorrow, Brown was not expected to be in his pulpit. An offer from his brother Edward (now pastor of the Baptist chapel at Twickenham Green) to preach in his place had been thankfully accepted. But on the previous day, just as the funeral of Archie's wife was starting, there came the news that Edward was suddenly ill and unable to undertake the engagement. So on the Lord's Day morning the people found their own pastor in the pulpit. He explained that he thought his brother's illness was perhaps God's way 'of letting me know that I had to crush personal feeling, and take my usual place here. I could not allow this morning's service to go by default for lack of a preacher.'

For the message he gave the sermon only his wife had heard the week before, later to be entitled, 'An Unintended "In Memoriam"'. In the course of the sermon he put the question:

Do you tell me that death is swallowed up in victory? Then why that hurried race down to Hastings in the early morning of last Lord's-day? Death swallowed up in victory? How is it that there are so many of you here who have the tokens of grief upon you? Death swallowed up in victory? Then why are not the gates of the cemetery closed? If death is swallowed up in victory, how is it that there is a grave-digger to be found? . . . Death is conqueror today. He conquers the fairest; he conquers the youngest; he conquers the wisest; he conquers the purest. You may fight year after year with death, but, at the end he will have defeated all your physicians. The coffin in your drawing-room will tell you what has been the result of the encounter. Does that look like death swallowed up in victory? Thanks be unto God, 'In that day' it shall be brought to pass that death is swallowed up in victory. And why? Because in that day the Lord shall come, and they that have fallen asleep in him shall be raised from the tombs, and, as Paul says, 'This corruptible shall put on incorruption, and this mortal shall put on immortality.' 'Then shall be brought to pass the saying that is written, Death is swallowed up in victory.'

And what is the next item? Not only will death be swallowed up, but, as you see, 'THE LORD GOD WILL WIPE AWAY TEARS FROM OFF ALL FACES.' When? In this day? It does not say so. In this age you cannot see much until you wash your eyes from tears. Depend upon it, it is often true that there is nothing so good for spiritual vision as a wet eye . . . How is it that the preacher has some tears on his cheeks while he preaches this morning? Is God true? Does God keep his word? Yes, God does keep his word; but he does not say that in this age all tears are to be wiped away. He says, 'in that day'; that is, in the day when death is swallowed up in victory.

In conclusion, the much-loved pastor told his hushed congregation,

I have found it far more difficult to preach the sermon this morning than I did last Lord's-day morning, when I took the loved one who is now with her Lord from one point to another, as I have tried to take you. There was not then the rustle of the leaves of a thousand Bibles. It was in the quiet room overshadowed by death.

Menton was a place of sacred memories for Brown and it was there that he went for a short break after February 10. We know of only one incident concerning that visit and it is worth recording. The error that if only a Christian is 'spiritual' they will always be blessed with health is not a modern one, and when a foolish man recommended that belief to him

at Menton, so soon after his bereavement, it was more than
he could calmly bear:

> I know of nothing more cursedly cruel than the doctrine
> that is somewhat in vogue just now, that you can judge of
> a person's spiritual standing by the amount of sickness that
> he has. When I was in the south of France I heard that said
> concerning some missionaries that had died on the Congo.
> Pointing to a hotel, not far off, I said. 'Do you know what
> place that is?' He said, 'No.' I said, that is the Hotel Beau
> Rivage. Do you know who died there?' 'No.' I said, 'A man
> named C. H. Spurgeon. He died there. There were millions
> of prayers going up on his behalf from all parts of the world.
> Are you going to tell me that he died because he was not liv-
> ing in close communion with God, and was lacking in faith?
> It is a cursed, cruel, doctrine. There was more grace in his
> little finger than there is in both of us put together.'

On the way home from Menton, Brown was to have a
happier experience. After fourteen hours of journey from the
south of France he arrived at a Paris hotel late at night: 'I
was somewhat weary; but I was not half as weary in body as
in heart, and I frankly confess that the thought of returning
home was a very painful one. Tired and depressed, I hastened
to retire to rest.' This, however, was at once hindered by a
clear and strong voice. It came from the next room, connected
to his own by a locked panelled door. It was soon apparent
to him that the person was not in conversation with someone
else but was reading:

> I had not to act the part of an eaves-dropper, for I could not
> fail to hear what was being read, and I heard these words
> coming through the panel: 'For we know that if the earthly
> house of this tabernacle were dissolved, we have a building of
> God, an house not made with hands, eternal in the heavens.'

So I quietly drew a chair to my side of the door and sat down, an unknown audience, as the reader read the chapter right through to his fellow traveller. As he read it, the very music of heaven made its way through the thin partition. God knew that it was what I needed, and that this chapter was more calculated to be a pillow for a weary heart than any material pillow could be for a tired head.

His wife's death gave AGB new light on his duty. As her illness had been the cause of the resignation, which had leaked to the press but had not yet gone to the church members, he now withdrew it, and, after a short break, took up all the work afresh.

* * * * *

Brown was now facing a difficulty that had never troubled his early ministry. We noted earlier how a critic, the Rev. G. S. Reaney, in the mid 1880s, speaking of Brown, said, 'The condition of things under the shadow of his own tabernacle were perfectly appalling.' While there was no doubt exaggeration in the statement, there was truth enough in it to hurt. The reality was that a massive change in population was taking place. In the early years of Brown's ministry there were many in his congregation who lived in the neighbourhood, both the 'well-to-do' people, and the majority, the 'artisan' class, who were qualified for full employment. Within twenty years this scene and the whole appearance of things had changed. Family homes were fast disappearing as their owners moved away to better living conditions, and in their place came occupants sharing rooms. Brown had commented on this situation in 1889:

It is the householders who are going, and room holders who are coming. The difference does not lie only in financial position. There is a difference in manners, tastes, and social life. Let the condition of our streets bear witness. We remember the Bow Road when it was a treat to walk along it, and when at night quiet reigned and all was respectable. Now night is made hideous, and sleep often an impossibility, by the gangs of boys and girls that go shouting and roaring their music-hall songs. All this serves to drive respectable families away, and with them goes the backbone of our churches. The suburbs are gradually sapping our neighbourhood. Twenty-three years ago, when we came to East London, the district of Bow was quite suburban, and well-to-do families abounded. Now London stretches out for miles beyond. We are fast becoming a central district. Only pastors placed in similar circumstances—and there are many—know how cruelly painful is the experience. Scarcely a week passes but someone you have learned to love comes to say, 'Good-bye pastor, we are going a little further out.'

This was a process of change which throws light on and explains the membership figures at the East London Tabernacle. While 4,800 were admitted into church fellowship by 1892, as already noted, in 1893 the figure on the membership roll stood at only 2,375. Many had moved to outer-London locations, and the number who still lived near the Tabernacle was much reduced. The newcomers to the area were commonly of a different type and this was a reason why, despite the mission work of numbers of evangelical agencies, the publication, *The Bitter Cry of Outcast London,* could say in 1883: 'We must face the facts; and these compel the conviction that this terrible flood of sin and misery is gaining upon us.'

A reporter from the *British Weekly* interviewed Brown in his home in November 1896, and his subsequent article is worthy of quotation:

The East London Tabernacle, as many of my readers are aware, is in Burdett Road, a turning off the main thorough-fare, but Mr Brown's own house is no. 22, Bow Road. From the drawing room window one can watch the endless streams of traffic which move constantly between Whitechapel and Stratford. As I waited for Mr Brown in the drawing room, I noticed on the table a bust of Mr Spurgeon, and in the study, where our interview afterwards took place, there were many memorials of the great preacher. Above the mantelpiece is a coloured portrait of Mr Spurgeon as a young man. The wall leading from the drawing room to the study is lined with books, and the study itself contains four or five large book-cases. Mr Brown writes at a large table, which stands in the middle of the room.

No minister in the East End has led a harder life than Mr Brown. But for the iron constitution with which he began his ministry he could never have endured the constant strain. At nine o'clock every morning he meets one or two of his missionaries and lays out plans for the day. With them he goes into cases of distress, emigration cases, and the thousand-and-one-problems with which the East-end minister has to deal. By 10 or 10.30 he is free for quiet study, and the morning is filled up partly with study, partly with correspondence. Before lunch he generally visits the boys' home and the girls' home in connection with the Church.

'In the afternoon', he said, 'I am usually occupied in preaching, either in London or the country. My average of services, when in full work, is nine a week. For many years I made the practice of giving Tuesday and Wednesday to outside work. I have gone all over the kingdom preaching for the poorer churches. On Thursdays I have my weekly services here. The early part of Friday is devoted to making up the accounts of our mission work and to settling other financial business. On Friday evening I prepare my Sunday morning sermon, but it has never been my custom to write my sermons.'

'I suppose there have been many changes since you came to East London?'

'Immense changes', replied Mr Brown. 'No one could form any idea today of what this neighbourhood was like thirty years ago. The Bow Road where you see the trams going up and down and endless rush of traffic, was then a country highway. There were no pavements, no stone-paved streets, and the Bayswater omnibuses only came as far as Mile End Gate. The inhabitants were chiefly well-to-do people, many of whom kept a brougham. The gardens of Tredegar Square, close by, were kept by a livery man. All this population has disappeared. For every Gentile family which leaves a Jewish family enters here. Bow is now to a great extent a Jewish locality. Twenty-five years ago my congregation was made up almost entirely of persons whose homes were in the neighbourhood; now at least 800 of our members come from east of Stratford Church, and that is, as you know, some distance from here.'

Mr Brown by no means shares the desponding views of many ministers with regard to the conversion of the Jews. He has himself baptised a large number of Jews, and he finds that in the East End this work has made most encouraging progress. At his prayer meeting on Saturday there is quite a Jewish colony.

Fuller information on the Jewish reference came into a sermon preached by Brown at the Metropolitan Tabernacle on September 13, 1896. In the course of speaking on the 'sprinkling of the blood of Jesus Christ', he said:

I know that in this building there is never a sneer at the word 'blood' . . . You do not live in such a Jewish district as I do. I live amongst the Jews and I have lived amongst them until I have learned to love them. This season of the year is the season which is important above all others in the Jewish calendar. The Jewish new year commenced last Monday, and next Thursday is the great Black Fast, the Day of Atonement. At the East London Tabernacle we always have a special prayer meeting for the Jews on the Saturday night before the Day of Atonement. Some persons who are now present attended that meeting last night. There were about a thousand people at the meeting, but the glory of it was that every brother that led us in prayer last night was a converted Hebrew, and you who were there will bear testimony as to how the blood was sounded out from Jewish lips. There is never any hesitation about a Hebrew Christian when he speaks of atoning blood. The blood saves from guilt.

The main reason for the above reporter's visit to Brown in November 1896 was the breaking news that he intended to close his ministry at East London Tabernacle on the first Sunday of the next year. Differing reasons for the preacher's decision had been discussed in the press, and the *British Weekly* wanted to hear the explanation first hand. He told the reporter:

I have been in the East End thirty years, and a period so long as this makes a great difference in a man. I have been conscious for some time of growing physical weakness. Family troubles have fallen upon me with peculiar heaviness, and since the death of my wife two years ago I have felt that my work was pressing too hardly upon me. A great dread of going beyond the thirty years has for some time past hung over me.

His reason for going was not any tiredness with the East End. 'I am', he declared, 'a thorough East-ender. The true East-ender knows little west of Aldgate, and you will perhaps be surprised to learn that it is many years since I was in Regent Street. I do not think I could find my way to Piccadilly, and the whole of West London is practically an unknown region to me.'

Other newspapers, making the same enquiry about Brown's decision, got a similar answer. Under the heading, 'Rev. A. G. Brown's retirement, Interview with the "East End Spurgeon"', the reporter of the *East London Observer* wrote:

> In answer to my opening question, the Rev. gentleman said: 'There is nothing wrong at Burdett Road, but for the past six years I have been in indifferent health, and added to this I have had much domestic trouble and affliction in the way of bereavement, and I don't feel equal to the great strain which the work imposes on me.' 'Have you sent in your resignation?' I asked. 'Yes', replied Mr Brown, 'but my dear people', he continued with some emotion in his voice, 'don't seem to want me to go. I am anxious they should know that I have never loved them better or more than I do now, and it will be a great wrench to leave them. However, I feel that a younger man should now take my place, and I don't think that after staying 30 years in one place anyone can accuse me of being fickle or erratic. I don't believe in taking a salary for the work of an office one feels one cannot thoroughly do.'

The first Sunday of 1897, January 3, marked the thirty years since AGB's first Lord's Day as pastor in Stepney, and it was his last in that role. The evening text was, 'He faileth not' (*Zeph.* 3:5). It was the old message, without anything personal until he came to the conclusion:

Although I am anxious that there should be nothing in these closing services to take your thoughts away from our all-glorious Lord, and turn them to his poor servant, yet I must bear my witness, and it is this: HE FAILETH NOT. That is the only explanation that I know with regard to the past thirty years. I have been failing all the way through, and always failing. There is not a worker for God who has not to make the same confession. What a marvel it is that, there should have been two texts for every Sunday, and another for Thursday, during all these years. How has it come to pass? Why, 'He faileth not.' And how is it, year after year, there has been found a multitude to hear the word? The explanation of that is not in this man. It is, 'He faileth not.' He has been pleased to honour his own blessed truth. If I knew my lips would never bear another testimony after tonight, my testimony, borne, God knows, from an honest heart is this, 'I, Archibald Brown, declare that I have proved for thirty years that God never faileth.' And I am certain that my dear brother, Dr Barnardo, who is sitting next to me, is ready to say that this has been just his experience too. Oh, the whole history of this church is just an explanation and illustration of my text.

AS A CHURCH BELIEVE THIS MOTTO, AND ACT ON IT: 'He faileth not.' Show that you believe it by acting on it. Have a holy fear of being led astray by the dictum of any wise man, or the advice of any merely earthly tongue. It is not for me to dictate, yet I would suggest, O church of God, that your wisest course will be to speak little and pray much. Get down before God. Multiply your seasons of prayer. Then look up, and remember 'He faileth not.' The pastor you have borne with so lovingly, and who never expects to be again so happy as he has been with you, has, in measure, failed. Long service and much sorrow have told on my strength; but how I have to praise God for keeping me these many years in such glorious health. But I want you to believe, dear church of God, that if health should fail in one, or integrity depart from another; if there should be collapse here or collapse there and failure all round, yet God faileth not. God wants you to trust him and he says to you now, 'Cast yourselves on me, the unfailing God.'

Despite the 'closing services' of January 3, 1897, the congregation were unready to accept their pastor's resignation. At a crowded church meeting on February 11 there was a unanimous plea, the *Freeman* reported, that 'he should take a long holiday, or have a co-pastor, but that the tie uniting pastor and people should not be severed.' A resolution to that effect included the words,

> They deeply sympathise with him in the experiences he has been called to pass through in his domestic life; these the church fully recognize, and regret that they have impaired his health, and they most affectionately and willingly tender him an entire relief from duty, and lovingly invite him to take a long season of rest in order that the same may be re-established. They would ask him to reconsider his proposed retirement from the ministry here.

At one point only did this meeting disagree with their former pastor. At an earlier church meeting when he had given in his resignation, among other reasons for it, he had expressed the belief that 'his style of preaching was not calculated to lay hold of the class of persons now living in the neighbourhood'. It was the conviction of the church that 'the evident token of God's blessing, and the readiness of people to listen to the gospel messages delivered by him' were proof that this was not the case.

The appeal of the church must have pulled at Brown's heart. The people certainly had no doubt of his continued affection for them. Although by February 1897 the routine of his duties was over, he kept the annual Thanksgiving Day in February, being in the vestry as usual from 7 a.m. to 7:30 p.m., when £430 was received in thank offerings. The *Freeman* (February 19) reported: 'The Rev. A. G. Brown this week spent what would be to him a quiet Sunday in the suburbs, preaching for the Congregationalists at Winchmore Hill in the morning, and for the Baptists of Enfield in the evening. Mr Brown will preach in his old pulpit both morning and evening next Sunday.'

But Brown's mind was made up, and he knew that February 21 would bring a final closure. Holden Pike had the same awareness as he made his way there that Sunday morning. He noted, as he did so, the change for the worse in the neighbourhood, now crowded with a class of people who were 'non-attenders at public worship'. Within the Tabernacle, however, every seat was taken, and 'by the time the service commences, accommodation is found for a large number in aisles and elsewhere. It is the ex-pastor's last Sunday, and the people seem to realize it, although in point of fact, they refuse to think of him as other than their pastor still.'

Intent that there should be no emotion, Brown began with prayer 'that all may know what worship means', and took the morning and evening services just as he would have done on any normal Sunday in former years. The texts were, 'According to the measure of faith' (*Rom.* 12:3), and, 'Messiah shall be cut off, but not for himself' (*Dan.* 9:26). There were no personal references and the East London ministry ended as it had begun, preaching Jesus Christ.

VISITS TO AMERICA
AND PALESTINE

Joppa from the south from J. Murray's *Illustrated New Testament*. The traditional house of Simon the Tanner is within the city, close to the wall on the south-west.

'The hope of the Gentiles lies in the Jew. The putting on one side of the Jew became the opportunity for the Gentiles. The "restoration" of the Jew shall be "life from the dead" [*Rom.* 11:15]. This the Word of God clearly teaches us. I must refer you, at your leisure, to the 60th chapter of Isaiah, and you will see that it is said concerning Zion, "Arise, shine, for thy light is come, and the glory of the Lord is risen upon thee; and the Gentiles shall come to thy light, and kings to the brightness of thy rising." The light which shines in Zion disperses the gloom of Gentile darkness. The Jews will become the great missionary power. Oh, may God hasten the time when all the intellect, all the power, and all the wealth of the Jewish nation is consecrated to the propagation of the kingdom of the Lord Jesus Christ!'

AGB, 'Jew, Gentile and the Church',
1 Corinthians 10:32,
May 20, 1894.

NEWSPAPERS are seldom always reliable and the report may be suspect that Brown was ordered to take 'a long rest' on his leaving the East London Tabernacle. It was hardly consistent with the fact that only days after the last service in East London, AGB sailed for New York on the *Aller* on February 24, 1897. The purpose of his departure had been previously announced and was commented on in the press. The *Freeman* (February 26) reported: 'Great interest is shown in Mr Brown's visit to the United States, especially as to the manner in which it was brought about, the undertaking of a month's mission services at Denver may be classed among the most striking adventures of his life.'

The truth is that it was not so much rest as relief from the incessant pressures of the East End that he needed most.

He had long loved the sea but whether what he now experienced was just what he had anticipated is doubtful. 'Have you ever seen the ocean when she has gone mad?' he would later ask others. 'Have you ever stood on the deck of a liner in mid-Atlantic when the gale has been let loose; when it is shrieking up there in the rigging; when piled up mountains of water crested with white foam are on this side, and abysses of deep green yawning gulfs are on the other, and the roar of the ocean is enough to drown thunder? A man who has ever seen the sea in its wildest mood, in my judgment will never want to see it again.'

Brown's first transatlantic visit was, in part at least, at the encouragement of Theodore Cuyler, who had retired in 1890 after a thirty-year pastorate in Lafayette Presbyterian Church, Brooklyn, New York. It was Cuyler who warned him that 'as he had not written novels he was not likely to realize thousands of dollars by lecturing'. But AGB was not thinking of money or of 'lecturing'. The *New York Times* for March 9, 1897, reported,

> The Rev. A. G. Brown, the English Divine, talked to a thoroughly sympathetic audience in Cooper Union, at 3 o'clock yesterday afternoon. The Rev. A. C. Dixon presided, and a number of clergymen occupied the platform. Mr Brown spoke on the need of complete consecration. Meetings will be held every afternoon this week, except Saturday.

Such was Brown's introduction to the United States and to a number of her preachers. He had already met D. L. Moody and probably Theodore Cuyler; it was a first acquaintance with A. C. Dixon, a minister who would re-enter the scene at a later stage.

From New York, Brown went on to New England where the *Boston Daily Globe* reported on March 15, 1897:

> Rev. Archibald Brown of London preached yesterday morning and evening at the Clarendon St Baptist church.[1] Despite the storm large attendances gathered to hear the English preacher, who made a deep impression by his earnest discourses. The [morning] text was from Chronicles, 'And when

---

[1] The former charge of the late Dr A. J. Gordon, to whose memory Brown paid tribute.

the burnt offering began, the song of the Lord began.' At the close of his services he held informal receptions at the communion rail and shook hands with the people as they were introduced by Mr McElwain. Mr Brown is decidedly unclerical in appearance. He wore a cutaway cut and black tie, and had a neatly cut moustache of white hair. His face is strong and his head is firmly poised on his broad shoulders. His arms are powerful and his hands large. He is evidently a working parson. He was a close friend of the Rev C. H. Spurgeon.

Arthur T. Pierson in his book, *Forward Movements of the Last Half Century,* recorded that while in Boston, Brown was asked to give some account of his work in London. In doing so, wrote Pierson,

> He attributed any success he had then enjoyed to two things: dependence on the Word of God and the Spirit of God . . . Pastor Brown might have added, if his modesty had not forbidden, that through the East London Tabernacle, thus educated and edified by Bible teaching, work was done for London and for far off lands, that any congregation might envy.[2]

How long Brown was in the States is not recorded. The month to be spent preaching in Denver, Colorado, was evidently the primary engagement. The newspapers termed it 'a mission', a title which the preacher himself had given up using. He would later record one incident relating to the visit to Denver which is best in his own words:

> When, some years back, it was stated in the papers that I was going to America, I received a strange letter from the West of England. A lady wrote and said, 'I see from the papers that

[2] A. T. Pierson, *Forward Movements of the Last Half Century* (New York: Funk & Wagnalls, 1900), p. 165.

201

you are going to America. I had a poor run-away son who went there, and I have heard that he died somewhere near Denver. Would you mind putting a wreath on his grave from his mother.' How could I refuse, but I confess I had rather a shock when I received a big wreath, about a foot-and-a-half in diameter, and thought, 'I shall have to carry this five thousand miles!' How wonderfully God works! When speaking to a crowd at Denver, remembering the mother, I said, 'Is there anybody in this crowd that ever knew so-and-so (mentioning the name); if so, will they tell me where he died and where he is buried.' Directly after the service a young man came up and said, 'Why, he was a chum of mine, and I was the only one that attended the funeral; I can take you to the place.' I am not ashamed to say that the tears were in my eyes as, alone in a big cemetery some miles out from Denver, I laid the wreath on his grave in the name of his mother who had followed him to the end.[3]

We also know that from Colorado he went further west to Arizona, where he told of driving by horse and buggy through a desert fifty-five miles wide. Half-way across they came to a little wooden shanty, and, pulling up and going in, found an old man 'reclining on a rickety sofa and reading a book very intently'. A closer approach revealed the book was a Bible, open at the Gospel of Matthew. 'Well', said Brown, 'you seem interested in your book.' 'That is a Bible', he replied, and asked the stranger if he was interested. When Brown affirmed that he was, the man went on to say how he was troubled by a printed sermon he had recently read, in which 'the parson says the world is going to get better and better, and what with education, and one thing and another, wonderful things are going to take place.' 'I said, "Don't you

---

[3] Luke 7:11-16, June 23, 1907.

think it is so?" I trembled with concern for his answer. It was three hundred miles from the nearest centre, and here was a man in the desert with no one to put anything into his mind; he just had his Bible. I said, "Well, dear friend, you don't think the world is getting better, do you?" He said, "No, I do not." Then I asked him what was his hope; and I can see the old man with his grey hair as he looked up and said, "I just sits and watches to see Him come over the desert." I took him by the hand and said, "That is just my view too. I am waiting to see Him come over the desert."'

While Brown was at times speaking to large numbers while in the United States, it is characteristic of him that the only detail he has left us concerned individuals.

* * * * *

A few years after this Brown was able to take the opportunity to visit Palestine which he had declined twenty years earlier. One of the missionaries who had been attached to the East London Tabernacle during his ministry, was Marcus S. Bergmann, a converted and gifted Jew. It was through this man, as the *East London Advertiser* once reported, that 'a number of Jews, mostly converted under his ministry, formed part of Brown's congregation'. He was clearly a man of similar spirit to Brown. One of his helpers in the Jewish work was Inspector Thomas Eveson, who kept a miniature Bible depot at the Leman Street Police Station.[4] The two Christians had met in unusual circumstances. One day when off duty, Eveson

---

[4] At his death in 1934 the East End Jewish community honoured Inspector Eveson with a page-long obituary (*Jewish Chronicle*, August 3, 1934). (He was a relative of Philip H. Eveson, Resident Tutor and later Principal of the London Theological Seminary, 1977-2009.)

was enjoying a bath in his cubicle at the Russian Vapour Baths in Whitechapel, when his attention was drawn to an earnest conversation taking place nearby. It was Bergmann who, after enjoying his own weekly bath, was proclaiming the gospel to a group of Jews. Inspector Eveson shouted 'Hallelujah', and the two men became lifelong friends and fellow-helpers. Eveson learned Yiddish, the language of all East End Jews, as well as Hebrew, and when Bergmann completed his second translation of the Bible into Yiddish in 1905, the policeman was an eager distributor. Eveson offered a reward of £5 to any Jew who could find a mistake in the translation from the original Hebrew. It was never claimed.

Bergmann's vision, however, was far wider than Stepney and Whitechapel. He wished he could provide every Jew with the Scriptures in language they could understand. This led to the proposal that he take Brown and five others with him to Palestine and Egypt for a month. Very little of the visit has survived in Brown's words, but Bergmann printed an account which tells us something of what it meant to them all.[5] They left England on January 13, 1906, and after travelling through Paris to Marseilles, joined a boat to Crete. Here, at Canea, they found about sixty Jewish families, and on the Sunday, Bergmann was permitted to preach to them in the synagogue, 'pointing out from the Old Testament Scriptures that the Lord Jesus Christ is the true Messiah promised to our fathers through Moses and the Prophets'. The service over, a long conversation with the Rabbi followed, Brown speaking to him in French and Bergmann in Hebrew. A number, including the Rabbi, asked for a Hebrew New Testament or a Yiddish Bible. No missionary had ever visited them before.

[5] God's Faithfulness: A Record of the Lord's Leading in the Life and Work of His Servant, Marcus S. Bergmann, by M. S. C. B. (London: Marshall, n.d.), pp. 67-90.

The party's first sight of Palestine from the sea was of the snow-covered peak of Mount Hermon in the distance. 'What a thrill passed through me', wrote Bergmann, 'on sighting the land of my fathers!' They landed at Haifa on the morning of January 23, and reached Nazareth in the afternoon. The competing 'sacred sites' of the Greek and Roman churches were of little interest to them, but the one Jew to whom they were directed made the time memorable, and again a Bible was requested and given. Brown fills in part of the story at this point:

We had slept the night at Nazareth, and starting at break of day we ascended the steep road which perhaps some of you may have traversed out of Nazareth on to the broad and extensive Plain of Esdraelon. We journeyed on and went through a little village bearing the name of Cana: I need hardly say with what intense interest we lingered awhile in that spot where our Lord performed his first miracle of changing the water into wine. Travelling over the rough road—in fact the road became indistinguishable, a road simply by name—the heat became oppressive, and towards eleven in the morning we called a halt for lunch, and encamped just by a large pool where a number of camels were being watered. It was a wilderness place; wherever you looked were boulder stones and rocks, interspersed with little patches of green.

After having looked at the camels being watered, and noticed the singular encampment that we formed at the al-fresco luncheon, I wandered a little way on, and saw an Eastern shepherd; there he was with his turban and loose garment, with the girdle round his loins, staff in hand—just as I had so often seen in pictures, for in the East nothing changes. And the thought that came into my mind was this: I would like to test the man and see whether the Eastern shepherd really has the power which is attributed to him of calling sheep by name. Is it, after all, only a pretty fable, an exquisite little fancy, a ministerial illustration, or is it a sober fact? A few coppers greatly helped us in our finding out, and then by means of signs—two or three had joined me—we got him to understand what we wanted him to do. Standing up he gave a strange cry—the Arab language always sounds strangely in a European ear—it was a call, and in a moment a sheep which must have been fifty odd yards away bounded for-ward, came leaping over the stones, and in a few seconds had put its nose into the shepherd's hand which had some crumbs of bread in it, and the sheep ate and went off. Directly after he gave another call, and from an opposite direction another sheep came; and so time after time until there was not the least room to doubt the fact that the shepherd knew his sheep by name, and that they perfectly understood their own name, and recognised his voice.

As I stood in that glorious sunshine watching this Eastern shepherd it seemed to me that I heard the Lord's voice saying, 'My sheep hear my voice; and I know them, and they follow me.'[6]

The friendly welcome the party had been receiving seemed assured when they reached Tiberias on the Sea of Galilee. But here were 3,500 Jews, and they soon discovered that among them were many akin to those who had opposed Paul in the synagogue at Corinth. When the visitors spoke in the syna-gogue 'a number of fierce looking Arab Jews rushed in with fury', claiming that their holy place was being desecrated. Certain Russian Jews were no less angry when they heard that 'Jesus of Nazareth, who was rejected by our nation, and crucified outside Jerusalem', was the Messiah.

---

[6] The words come from a sermon on that text, John 10:27, preached at Chats-worth Road Chapel, February 25, 1906. He told his hearers, 'The sermon I want to preach to you this morning was really picked up in the neighbourhood of the great Plain of Esdraelon.'

All was peaceful the next morning when a Jewish fisher-man took them the length of Galilee by boat, after which they had to take to horseback, for the first time, to continue south to Jerusalem. They found the city in a sorry condition under Turkish rule, and the people heavily taxed. The 'Christianity' that existed seemed to do more harm than good. One Jew, on hearing Bergmann was there as a missionary said: 'That does not matter, for I see you want to do us good; but what we do not like, is the idolatry of these Christians who have set up everywhere in Jerusalem these hateful abominations.' The one bright exception in Zion's once noble city, was 'an iron building, plain and simple', where they found to their joy 'a goodly number of Jews and Moslems gathered for a simple gospel service'.[7]

Visits to other places followed. Not a single Jew could be found on their visit to Bethlehem. At Joppa they were shown the building believed to be the house of Simon the tanner, and thought there was reason to believe the claim was genuine. Among journeys from Jerusalem none was more memorable than when they rose at 5.30 a.m. and set off for the Dead Sea. By dawn they had progressed far enough to see the sun rise over the mountains of Moab. Brown shared a 'rough vehicle' with Bergmann and two others. At some points they found faster progress could be made on foot, but at others mud so clung to their feet that walking was impossible. At last they reached the shores of the Dead Sea and everything they saw lived up to its name. 'The water was quite warm, but it had a nasty slimy feel, and was difficult to wipe off.' After talking with a few Jewish traders, they proceeded to the Jordan and then to Jericho on the way back to Jerusalem. The last part of

---

[7] This was the Jewish mission, a work led by an American by the name of Thompson, 'a dear man of God'.

the journey, all uphill on a rough road, was the most arduous of the day, and seventeen vehicles made up the party, Brown and Bergmann being in the thirteenth. 'It was nearly eight o'clock', the latter would later write, 'before we came near to Jerusalem. I had here a most startling experience. A little distance outside the city there were three men waiting in the dark with a carriage, who held up each of our conveyances in turn, shouting my name, until they reached the one in which I was. On hearing my name called, I shouted out, "Yes", when two men, merely saying, "We want you", literally lifted me from my seat, and dragged me into the carriage that was waiting, and before I could realize what had happened I was being furiously driven off.' It would seem Brown's alarm at his friend's disappearance was not relieved until later that evening. The explanation was that Bergmann had promised to address a meeting at 7 p.m.; his 'captors' had been sent to find him and bring him straight there! 'I was decidedly not fit to address a meeting', wrote Bergmann, 'but when I entered the hall, and saw it well filled with Jews, I forgot my weariness and hunger, and felt only the joy of proclaiming the blessed gospel.'

In another later sermon Brown spoke of another impression made on him in these weeks:

Palestine is in the very centre of the volcanic region, and one cannot visit the Holy Land without being impressed with the fact that the earthquake fiend has been busy there for ages. Who can go along that awe-inspiring gorge down Jericho way, or walk along the ravines where the Jordan flows, without feeling that the plough-share of earthquake has been driven all along here. You stand by the Dead Sea, and behold a weird argument for it, for all round about there is lava and pumice stone, and on every hand you see proof that the mighty powers within the bowels of the earth have shaken that district through and through. In fact I think I am correct in saying that travelling from North to South of the land you are hardly ever out of sight of some manifestation of earthquake power; there are ruined cities on every hand, and today there are the waters bubbling up at Tiberius too hot for the hand to bear. It would be a strange thing, then, if a book written in and about this district had nothing to say about earthquakes. It has, however, a good deal to say on the subject. Someone may say, 'But those Jews saw God in everything.' Well, if that be a mistake, it is a very blessed and a very comfortable mistake, and a very poetical one too. That is a wonderful idea of the psalmist in the hundred and fourth psalm, when he says, 'Thou lookest upon the hills and they quake: thou touchest the hills and they smoke.' To the Hebrew mind God was always to be seen magnificently in the phenomena of nature.[8]

On leaving Palestine they made a short visit to Egypt and the Pyramids before they began the homeward voyage. This was not uneventful, as Bergmann wrote:

For about four days it was fearfully stormy. On Sunday, February 11, we had it very stormy, but in spite of it again we had a blessed time on board. The morning service was conducted by the clergy. In the evening Pastor Archibald Brown took the service, in which Mr Berry took part. The sermon preached by Mr Brown was a most powerful one on the transfiguration of Christ. I may here remark that the dear pastor was hardly fit to preach, having been in bed the whole day, but we all realized that the Lord made his strength perfect in the weakness of his servant.[9]

[8] 'What the Bible Says About Earthquakes', A sermon on Matthew 27:54, *Metropolitan Tabernacle*, January 10, 1909.
[9] *God's Faithfulness*, p. 90.

IN SOUTH LONDON AGAIN

The interior of Chatsworth Road Chapel, with AGB's choice of text on the pulpit wall: 'Surely I come quickly. Amen. Even so, come, Lord Jesus' (*Rev.* 22:20).

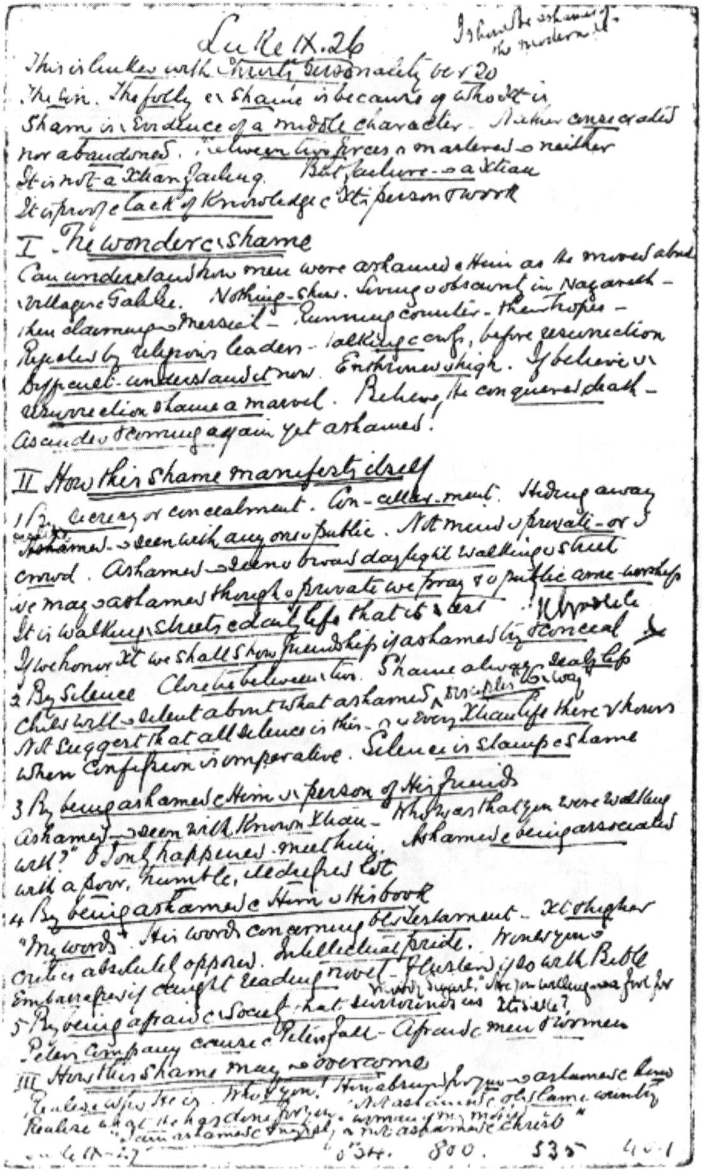

Luke IX.26

This is linked with Christ's personality ver 20

The sin. The folly of shame is because of who Xt is

Shame is evidence of a middle character. Neither consecrated nor abandoned. Between two forces & mastered of neither

It is not a Xtian failing. But failure of a Xtian

It is proof of lack of knowledge of Xt's person & work

I. The wonder of shame

Can understand how men were ashamed of Him as He moved about villages of Galilee. Nothing-show. Living obscurely in Nazareth – then claiming Messiah – running counter to their hopes – repudiated by religious leaders – talking of cross, before resurrection. Different – understand it now. Enthroned on high. If believe in resurrection shame a marvel. Believe He conquered death – ascended & coming again yet ashamed!

II How this shame manifests itself

1 By secrecy or concealment. Con-cellar-ment. Hiding away. Ashamed to be seen with any one in public. Not mind in private – or in crowd. Ashamed to be seen in broad daylight walking the street. We may be ashamed though in private we pray & in public join in worship. It is walking streets of daily life that is the test. If we honour Xt we shall show friendship. Hypocrite is ashamed to conceal. Shame always dearly lip.

2 By Silence. Christ be between us. Children silent about what ashamed. Disciples in every Xtian life there shows. Not suggest that all silence is this. Silence is stamp of shame when confession is imperative.

3 By being ashamed of Him in person of His friends. Ashamed to be seen with known Xtian – "Who was that you were walking with?" Ashamed of being associated with a poor, humble, illdressed lot.

4 By being ashamed of Him & His book. "My words". His words concerning Old Testament – Xt's higher critics absolutely opposed. Intellectual pride. Embarrassment if caught reading novel – flustered if so with Bible.

5 By being afraid of Society – that surrounds us. Peter's company cause of Peter's fall – Afraid of men & women

III How this shame may be overcome

Realise who He is. Who you. Realise what He has done for you. "I am not ashamed of Christ"

Luke IX-27 … 534. 800. 535 401

AGB's sermon notes of 'Ashamed of Christ'.
See Appendix 4.

AFTER his months in America in the early part of the year 1897 Brown had a special reason for looking forward to the return home. In June 1897, at the age of fifty-seven, he married for the fourth and last time. His bride, six years younger, was Hannah Gearing Hetherington, a former hospital matron. They began their twenty-five years of happy married life living in country seclusion at Staplehurst, Kent.

The Browns cannot have been long at this location in 'the garden of England' before he was being sought by churches with invitations to preach. One of these churches was Chatsworth Road Baptist Church in West Norwood, South London, a congregation without a pastor. At a deacons' meeting of this church on June 9, 1897, it was recorded: 'Mr Arnold kindly undertook to write and ask Mr Archibald Brown if he can take the services in July and August.' Abraham Arnold had formerly been the elder of the church, and, although no longer a church officer, his presence was sought by the deacons at all their meetings. At his death the Minutes of the Church Meeting would speak of him as an 'earnest and devoted Brother, who by his large-heartedness and loving Christian influence won the hearts of all those who knew him.' Brown's reply to the invitation from the deacons was that he could only offer a Sunday in September. Perhaps no one thought much about it except Arnold who, on his own initiative, took himself off to visit Archie at Staplehurst. The result was a 'Special Meeting of the Deacons', July 17, at which they were given some surprising news. The minutes of that meeting read:

> Being an old friend of Mr Brown's, Mr Arnold had this week spent a day with him at his temporary house in the country, and had opportunity of ascertaining Mr Brown's plans for the future. He was intending to settle down in a pastorate again, and probably in October, for he had already several invitations before him. Mr Arnold had then opened the subject of his coming to Norwood and discussed the whole situation, past and present. Evidently Mr Brown was very favourably disposed, for he had special ties with the neighbourhood, he was converted at Palace Rd, he afterwards selected the site for the Chapel and preached the first sermon in it.[1]
>
> All present were of one mind—*viz.*—that if Mr Brown could be secured it would by God's blessing be the making of the place. It was felt that not a moment should be lost in sending an earnest invitation to Mr Brown.[2]

This was done, and in response Brown wrote, 'I frankly acknowledge that the invitation has considerable charms for me.' But he wished to see an invitation from the church as a

---

[1] The history of the Chatsworth Road Church states that in 1876, 'The acquisition of the site was due to the admirable choice of the Rev. Archibald G. Brown.' He was probably acting on behalf of the London Baptist Association. *Chatsworth Road Baptist Church, West Norwood, a Brief Record* (privately published, 1927), p. 9.

[2] The history of the church, written thirty years later, gives a more exciting account of how this deacon's meeting began: 'Mr Arnold, the Church elder, burst upon them one evening so agog with tidings that he couldn't tell them out!' Arnold died on March 11, 1898; in view of the major part he played in the call given to his friend, one sees the providence of God in his not dying nine months earlier. As Brown used to say, 'God's time is perfect.'

body, and when this was supplied by a unanimous church meeting (July 23), he proposed a meeting for discussion with the deacons and the 'church committee' (presumably men selected to serve with the deacons in finding a pastor). Under a heading, 'Rev. A. G. Brown's Conditions', the minutes of this meeting held on August 17 read:

> Mr Brown examined the Trust Deed and Rules of the Church, was glad to have met the Brethren, and stated the Meeting should thoroughly understand (1) he was compelled to give up the enormous work at the East London Tabernacle entirely thro' ill health, (2) that he took his stand on the Bible and the preached gospel, (3) that he did not believe in the Church providing amusements (so-called), (4) that providing he did not neglect his Church work, he should feel at liberty to preach here and there where Churches required help, (5) that he could not take part in the financial affairs and monetary business of the Church.
>
> The Meeting acquiesced and agreed to all these conditions. Mr Brown stated that he could not decide that moment, as the Church at Folkestone had also unanimously invited him, he would, however, send a definite reply in a few days.

But, after reflection on what he read in the Church Rules on the necessity of any prospective pastor preaching on two occasions at the church before a call is given, he postponed any decision until he had fulfilled preaching engagements at Chatsworth Rd in September. Thereafter he wanted the church to meet again to confirm their earlier decision as the rules required. On September 24 the Church Secretary received the telegram for which they were all hoping, followed by a letter:

Staplehurst, Kent
Sept. 24 /97

My Dear Friend,

It will be two months on Monday since I received the unanimous invitation of the church at Chatsworth Road to become pastor. Since that time the subject has been constantly on our heart and in our mind. The two Lord's Days spent in your midst have greatly impressed me with the conviction that the call is from 'Himself'. I am willing therefore in absolute dependence upon 'the partnership of the Holy Spirit' to come and labour in your midst. I earnestly beseech you as brethren not to let your faith stand on anything that is of man but simply on the power of God.

While praising God for having sent numbers to hear the word, let not 'numbers' be overestimated or made the chief thing sought, but let us desire with a holy ambition, that Chatsworth Road may become a monument of praise unto the name of the Lord and the power of the gospel.

I cannot do anything, but the 'Partner' can do all things through the weakest.

Even now if the church has any doubt as to the wisdom of the call I will gladly step aside. It is only right to say that I cannot attempt more on the Lord's Day than the two services. Sunday afternoon work I cannot venture. All details of service can however be left to a future meeting.

Now may God himself, even our own God, make clear that all is according to his own purpose.

With much love to the brethren and all the members of the church,

Believe me, yours in Christ,

Archibald G. Brown

This news was given to a church meeting on October 10, and a ballot of members taken to confirm the call: 'The result was declared to be that the Rev. A. G. Brown had been unanimously elected, and the meeting at once rose and sang the Doxology.'

Thus, at the building where he had preached on the first Lord's Day after its opening in 1877, Brown took up his ministry on November 7, 1897, with the text Jeremiah 32:17, 27, 'Is anything too hard for the Lord?' Against this entry, he wrote in his preaching record, 'My first sermon as pastor.' This record, which had been laid aside since November 22, 1874, was now taken up again. In it he explained the long absence of entries in the words, 'Here comes an interval of 23 years. I became too busy to keep up the record.'

In the years since the beginning of the work at Chatsworth Road, the pastorate had been well served by William Fuller Gooch whose settlement had been encouraged by Spurgeon. Gooch had taken Spurgeon's part in the Down Grade controversy, but in the early 1890s he went further than either Spurgeon or Brown in deciding that there ought to be an end of denominations altogether. Maintaining denominational distinctive, he had come to believe, 'fettered the catholicity of the one Church of Christ and threatened its witness to revealed Truth'. As Chatsworth Road belonged by its trust deed to the Particular [*i.e.*, Calvinistic] Baptist churches, Gooch's biographer says, 'Christian honour and consistency compelled him to relinquish what he might have wished to retain.' Accordingly he told a farewell meeting at Chatsworth Road, on May 5, 1892, 'He desired perfect freedom to express his convictions on Church government and other matters.'[3]

---

[3] H. M. Gooch, *William Fuller Gooch, A Tribute and A Testimony* (London: World Evangelical Alliance, 1929), p. 51. Gooch's position on Christian unity seems to have been close to that of the Brethren who believed that 'denominations were to be annihilated and not to be replaced by another denomination'. For another understanding of church and denomination, see Spurgeon, 'Unity and How Not to

Gooch's ministry had been of great help to many; with the consequence that when he left to begin a new work not far away at Lansdowne Hall, Norwood, he took 'nearly everybody' with him into 'The Evangelical Free Church and Fellowship'.[4] Not surprisingly, his successor, James L. Stanley, found the church at a 'somewhat low ebb'. [5] Stanley moved on in June 1897, at which time there was a 'small community of some 200 members'. The financial situation was evidently not healthy, for a deacons' meeting of July 9, 1897, noted, 'the church funds being very low' interest free loans of £50 and £20 were accepted with 'very warm thanks'. They were more cheerful after Brown's acceptance of the call, resolving 'to carpet the Pastor's pew and also the Vestry', and to print 2,000 programmes for the Recognition Services.

While the church was happily surprised at Brown's willingness to come to a work so much smaller than his last charge, they were not altogether without an explanation on the human level. The history of the Chatsworth Road Church, expressed the belief that 'to live without preaching was as impossible to Archibald Brown as to have a church with no prayer meeting'. The comment is not quite adequate for it would have been possible for Brown to preach regularly at many different places; what he was missing as a pastor was his own people.

Among those who sent greetings for the Recognition Services was the following:

From a band of believers assembled for prayer in the Metropolitan Tabernacle on the evening of Monday, November

---

Promote It', *S&T,* 1886, p. 516.

   [4] I quote from the MS of an interview with Brown undertaken by an unnamed person, on behalf of a Mr Booth who was presumably an editor. It is dated December 11, 1900.

   [5] *Chatsworth Road Baptist Church,* p. 14.

8, 1897. To their friends and fellow workers at Chatsworth Road, West Norwood,

GREETING

We desire to assure our dear brother Archibald G. Brown, your Pastor, of our prayerful interest in the new work to which he is now setting his hands and heart.

We rejoice greatly at every remembrance of him, and of his God-honouring career, we recall with pardonable pride the fact that he trained in the Pastors' College, founded by our late loved Pastor, C. H. Spurgeon, and that he was, so long as the honoured President lived, his faithful friend and helper, while we cannot refrain from sympathising with East London's loss, we rejoice in the great blessing that we feel assured will come to Norwood and its neighbourhood through our dear brother's ministry, accompanied by the zealous efforts and holy lives of those who labour with him.

The Browns now settled into their new home, 'Tredegar', on Idmiston Rd, West Norwood, in November 1897. At first, it seems, the pleasant situation did not make up for the conditions he missed in East London. On that, and other points, a record has survived, written by a visitor who came to interview AGB in December 1900:

After a short preliminary talk, I asked, 'What were your first impressions, coming from East London?' He replied: 'Dull respectability; unable to kindle a spark of enthusiasm. For the first six months it was terrible. The people are middle class—'villadom', managers, merchants in the City, not wealthy. What I miss is the working class—no artisans— nothing between villadom and dirty poverty.'

The poverty to which he referred existed in a corner of the district, but instead of the honest poverty he had known in the East End, it was the 'preventable' type, the result of careless living and of drink by men who sought no steady employment. 'He emphasised the absence of the sturdy working element, "like engineers".'

On the condition of the Chatsworth Road congregation in 1897 the visiting interviewer wrote: 'When Mr Brown came the church was in a bad way. The galleries were closed and only a handful of people were left.' 'A handful' scarcely matches the figure of 200 belonging to the church already quoted. In contrast with the size of the building that number would look small, and no doubt it contained a mixture with regard to the degree of individual commitment. Some from among them, it seems, were responsible for anonymous letters to Brown advising, 'that if he imagined the gospel he had preached at the East would do good for this neighbourhood, he was mistaken'. Brown's judgment of the attitude of the neighbourhood, he told his interviewer, was that it was not antagonistic: 'It is sodden by the gospel and not saved by it. It has had the wonderful testimony of Fuller Gooch for twenty years and a magnificent testimony it has been.'

The church minutes, and his sermon record, show that Brown was not long in seeing the work reviving in his new charge. At a church meeting at the end of February 1898 it was noted: 'With such manifest tokens of God's blessing upon the church and upon the Pastor's faithful work as evidenced by the unprecedented large numbers of friends joining the church, and by other spiritual blessings, the meeting at once rose and praised God.' Later that first year Brown wrote to the people, setting a date for a 'Thank-Offering Day' in the light of 'no little blessing'. He would be at the church for lengthy periods between 8 a.m. and 9 p.m. His letter included this paragraph:

No amounts will be announced, and the little gift of the poor will be as welcome as the larger donation of the wealthier brother. I hope that the children will bring their contributions. Do not simply give them something for them, but let them bring their own little gifts to the Lord's house. It is blessed training for them.

At a subsequent church meeting he said it had been 'a day of blessing and joy', when about 600-700 people had visited him and donations had amounted to £204, 'which would pay the cost of the installation of the electric light'. On the same occasion, a year later, the giving amounted to £740, and it was recorded that by the end of the second year of the new pastorate, 358 had come forward for fellowship during that time.

By the end of 1900 the pews, which seated 1,100, were more than two-thirds occupied on a Sunday morning and quite full in the evening. Sometimes, the same interviewer quoted above was told, 'We have a difficulty in seating the people. There used to be two distinct congregations, but people who never came twice, do come in the evening now.'

Brown had the enthusiastic support of his seven deacons, six of them being regularly at the prayer meetings. While at his settlement the church had a Saturday night prayer meeting, there had been only about six to twelve people in regular attendance, and the opinion was offered that this could not well be changed: 'It was all very well where the people had no comfortable homes and were glad to go out.' To which AGB responded, he 'believed and had proved that where the Spirit of God is the results will be the same.' By the end of 1900 there were 150-200 present at the Saturday meeting, and for the Wednesday service 20 had grown to 300. 'Week night services are a strong point with Mr Brown', the same interviewer noted, and he recorded Brown as saying: 'I never trouble about Sunday. Some only think about the Sunday service. I go in for week nights. If the people come on a week night they are sure to be here on Sunday.'

By 1900 there were 500 additions to the church. In commenting on that number, Brown believed, 'Many have come from the world, and we also get a large number of backsliders whose church membership had lapsed—people who had left the church and made money. This is a locality of backsliders. People get respectable and lose their standing. You never lose members through the stress of poverty and hard work.'

Questioned by his interviewer whether the church programme included any social activities, the answer was, 'They find their recreation in Christ. They don't want them.' On which the interviewer noted: 'Mr Brown is very strong on this point. He holds that the church should not mix itself up in social matters as a church, believing this weakens its influence.'

At the outset the deacons had agreed to Brown's proposal that he should have two days a week to help other churches, and his wider interests remained. Perhaps he was on holiday and not preaching on the Lord's Day, August 4, 1901, when the entry in his sermon record noted, 'Had a miserable day in Boulogne.' On January 1, 1902, he notes, 'Spent day at ELT on behalf of Christian Buildings.' There is a poignant comment for 'Lord's Day, March 27, 1904. Preached at Met. Tab. From 2 Cor. 1:19. The Met. Tab. is not what it used to be. It makes me sad.'

There would have been more than one cause for his sadness. Part of it would be connected with the memory of what had happened on Saturday, April 20, 1898. That was the day of the annual Pastors' College Conference. Brown was there, along with 400 other men, and one of his deacons from Chatsworth Road, John Pearce. Pearce accidentally played a significant part in what happened that disastrous day. From a background of childhood poverty, he had prospered in the catering business and become the owner of fifty-four John Pearce Restaurants. It was his staff that were responsible for the dinner to be provided for the College Conference. Perhaps, because of the numbers expected, the fires in the kitchens beneath the Metropolitan Tabernacle roared as they had never done before. All unknown to Pearce, there was a beam high in the roof, in proximity to a flue, and this caught fire. It could not be reached, and once alight the flames spread until the whole great building was engulfed. Efforts to stop the fire were futile and had to concentrate on preserving the College and surrounding buildings. For the men who came to encourage one another the burning Tabernacle must have been one of the saddest sights they ever saw.

A new Tabernacle had been opened in 1900, shorter in length, and designed for a maximum of 3,000 rather than the 5,000 of the original building. It is unlikely that it was simply the changed building that made Brown sad on that Sunday in 1904. After a good deal of discussion and some differences, as already mentioned, Thomas Spurgeon had been given the unenviable role of continuing his father's work. Not surprisingly this was proving difficult and some of Spurgeon's trusted deacons were no longer at hand to guide the son.

The prosperity at Chatsworth Road meant that they were not only able to contribute to the new Metropolitan Tabernacle building, but to undertake extensive improvements to their own premises. Electric light was installed in the re-decorated church, and a platform replaced an antiquated pulpit. Behind the church a dilapidated Lecture Hall came down, and a vestry and a fine new building for the Sunday School and for other purposes, was built on two floors, at a total cost of £6,000. On the first Sunday the new building was used, there were 310 children in the Sunday School and 33 teachers. The very fabric of the building showed the church's ties with the old Metropolitan Tabernacle for the stone steps from two staircases were brought and became part of the structure.

John Pearce was one of the generous donors for the new building. 'The present beautiful hall', Brown would later say, 'is largely a monument of his devoted spirit. Grateful for mercy received he gave a "thank-offering".' It is said that on one occasion Pearce was speaking with Brown in his vestry when word came of an enquirer anxious to speak to the pastor. Pearce at once said, 'I will see you some other time; you go and see the enquirer whoever he may be.' It turned out to be Pearce's own son. Brown could never have done what he did without men such as Pearce, whom he described as, 'devout in spirit, retiring in disposition, simple as a child in character, strong in conviction, and keen and punctual in business'.[6]

While Brown was the only paid servant of the church, he saw to it that he was not the only worker. He pursued his old policy of leading others to take initiatives which included visitation and open-air preaching. He did not visit himself except in cases of sickness; social visiting had never had any part in his schedule. There was regular correspondence for

---

[6] James J. Ellis, *Pluck, Patience and Power, the life story of John Pearce* (London: Allenson, 1910), p. 113.

him to deal with, and to which he replied by hand. His published sermons prompted all kinds of questions, including one from a Londoner who wanted the precise location of the spot where he gained assurance of his salvation in April 1861. His reply has survived:

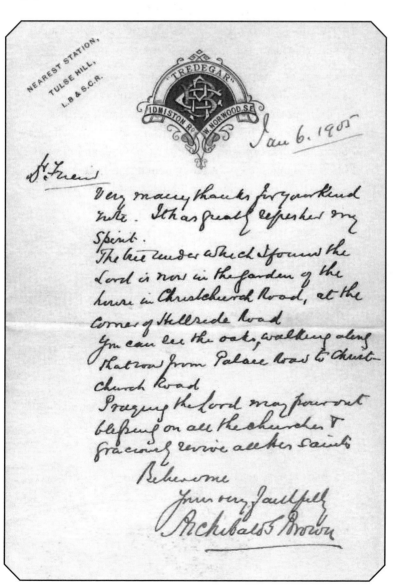

The church records reveal the abounding affection of the people for their pastor. 'The work', he could say in 1900, 'had been carried on without a jarring note; if there had been any feelings of petty jealousy he had not heard of them; there was great love in the church, without which the Holy Ghost would never work.'[7] A resolution of the church, dated June 21, 1901, and sent to the 'Beloved Pastor', shows something of this spirit. I quote the opening sentences:

> The church of Christ worshipping at Chatsworth Road take this opportunity to express devout thankfulness to God for the public profession by baptism forty years ago of their present Pastor, Archibald G. Brown; the token of a change to him which has brought, by the grace of God, an infinitude of blessed changes to multitudes whom he has been made the means of bringing to our Lord Jesus Christ to the salvation of their souls.

* * * * *

Preaching was ever AGB's first calling and the entries in his sermon record tell much of what it meant to him. The following are representative samples:

Isa. 60:13. 'The place of my feet'. A glorious subject and full of teaching.

Deut. 9:17; 10:5. 'The tables of stone and the Ark'. One of the very best gospel subjects.

2 Sam. 6:22. 'I will be more vile.' Happy as a bird.

Titus 2:11. 'The grace that brings salvation'. One of the very best seasons yet.

---

[7] *Norwood Press*, April 28, 1900.

[The last was a Sunday morning sermon. The next was a Thursday evening.]

Titus 3:4-7. 'The kindness and love of God'. Followed very sweetly on Sunday morning.

The Sunday after this he was in his old pulpit at East London Tabernacle, taking the Titus 2:11 and his 'Manasseh' sermons.

Isa. 53:10. 'Yet'. Fine theme but not happy.

John 10:28, 29. 'Eternal security'. A sermon arising from a great deep of depression.

Isa. 9:6. 'Wonderful'. We had a wonderfully good time on a Wonderful Saviour.

Ezek. 47:11. 'Hopeless Marshes'. One of the most solemn services we have had. Full house.

1 Cor. 1:2. 'Who God's church consists of.' A good doctrinal theme, much needed now.

* * * * *

At the end of nine years at Chatsworth Road Chapel, Brown reflected on them as he began his tenth year:

To some of us it seems an exceedingly brief period, and to the speaker specially so. It often seems to me as if I had just stepped into your midst, for nine years seem little more than a postscript at the end of the long thirty years of a previous pastorate. And yet as things go, nine years is far from being a brief pastorate: it might almost be considered a fairly long one; and in these years we have seen much, and I trust we can add, we have learned not a little. There are certainly

lessons to be gleaned by a Christian worker out here in a
South London suburb, which he could never learn in East
London—perhaps some of the most humbling lessons possible. We have had experiences here that were absolutely
unknown to us until we came into your midst . . . they have
been nine perfectly happy years; there has been love, joy,
peace and a holy brotherhood amongst us; and we have seen
God working on the right hand and on the left.[8]

Clearly, the work of the church had steadily progressed.
By the year 1907, 1,300 people had come into membership,
'most of them having found the Saviour there'. He described
the congregation as 'the most consecrated company of saints
it has ever been my joy to live and labour among'. But events
in April 1907 came as a sudden indication that this period
seemed about to end. Brown received two calls, one to go
back to his old charge at East London Tabernacle, the other
to the pastorate of the Metropolitan Tabernacle.

The call to the Metropolitan Tabernacle had arisen out
of the resignation of its pastor, Thomas Spurgeon, in March
1907. Then, at the call of the church, Thomas withdrew the
resignation on the understanding that he could have a year's
furlough for the recovery of his health; at the same time, in
a letter to the members of the Tabernacle (April 20, 1907),
approved by the deacons, he had recommended that 'a sound
and powerful preacher' be secured to serve in his absence,
with the hope that this person would 'remain after my return
to share the burden with me'. He went on:

> Now, it has occurred to me and others, that such an one (if
> we can only secure him) is our dear and honoured friend Pas-
> tor Archibald Brown. He is of our way of thinking on matters

---

[8] 'The Battle is the Lord's', 2 Chron. 20:15, November 4, 1906.

that are to us of vital importance. He was my father's loved and faithful friend. He has been my friend and the friend of the Tabernacle Institutions all these years. We know how faithfully and earnestly he proclaims the old gospel, and what good success God has given him in winning souls.[9]

Without delay the members of the Metropolitan Tabernacle acted on this proposal and called Brown as a co-pastor.

With an emotion he could not suppress he broke this news to the church at the close of a communion service, asking for their prayer, and assuring them that he had not the least desire to move, enjoying, as he was, 'everything a pastor could desire'. But, as he also told them, the pull to the Metropolitan Tabernacle was strong: 'I cannot forget that I was originally a member of that church, that my father was a deacon, that I was a son of the College in its earliest days, that I had the priceless privilege of being one of the most intimate friends of dear C. H. Spurgeon, a man for whom I often felt I could lay down my life.' The fact that it was to be a co-pastorate, if he accepted, was an appeal rather than an obstacle for it meant that, after one year, he would have a friend with whom to share the weight of responsibility.

At a meeting of the Chatsworth Road Church on April 29, 1907, a unanimous resolution was passed which included the words, 'Whilst these longings prompt us one and all to constrain our beloved pastor to abide with us, we dare not, we would not, disregard the possible fact that God in infinite love and wisdom may be calling his servant to a wider sphere of service.'[10] On that same evening, at a meeting of the Sunday

---

[9] *S&T*, 1907, p. 282.

[10] Quoted by Ellis, *God's Full-Orbed Gospel*, p. 22. A MS letter of Brown's to an unnamed recipient—probably the church secretary at Chatsworth Road—dated April 13, 1907, read: 'Accept my warmest thanks for your kind note conveying the

School teachers, another resolution was unanimously passed, 'expressing sympathy with the Pastor at this most momentous period of his life, praising God for all that he had permitted him to do at Chatsworth Road and for the many souls won for Christ through his instrumentality: also expressing the earnest and sincere desire and longing of each Officer and Teacher that if it be in accordance with God's will the Pastor might continue his work in West Norwood.'

Brown had not yet made up his mind, as he wrote to the teachers the following day: 'My whole heart clings to Chatsworth Road. There is no desire to leave . . . nothing but a deep conviction that I have received an imperative call from God could induce me to. I am waiting to know his will and it is not yet revealed.'

At the Sunday evening service on May 5, Brown preached on 'God's word and a worm', from Job 25:6; Psa. 22:6; and Isa. 41:14, 'Fear not, thou worm Jacob, and ye men of Israel; I will help thee, saith the Lord.' Against his sermon record for that night he wrote, 'It was *Isa. 41:14 that decided me to accept the call to the Met. Tab*' (his italics). He announced to his people that night his acceptance of the call to the Metropolitan Tabernacle, and the letter of his acceptance, dated May 4, was later printed for all to see. It began:

TO THE MEMBERS OF THE CHURCH OF
THE METROPOLITAN TABERNACLE
My dear Brothers and Sisters in Christ, Never have I written a letter that is the outcome of so much soul travail and sore agony as this. God only knows what it costs.

---

essence of the resolution paper at the church meeting last evening. I greatly prize it. Never did I need its promised prayers more than now. Yours gratefully, Archibald Brown.'

My happiness among my people here is perfect. We all live in love, and our heart-strings are interwoven . . . I recognise the stupendous difficulties of the sphere to which you call me, the complete change in the neighbourhood, the apathy just now of the masses, and the spirit of infidelity that is abroad. To maintain a faithful witness, rather than a popular ministry, is the limit of my expectation.

What this decision meant to Brown is borne out by a note in his sermon record for the following Sunday evening when his theme was 'The Story of the Father's love', from Luke 15:11: 'I was able to forget the heart-breaking experience of the past few weeks.'

With the knowledge of the short time left for Brown at Chatsworth Road, the numbers and the attention to his preaching were greater than ever. On successive Sundays he noted, 'Great crowd', 'Tremendous crowd', and even on Wednesday, May 29, when he baptized 26, 'About 600 present.' On his last Sunday morning, June 2, his sermon was on 'Make your calling and election sure' (2 *Pet.* 1:10, 11). In the evening he took, 'Paul's desire as to the finishing of his course' (*Acts* 20:24), and noted: 'Overwhelming crowds. Had to begin before 6.30. Hundreds shut out.'

At his last deacons' meeting on May 24, it was noted, 'how much they regret his leaving us especially so after the nine-and-a-half years of Deacons' Meetings, all of which have been as happy and natural as it was possible for them to be, the Lord having given his blessing upon the gatherings all along.' On Wednesday June 5, the Farewell Meeting was held. Brown evidently sought to relieve the emotion of the occasion with an element of humour, as he thanked the church for a cheque for one hundred guineas:

He called it a sensible present—it was what his wife was always asking for. He thanked them with all his heart, and knew not whether to cry or laugh, but he had a great objection to the former. When he reviewed the dealings of God with them, it seemed little short of a miracle; he had been so perfectly happy there, not a passing shadow, not an unkind word, nor he believed an unkind thought. The years had flown by so swiftly that he hardly realised the time had passed. He had not the least wish to go, for he was as happy there as a mortal man could be. But it was of no use to preach about doing the will of God unless it was carried out in the life. He might tell them he decided to decline the call, and even sketched out the letter to be sent. But the thought, 'Am I doing the will of God?' so came upon him that he felt so ashamed and cried, 'Lord, take my few remaining years if thou wilt.' He has thought for some time of the little cottage on the cliff, where he might retire and peacefully end his days, and his wife had even been looking about for one. His dreams had been upturned, but he had an inner consciousness that he was doing what God wanted him to do, and what more could be desired. He saw before him then, those who, a short time ago, were found at the opera, the theatre, the race meeting, who now delighted to be present at the prayer meeting. And what God had done he could do, and whoever might stand in the pulpit, might the testimony ever be to the saving grace of God. 'You gave me up for Christ's sake, and I give up the remainder of my days to him.'[11]

A hymn, specially written for the occasion, had for its last verse:

> The Lord's rich grace upbear thee
> In paths Himself doth choose;

[11] Ellis, *God's Full-Orbed Gospel*, pp. 24-6.

For His great work prepare thee,
  To His great glory use.
God lives—what'er befalleth,
  God loves—His will is best:
God speeds whomso He calleth
  Thou shalt be surely blessed.

When Brown got back to the quietness of his study, he noted against 'Farewell Meeting',

> I felt humbled to the dust. It is all through expounding the Word. To God be the glory for these beautiful years of blessing spent at West Norwood. God go with me, as I do what I can only believe to be his call, to the Metropolitan Tabernacle.

James Ellis has recorded how, on Brown's last Sunday at Chatsworth Road, ' a passer-by noticing the crowds thronging into the beautiful sanctuary, and remembering how deserted it had been before Mr Brown's advent, remarked: 'What a testimony to the value of simple Bible teaching; he is an example of what the people want.'[12]

Chatsworth Road Baptist Chapel.

---

[12] *Pluck, Patience and Power*, p. 112.

THE UNEXPECTED AT THE
METROPOLITAN TABERNACLE

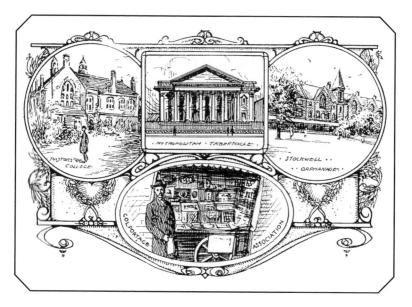

Metropolitan Tabernacle Institutions.

'The Deacons met the Elders in their room on Monday evening April 15th 1907, to consult them in regard to a proposal to ask Pastor A. G. Brown to accept a Co-Pastorate with Pastor Thomas Spurgeon of the Metropolitan Tabernacle. After conference and discussion it was unanimously decided to ask Mr Spurgeon to interview Mr Brown in regard to the matter, and to submit the proposal to a Special Church Meeting to be called at an early date.'

From the Minutes Book of the Deacons
of the Metropolitan Tabernacle.

THE call to the Metropolitan Tabernacle did not require the Browns to remove from their home at Idmiston Road, West Norwood. But, apart from keeping the same home address, little remained the same. The new work at the Elephant and Castle constituted an enormous difference. It is true Archibald Brown was only 63 when he became a successor to Spurgeon, and co-pastor with his twin son in June 1907, but in the forty and more years since he had entered the Christian ministry he had not faced a situation such as that now before him.

It was not that he was unused to serving large numbers; in fact, by 1907, the attendance at the Metropolitan Tabernacle had fallen to figures similar to those he had known at the East London Tabernacle. Previously, however, his experience had been to see numbers grow around him, so that individuals were all known to him personally. Now he was among a great many whom he did not know. Something else was also new to him. Never before had he served a numerically declining congregation, as was now the situation at the Metropolitan Tabernacle fourteen years after Spurgeon's death.

After the initial differences in the church, it was Thomas Spurgeon who had been called to that pulpit in 1894. With something of his father's spirit, yet not possessing all his father's gifts, the son had undertaken the responsibility bravely, but not without much strain. The destruction of the old building in 1898 was among heavy disappointments through which he had to lead the people. His mother had died in 1903.

Despite Thomas Spurgeon's labours, numbers fell. One consequence of that fact would not immediately occur to us, namely, that the Metropolitan Tabernacle supported a whole range of agencies and institutions (of which the College and the Orphanages were only three). The maintenance of these depended in part on the income of the church. Even at the height of C. H. Spurgeon's extraordinary influence, the financial responsibility for these agencies could weigh heavily on him. After his death, reduced numbers meant reduced finance, and a still heavier burden for his successors. In the course of time the retrenchment of these agencies would be inevitable; some would close, others—as the College—would become slowly independent. But in 1907, in the after-glow of Spurgeon's ministry, when there was little readiness to give up anything he had begun, the attendant ministries were still being maintained. For the pastor of the Tabernacle this meant that, as well as the responsibility for three services every week, there was a wider degree of support expected.

The range of Brown's new duties, additional to the full schedule of preaching, was extraordinary. He was a Vice-President of the College; President of the Colportage Society (a vigorous organisation of men for the distribution of Christian literature); he presided at Missionary meetings, Sunday School anniversaries, the Metropolitan Tabernacle Evangelists' Association, and much more; he was expected to speak on countless occasions—from watch-night services and thanksgiving days, to his two-hour long address on his visit to

Palestine (so popular that he had to give it twice). It is true he had the help of assistant pastors, first C. B. Sawdray, then T. L. Edwards, both faithful men; but for the first year, according to the arrangement made with Thomas Spurgeon, now on sick leave, Brown was expected to preach at all services.

On his first Sunday, June 16, 1907, his subjects were, 'Things new and old' (*Matt.* 13:52), and 'Whom we preach' (*Col.* 1:28). The preacher noted in his sermon record: 'There was a great congregation and I trust the power of God was present. Place filled. Felt much liberty and joy.' The next day a tea of 'gigantic proportions' was served before a Welcome Meeting began at seven o'clock with the singing of Psalm 100, 'All people that on earth do dwell', to the tune 'Old Hundreth'. A letter was then read from Thomas Spurgeon, who was on the Continent seeking better health, and 'the loudest applause ensued when the hope was expressed by the new Co-Pastor that ere many months had passed he and his beloved brother would be working side by side in the service of the church'.

When the Browns had left Chatsworth Road, his wife, Hannah, had been given a presentation by the church and light-heartedly addressed as 'co-pastor'. Her reputation had gone before her, and in a letter to her from 'All the members' at the Tabernacle's Welcome Meeting, it was said: 'We have heard how gracious your service has been at West Norwood, and how much you are beloved by the church there; nor are we unmindful of the loss our brethren and sisters have sustained in parting with you.'[1] One could wish we knew more of all that Hannah meant to her husband's life and ministry.

---

[1] The Tabernacle agencies were not slow in making use of her gifts. At the Metropolitan Tabernacle Mothers' Meeting, on December 2, 'Mrs Archibald Brown gave the mothers an earnest gospel address.'

A report of the Welcome Meeting says it was not until a 'late hour' that 'Pastor Archibald G. Brown rose to respond to the many kind wishes that had been expressed on his behalf.' That is hardly surprising for, besides other speakers, no less than twenty-nine 'Missions, Societies, Institutions, *etc.*, connected with the Tabernacle' had given their 'half-minute greetings'. That all kept to the time allotted may well be doubted.

Brown's sermon record for the following months reveals that he did not find the adjustment to the new situation an easy one. On his second Sunday evening he preached on the text of Luke 7:14, 'An Interrupted Funeral', which had been attended with such consequences at Stepney Green. On this occasion he noted only: 'Large gathering. Did not feel at home. Conscious of lack of power.' Over the next weeks the comments varied between, 'Did not feel happy', and 'Felt wonderfully at home. God was there.' It should be said that the purpose of these comments was not so much to record his feelings as to note his assessment of the helpfulness of the subjects which he took, hence such comments as 'Interesting theme', 'Makes a glorious subject.'

He had only taken a short break before taking up the work at the Tabernacle, and he went on preaching three times a week through the summer of 1907. There were also about 500 present for the mid-week service he took on Thursday evenings. The pace caught up with him. *The Sword and the Trowel*, September 1907, after noting that Pastor Brown was 'being greatly helped in his ministry', reported that 'he is, at the time of going to press, indisposed . . . but his trouble, we are glad to know, is not serious; it is a kind of malarial fever which attacks him almost annually in the spring-time—this year it has come in the autumn.' He intended to take 'a well-earned holiday next month', and be back in the pulpit on October 27.

He was back on that date, and immediately into additional duties such as presiding after the evening service at the meeting of the Lambeth Auxiliary Sunday School Union. The next month saw him presiding at such gatherings as the Annual Meetings of the Pastors' College and the Zenana Mission.

The copies of *The Sword and the Trowel* after Brown's arrival show one significant difference from the content of the magazine in C. H. Spurgeon's time. After Spurgeon began that monthly in 1865 he had remained its editor, as well as being President of the College and the other Tabernacle institutions; understandably his ministry had always been prominent in its pages. When Brown came, Thomas Spurgeon, although absent, continued to be the editor of the magazine, with major assistance from Dr A. McCaig, Principal of the Pastors' College. Thomas Spurgeon was also President of the College. For whatever the reason, in the six months after Brown's arrival at the Tabernacle comparatively little about him, or from him, was to find its way into *The Sword and the Trowel*. The new co-pastor contributed virtually nothing to its pages, and notice of his ministry is only to be gleaned from paragraphs under a heading of 'Tabernacle Tidings'. I do not believe that there was any intentional side-lining of AGB, and the omission was to some extent rectified the following year.[2]

---

[2] The *S&T*, 1907, did give a short account of Brown's life to mark his arrival, speaking of him as 'greatly beloved by the Tabernacle members for many years', but the presence of some who would scarcely know Brown may have prompted the article. The index for the 1908 volume lists one sermon and one address, and there also began a series containing summaries of some of his sermons, 'set forth by his son Pastor Douglas Brown'. This was hardly enough. Perhaps an awareness of this fact was being recognized in Thomas Spurgeon's words in his Preface, written after the conclusion of the 1909 volume, 'Our magazine has always recorded matters of interest at the Metropolitan Tabernacle. Henceforth it will be able, we hope, to devote more space thereto' (p. iv).

Understandably, the congregation still looked to Thomas Spurgeon as their main leader and were expecting the resumption of his role.

* * * * *

In the Christian ministry, as everywhere else, serious difficulties come unexpectedly, and it was little more than six months after his settlement that Brown faced one. In part it was occasioned by what was happening in another London church, the City Temple, where Joseph Parker had been succeeded by R. J. Campbell. This church belonged to the Congregational Union, and Campbell proved how far liberal unbelief had advanced in that denomination. His preaching—publicised in his book *The New Theology*—owned no dependence on Scripture, and distinguished 'the Christ of experience' from 'the Jesus of history'. He identified 'the Christ idea' as 'a living factor in the spiritual evolution of mankind'. It was a sign of the times that before Campbell's settlement in London he was described as 'the most popular minister in Brighton'.

It was customary for the Baptist Union to use the large premises of the City Temple for their annual president's address, but in 1907 neither the president or other Union officials wished to appear to be condoning Campbell's teaching, and the possibility of their hiring the Metropolitan Tabernacle for their meeting in April 1908 was raised. At that meeting the presidential address would be given by Charles Brown, no relation of AGB's but a definite evangelical. Before any request was made to the Metropolitan Tabernacle, a Baptist minister raised the possibility informally with Archibald Brown, who responded that 'as far as he was personally concerned there would be no difficulty, but that when the application came, it would rest with the deacons to decide and reply'. Such was the wording recorded in the Deacons' Meeting of December 2, 1907, to be followed by this:

> The Court expressed the unanimous opinion that as no question as to joining the Union was involved, and that it was merely a case of lending the Building for a specific meeting and for which a charge could be made, it is desirable to accede to the request when it is made.

It was an additional suggestion at the Deacons' meeting that led to trouble. Understandably, a senior deacon proposed that Pastor Brown write to Pastor Thomas Spurgeon at Meran, Austria, for his approval. A letter was duly sent, and the response (December 9) was, in Spurgeon's own words, 'emphatically in the negative'; he added, 'the onus of the refusal I am willing to bear alone'. By the time of a Special Deacons' Meeting (December 16), the request from the Baptist Union for the hiring of the building had arrived and, after AGB had placed his colleague's letter before them, it led to this statement by him:

> As Mr Spurgeon's colleague he would, in the event of a refusal being sent to the Baptist Union, have to join in the refusal but as a Christian man, he could not endorse an act which he should consider lacking in Christian courtesy. Seeing then that he could not acquiesce in the reply which must follow the adoption of Pastor Thos Spurgeon's verdict and he should refuse to act in any way that was in opposition to his brother in the ministry, he had no alternative but to tender his resignation to the Deacons. His hope was that Mr Spurgeon had misunderstood the purport of the request, and had supposed that this was in reality a move in the direction of membership of the Baptist Union. As regards that matter,

he had at some cost joined the late beloved C. H. Spurgeon in his great protest, and although the present membership of the B.U. was entirely different from that of which it was composed in C. H. Spurgeon's lifetime, he had no desire to rejoin and should in all probability remain outside to the end of his life. In the refusal however to lend the building for the holding of an Annual gathering of the Ministers of the denomination he could not co-operate. Especially as similar facilities had recently been granted to the Baptist Missionary Society, the Sunday School Union and others.

The deacons shared Brown's opinion of a misunderstanding on the part of Thomas Spurgeon and decided that three brethren should draw up a letter to the absent co-pastor. By the next day the draft letter was written and brought that evening to another Special Deacons' Meeting (December 17), where Brown was not present. It was now thought best that on such a sensitive issue Dr McCaig should take the letter personally and discuss the difficulty with Spurgeon. It was also agreed that McCaig should take the letter subject to Brown's approval of its content.

For the third night in succession, another special meeting of the deacons was held on December 18, Brown being absent on account of other duties in the Tabernacle. At this meeting it was noted that the draft letter to Thomas Spurgeon had not been approved by AGB, and it was cancelled. One of the members reported that in a private conversation with Pastor Brown earlier that day, 'the Pastor had said that his resignation, which he had submitted by word of mouth on December 16 must be considered seriously.' At that point it was considered urgent enough to ask Brown to interrupt his interviews with candidates for membership (taking place in the adjoining vestry) and to join them. On his arrival, the record reads:

The Chairman then expressed the deep concern of the Deacons that after so rich a time of blessing anything should have occurred to mar the harmony, and their confident expectation that all would end satisfactorily. With regard to Pastor A. G. Brown's resignation, they hoped that the Pastor would allow this to stand in abeyance, and that it go no further than the Deacons' Court for the present. To this the Pastor cheerfully assented.

McCaig, armed with the latest information from this meeting, left the next day for Austria. After two days with Thomas Spurgeon, he wrote two letters back on December 24, the first to all the deacons and the second a 'personal word' to one of them (F. H. Ford). The next day Thomas Spurgeon wrote at length to Brown. It was a cordial letter—for the relationship between the two men had always been good—and summarised well the reason for his disagreement. It lay in no personal quarrel with Charles Brown or individual members of the Baptist Union, but in the fact that the Union had not rescinded their censure of his father when

> he stood for the Evangelical Faith—he asked only that a simple creedal basis be adopted. There has been no expression of regret, no acknowledgement that his indictment was true, and his protest justified . . . If it be urged that by lending the building we do not at all identify ourselves with them, I can only point out that, on the same reasoning, the B.U. does not identify itself with the teaching of Mr Campbell by taking the City Temple. I could not conscientiously consent to lend the building so closely associated with C. H. Spurgeon to an organization which has so treated him. I feel—and O my dear Brother, I can assure you that this is one of the most solemn convictions I have ever had—that I must continue, at all costs, to be absolutely loyal to his dear memory. To

accede to the request commends itself to me, of course, as an act of courtesy, but, since it appears to me to infringe upon my fidelity to CHS's memory as my much loved father, and as the Champion of God's truth, I must sacrifice the courtesy. I can do no other.

I will only add that I could wish you and the deacons saw with me and shared my feelings, but I do not fail to recognize that if you do not and cannot, you have a right to act accordingly to your own conscientious views.

These letters did not fail to make an impression when they reached London. Also preserved in the Deacons' Minutes is McCaig's personal letter to Mr Ford, and, given the united affection for Thomas Spurgeon, it may have been the closing paragraphs of this letter that had most effect:

I am also sorry to find that this affair with the B.U. has greatly troubled him and has distinctly thrown him back [in his health]. Of course, one of the essential things that his doctors have insisted upon was that he should be kept free from worry. Personally I feel very sorry that the matter has arisen at all, and if as he so strongly seems to think he will not be able to resume the ministry at the Tabernacle it would appear a great pity to cloud the closing days of his pastorate by doing what would give him pain, so that I should be glad if Mr Brown and the deacons saw their way to agree with him in this B.U. business.

All three letters were before the deacons when they next met on December 30, and they noted:

From these it was clear that Pastor Thomas Spurgeon had conscientious objections to the visit of the Baptist Union. Pastor A. G. Brown stated that although in common with the Deacons he had no fear of any misconception arising from such a visit, and could have wished that Pastor Thomas

Spurgeon had seen his way to join in the approval, he would not on any account act in opposition of his Colleague, and in the event of the Deacons desiring to refuse the loan of the Building in order to meet the views of Mr Spurgeon, he was prepared to withdraw his resignation and act in concert, stipulating only that his personal feeling in the matter be made clear to the Baptist Union. The protest having been made, the whole incident would be obliterated from thought and buried with a Memorial Stone. This course was unanimously adopted.[3]

A deputation of three was appointed to meet the Secretary of the Baptist Union and to ask that the application for the loan of the building be withdrawn. They subsequently reported back that Dr J. H. Shakespeare, the Secretary, while acceding to their wish, 'expressed his extreme regret that it had not been found possible to give them the opportunity they had sought of making a public protest by leaving the City Temple and holding their meeting at the Metropolitan Tabernacle, the recognized centre of Evangelical Truth'.[4]

There the matter rested, but there was a statement on another subject in one of McCaig's two letters from Austria that Brown would not have missed. It read: 'The beloved President [of the College] has for some time been feeling that

---

[3] In a brief reference to this disagreement, W. Y. Fullerton wrote that Thomas Spurgeon said to Brown 'The Baptist Union almost killed my father.' To which Brown is said to have replied, 'Yes, and your father almost killed the Baptist Union.' *Life of Spurgeon*, pp. 307-8. But this conversation did not belong to this time when there was no possibility of personal discussion.

[4] Dr Shakespeare was hardly authorised to speak for all the Baptist Union, given that at least some of its members (Dr Clifford notably) were of known sympathy with the teaching of R. J. Campbell. It would also seem regrettable that the deputation only stated the opposition of Thomas Spurgeon in terms of his 'not being true to his father's memory in agreeing to the proposed visit'. I will comment further on Brown's part in this below.

the state of his health would not permit of his returning to the Tabernacle work. He tells me that he has been intending to let the deacons know that his resignation must be made absolute.'

If it came as a shock to the church when, on February 8, 1908, Thomas Spurgeon wrote from Austria to say that he had to stand by his original resignation, it cannot have been to Brown. While thankful for the furlough and the rest that he had been given, Spurgeon wrote, 'I do not, I regret to add, feel that I am sufficiently strong to resume the work at the Metropolitan Tabernacle, even with the able co-operation of Pastor Archibald Brown . . . It is a comfort to me to know I now leave the work in such good hands.'

The surprise to the church was quickly followed by a second one. Thomas Spurgeon's assumption that the pastorate would now continue in Brown's hands was based on the stipulations of the Tabernacle's Trust Deed which stated that, in the event of there being co-pastors, on the death or resignation of one, the other remains as the sole pastor. But without prior discussion with church officers, Brown announced at a Sunday service that he 'absolutely relinquished the legal rights to the Pastorate and would only consider an invitation from the Church which was practically unanimous'. When the deacons met on March 9, 1908, he repeated this statement: 'He desired to make it perfectly clear that he was not seeking the position.'

In the light of this development, the deacons immediately proceeded to frame a resolution in which they 'heartily and candidly invite him to become their Pastor, believing that the Church was led of the Holy Spirit to call him to the Co-Pastorate in April last by a unanimous vote. They desire to record their devout thankfulness to God for the blessing which has attended his ministry amongst them during the past ten months and the manifest power which has accompanied the exposition and preaching of the Word.'

On March 11, 1908, two nights later, at a special church meeting where Brown was not present, a vote was taken on this resolution, and when the chairman announced it was carried without a single dissent, 'the audience rose and sang the doxology with much fervour'. A deputation was sent at once to the Pastor's home with this news. Yet there was no immediate response, and uncertainty remained when the April issue of *The Sword and the Trowel* had to go to the press. Under a heading, 'Personal Paragraphs', the thankfulness of the congregation was expressed that God 'has so graciously provided for the needs of the Tabernacle work in sending Pastor A. G. Brown among us . . . if, as we all hope, he consents to remain as Pastor we trust that great blessing will crown his ministry and bright days await our historic church.'

At a deacons' meeting on March 17, Brown did consent (too late for the news to be in the April magazine), but only after further discussion in which he plainly stated his concerns:

> He felt the tremendous responsibility of the task especially as he was not a young man and moreover his personal inclinations were toward a retirement from the more public offices of the Ministry. He suggested that he should be allowed to fill a more temporary position. The brethren pointed out that the leadings of God's Spirit appeared so unmistakably to direct that he was to be the permanent Pastor of the Tabernacle Church . . . After further deliberation, Pastor A. G. Brown said that in dependence upon the Lord he would accept the responsibility of the position.

At a special meeting of the members of the church on March 26, this was made known to them, and a letter read from AGB, perhaps the most open-hearted and poignant he ever wrote:

Dear Brethren and Sisters in Christ,

Before giving an answer to the solemn and momentous call to the Pastorate of this Church, permit me in a few sentences to give its history from my standpoint. The same thing may appear so different when viewed from opposite positions. Most of the misunderstandings in life arise from this—that we do not attempt to place ourselves in the position of the one with whose judgment we do not agree.

Your perfectly unanimous call precludes the idea of any differences on your part, and is to me the weightiest of arguments. Yet allow me for a few moments to bring before you the history of the past year as it has concerned me personally.

Twelve months ago I was in the midst of the most loving, united people any pastor could desire. The blessing of God was on us all, and I was supremely happy. No thought of change of sphere troubled me. The only dream of the future was an ultimate retirement into seclusion, to spend my remaining days in the quiet of the country, in the study of the Word and the joy of preaching the gospel in various places without any burden of a pastorate.

I cannot charge myself with any sin in this desire after forty-four years of service in London and its suburbs, and I acknowledge frankly that my natural leanings are still in that direction.

It was on the 14th of April last that I first heard of the proposition to call me to the Co-Pastorate of the Metropolitan Tabernacle. It was a bolt from the blue, utterly unthought of as well as unsought; it shattered all my pretty dreams of future seclusion.

The call came and my first instinct was at once to decline it, and I should have done so, but, having prepared a sermon to preach on May 5th from the words, 'Fear not, thou worm Jacob', I was condemned by my own sermon. I saw that I was actuated more by fear than by a desire to do God's will. That Sunday night service settled the matter. Though feeling in myself as weak and as unable for the task as a worm, I relied on the promise, 'I will help thee', and surrendered the pastorate at Chatsworth Road, and accepted your call to become co-worker with Pastor Thomas Spurgeon.

My idea and hope was, that, though the work was heavy, there would be two to share it, and that the preaching would be equally divided, and that therefore both of us would have a measure of relief and restfulness.

Of the months in which I have served you I need not say anything. I have endeavoured to be loyal to the Lord and his Word, and have sought only the ingathering of souls and the building up of Christ's church in the faith.

Then through the resignation of Pastor Spurgeon, compelled by his feeble health, I was suddenly placed in a new and trying situation; I felt it only right, at once and openly, to relinquish any and every claim to the Pastorate based on the fact of being already Co-Pastor.

Your remarkable meeting on the 11th of this month, in which with absolute unanimity I was called to the Pastorate, was to me more startling than the call to the Co-Pastorate. Since then I have suffered a mental agony, being well-nigh rent in heart by conflicting emotions.

There was a natural and intense shrinking from the undertaking at my time of life so huge a work, and there has been a deeper dread of resisting the will of God. If, in obedience to what seems to me a direct call from the Lord, I sacrifice all my dreams of a quiet sunset, and gird on afresh, as though I were young, the armour of battle, I think I may rightly claim the whole-hearted fellowship of every member of the church whose call I now accept.

Bear with me as I remind you of a fact that must be patent to all, that this Pastorate cannot be, as in the case of many of my predecessors, one of long years. There is a 'time limit' which nature will not allow to be unduly extended. At the best it can be but a parenthesis; but in that parenthesis God is able to pack abounding blessing which shall extend its influence for years to come, making a brief term practically long.

I would earnestly plead that any 'differences' or feelings of 'partisanship' be from this night reckoned dead—to paraphrase a well-known line—

Let none be for a party, but all be for the Church.

Both by nature and grace I am so constituted that an atmosphere of coldness,—not to say 'contention'—paralyses my activities in Christian service. With one heart and one soul, bearing and forbearing, let us seek alone the glory of the once crucified but soon coming One.

I cannot do better than close these lines by quoting words that were uttered this very month, forty-seven years ago, by him whose name will ever be a sacred heirloom of this Church:—

'I propose that the subject of the Ministry of this House, so long as this pulpit shall stand shall be the PERSON OF JESUS CHRIST. I am never ashamed to avow myself a Calvinist; I do not hesitate to take the name of Baptist, but my creed is Jesus Christ.'

These words I repeat as expressing my own personal position as I now accept your call.[5]

---

[5] *S&T*, May 1908, pp. 233-5. I have omitted a few sentences incidental to the main theme.

Only those who cannot appreciate the weight of the responsibility in pastoring such a congregation as that of the Metropolitan Tabernacle may wonder at Brown's hesitancy at this juncture. Thomas Spurgeon was a dozen years his junior, and yet it was nervous stress more than anything else that had broken his health.[6] Brown was now sixty-three, with long years of constant public labour behind him. He was only at the Tabernacle, as he said, because of his expectation that the work was to be equally shared. His hesitancy was not because he distrusted others; he distrusted himself.

Added to this there were undoubtedly aspects of the church life at the Tabernacle that caused him concern, and not without reason. Statistics showed that in the year to January 1, 1908, 108 individuals had been added to the membership of the church, and the church roll stood at 2,893. But this did not mean there had been an increase. On the contrary, there was an overall decrease of 142 for the year, made up of: 57 transferred to other churches; 22 joined other churches without letters; 7 withdrawn at own request; 104 erased for non-attendance; 1 excluded; 59 deaths.

At the church meeting of February 27, 1908, Brown 'called attention to the seriousness of so large a number being struck off the Roll for non-attendance.' He had never experienced such a situation before. And, more important than the figure, he believed the level of spiritual life in the congregation was not what it had been. An appeal, at a later time, that the members' support on a Thanksgiving Day, 'would be such a glorious evidence that I live in your affection', is perhaps suggestive of one need. Certainly there was a loyal and

---

[6] A consultant's report on Thomas Spurgeon's health, given to the deacons in March 1907, said that while there was 'no evidence of actual organic disease . . . he shows a great deal of nervous depression.'

considerable number at the heart of the church, and they were not without the sense of God's presence at prayer meetings, but unity may have weakened and support for the mid-week meetings had decreased. Thomas Spurgeon's letter of greetings, read at Brown's Welcome Meeting had urged on the church 'a fresh starting point. Some of you can hardly be more diligent. God knows your faithful, self-denying labours. Oh, that all were thus. The luxury of doing good is not for a favoured few.'

* * * * *

Very few prayers of Archibald Brown were recorded, but the following has survived from 1908. It came after the reading of Titus 2:1-15, and before his sermon on 'The Beautiful Love of God', from Titus 3:4.[7]

O our God, we do praise Thee for having already come to meet us in Thy courts. We bless Thee for the privilege of singing Thy praise, and if there has been any music in our hearts, of Thine own have we given Thee, for Thou has put the music there. We thank Thee Lord for the words that have fallen on our ears [*Titus* 2:1-15], and if one may speak for the many, they are words that search us, and words, too, that carry with them an element of rebuke. They are words that make us feel how often we fall short of the true standard of the Christian. We bless Thee for as many here this evening as can say, 'He saved us.' O our God, did mortal tongue ever utter three more blessed words than these, or words with more infinite meaning? If we can say these words, the very

---

[7] At the Metropolitan Tabernacle, Sunday night, December 27, 1908. In his sermon record he noted: 'Snowy night. Felt joy and liberty in preaching to a diminished congregation.'

joy of heaven shall be within our souls. Lord, all the salvation is Thine. We have nothing whatever to do with it. We fought against being saved, but it was Thy love that triumphed. Oh, let the crown be put upon the right brow. Not 'we saved ourselves', not 'we helped God to save us', but 'He saved us', and unto Him be all the praise. O our Father, we thank Thee also for those other five words, 'He gave Himself for us.' Blessed Lord, we want to know not only the salvation, but the wonderful channel through which that salvation has come to us. O Eternal Father, Thou Fount of life, and love, and salvation, we praise Thee because Thou hast revealed Thyself in Thine own dear Son, and, gazing into His face, we see Thy glory. We praise Thee, Thou blessed Son of God, for having given Thyself a sacrifice for us, and now we pray that we might realise the object of our salvation. We pray Thee, teach us how to adorn the doctrine, how to make the doctrine beautiful, because we incarnate Jesus Christ in our every-day life.

Now, our Father, if there should be any here this evening who have not yet passed over the line into Thy salvation, save them tonight. May this last Sunday of the old year be the last Sunday night that they shall be rebels against God. Oh, come into our midst, and may the very simplicity of the theme be both its sweetness and its power. We trust Thee absolutely. Come and breathe an evening blessing into every soul, for Christ's sake. Amen.

13

BEING FAITHFUL
WITHOUT REVIVAL

Faithful women:
Hannah G. Brown (1850-1922) and
Eleanor ('Nellie') Brown (1869-?).

We have not been deceived. Jesus does give rest to those who come to him, he does save those who trust him, he does photograph his image on those who learn of him. I hate the Christianized infidelity of the modern school more than ever, as I see how it rends away from sinful man his last & only hope. Cling to the gospel of forgiveness through the substitutionary sacrifice; spread it with all your might, each one of you, for it is the only cure for bleeding hearts.

Peace be unto you as a whole; & peace be to each one! I greet with whole-hearted gratitude my brother Dr Pierson, & with unfeigned love each deacon, elder, & member, & worker, My own dear brother in the flesh is also ever watching over the concerns of our great work. May the Lord himself keep watch over all. To Mr Stott I wish a long & prosperous ministry where the Lord shall direct him

Yours ever lovingly

C. H. Spurgeon

From a letter of C. H. Spurgeon to his congregation, January 10, 1892. For full text of this letter see Iain H. Murray ed., *Letters of C. H. Spurgeon* (Edinburgh: Banner of Truth, 1992), pp. 207-8.

BROWN had spoken to the main need of the church in a letter to all the members at the beginning of 1908, headed 'Remember Jesus Christ' (2 *Tim.* 2:8). In it he wrote, 'Is there nothing that will preserve holy boldness, enthusiastic activity, and overflowing joyfulness? Yes, there is. The recipe is found in remembering the living Jesus.'

Even while he sought to preach that truth to himself, he was not wholly able to dismiss from his mind the crisis in which he had suggested his resignation to the deacons in December 1907. The stress that had been present in the closing years of his ministry at the East London Tabernacle was recurring. There was less of the buoyant spirit that marked earlier years and a lack of confidence—never previously one of his characteristics—began to appear. At the deacons' meeting of October 13, 1908, it is recorded: 'He reviewed the events since the time of the invitation to him to become Co-Pastor with Mr Thos Spurgeon and expressed his willingness for a revision of the present position if the brethren had any doubt as to the confirmation by the Holy Spirit of his appointment to the Pastorate.'

When the assurance he looked for on this occasion was immediately and emphatically given, 'he expressed his

gratitude to the Lord for the help given in the trying circumstances of the commencement of his work.' To underline their
united support, the deacons went on to record this resolution:

> We do most heartily thank the Lord for his goodness in deliv-
> ering the Church in the time of her great trouble and we
> record our affection and esteem for our beloved Pastor and
> our joy that we are permitted to co-operate with him.[1]

But Brown's sense that he was not to be long in this role
did not leave him. At the deacons' meeting on May 3, 1909,
when it was proposed that the second anniversary of his pastorate 'be observed by a Public Meeting', he said that this was
not his desire. A few weeks later the brethren (deacons and
elders) received this letter from him, written on May 26:

> My dear Brethren,
>   Next month I complete two years of service at the Taber-
> nacle, and after much thought and prayer I have been led to
> the decision not to prolong the same. I can honestly say that
> 'I have done my best.' From the commencement however
> there have been difficulties that I never dreamed of and the
> conviction has been deepened during the past few months.
>   My heart-felt wish and prayer is that God may send you
> some man unburdened with my 'years' and equipped with
> special grace for the great work.
>   For all blessing bestowed during the two years I devoutly
> praise God and give him the glory. For the many kindnesses
> received from you, personally, and also by my dear wife I
> return deepest gratitude.
>   Believe me, yours most faithfully,
>   Archibald G. Brown.

---

[1] 'Her great trouble' would appear to refer to the disagreement of December
1907.

At a deacons' meeting on June 7, 1909, the letter was taken up and amplified by Brown, 'laying particular stress upon what he deemed to be the lack of enthusiasm in the Church as indicated by the comparatively small attendances on Sabbath mornings and also the fewness of candidates for membership'. After much to the contrary was said by the deacons, who instanced the many blessings being experienced under his ministry, Brown agreed 'to consider the matter carefully, and to give an answer after his holiday'. He was to have four Sundays off the next month, to which the deacons added a further two Sundays, 'as Pastor A. G. Brown had recently passed through a severe family trial and was in a low and depressed condition of health'.[2]

Such was the concern and sympathy of the deacons that they met, together with the elders on June 21, to discuss the situation further. Once again, support for Brown was unanimous and five of them were asked to draw up a letter to him. This was done the next day and warrants being given here in full:

June 22, 1909

Beloved Pastor,

We the Elders and Deacons of the Metropolitan Tabernacle Church send you our most cordial greetings in the Lord.

We know your objection to long and wordy communications, but we must ask your patience while we say to you what is burdening our hearts.

You have expressed to many a feeling of dissatisfaction with the condition of things at the Tabernacle since your acceptance under such trying circumstances of the Pastorate of the Church and you have so plainly declared your discomfort

---

[2] 'The severe family trial' refers to a great disappointment Brown had over the conduct of one of his children.

and uneasiness, that we cannot quietly stand by and see you suffer in mind as we know you are doing. Now it is no exaggeration nor fulsome flattery to say that since you have been our Pastor you have bound to yourself very closely the heart of the Church—both Officers and members. Your election was unanimous and after your two years of gracious ministry, the choice of yourself as our Leader would be even more enthusiastic now. But this is a small thing compared to the more important matter we now mention, God has set the unmistakable seal of his Divine favour upon your work among us. We know you rejoice in the frequent additions to the membership. Moreover the testimony of experienced Christians in the Church, and of workers not only in the Tabernacle and its Schools, but in its Missions, is repeatedly heard to the effect that your expositions of the Divine Word feed their souls and establish them increasingly in the faith.

We fear you hardly recognize the extent of the blessing which our gracious God has vouchsafed.

We cannot live in London today without being too well aware of the decreasing attendances at the Places of Worship and the growing dearth of conversions. Is it not for us all to magnify the grace of God in your ministry which yields such results, rather than to look upon discouragements which do but slightly reflect the state of things all around us. But even more than all this: you are called to a great task at an age when most men are seeking rest. You are filling a position which the greatest preacher of his day, when younger than yourself, found a heavy burden. But the importance of the position is as honourable as the work is arduous. The Church at the Metropolitan Tabernacle needs your wise strong guidance and powerful exposition of the Word, more than language can express. We entreat you do not let disappointments of any sort or size, blind your mind to the clearly Divine Call to one of the highest places in the field, for which your past experience and God-given powers have so exceptionally fitted you.

The fight will thicken before victory is assured; and Oh! how necessary it is for such accredited leaders as yourself to hold the fort in the face of the rising tide of infidelity and materialism.

Satan will weaken God's hosts and steal the heart from the bravest if he can. He will multiply temptations and inducements to surrender; not only our field of service, but our homes and our social circles will yield him arguments to hinder us, at the time when our Lord needs us the most. Will you not hearten us by a new manifestation of prayerful faith and the zeal you have exhibited ever since your early ministry, to do battle more vigorously with the powers of evil?

The Master we adore and love is by your side! Your Church is with you! Difficulties of every shape and complexion are but tests of holy courage. There is a sound of a Divine 'going' in the congregation![3] Sinners are being saved! Saints are reviving in faith and zeal! Dear Pastor, accept our affectionate assurance that we believe God has chosen you to stand for him in this mighty war.

We shall not fail to bear you up in daily intercession, earnestly crying to God that he will incline your heart to continue as the beloved Pastor of this great Church.

With our united love,

We are, dear Pastor, on behalf of the Officers of the Church.

To this fine letter Brown replied on June 24:

Words cannot tell all I feel in the way of loving gratitude for the letter received from the united courts of the deacons and elders.

---

[3] 'Going', an allusion to the words of 2 Samuel 5:24 in the King James Version.

Your verdict on the two years of work is such a contrast to that passed by my own heart that I am staggered. Let me in quiet think over the letter when mental weariness, the result of heart depression, shall have passed away through a little rest.

That God may reward you all for your loving consideration is the heart-felt prayer of yours most gratefully.

At the deacons' meeting on September 6, 1909, the first after Brown's return from his summer break, he raised a significant question before speaking of his decision. He wanted 'to know the views of the brethren in respect to the duties comprised in the office of the Pastor, and asked whether these included any responsibility in regard to the oversight of the Institutions'. He was assured he had no responsibility, except for the Colportage Association. The College and the Orphanage were managed by separate bodies of trustees. All that was expected was that he kept 'in close touch' with the Institutions. It was then minuted that 'the Pastor's duties comprise the preaching of the Word, and looking after the spiritual interests of the Church'. On this understanding he said he was willing to continue in the work.

They must have seemed long years since his arrival in the summer of 1907 and not ones he would have wished to live again. When the interviewer, already quoted, met Brown in the vestry of Chatsworth Road Baptist Chapel in December 1900, he said of his appearance: 'Mr Brown has changed little in recent years save that hair and whiskers have assumed a decidedly grey tinge. The same erect, broad-chested figure, frank manly face and clear eye.' Not all that could have been repeated ten years later when his hair had changed to silver white. He had been through the most testing period of his ministry.

* * * * *

It is to the credit of the deacons and elders that the troubles repeatedly discussed in their courts never reached the ears of the members of the church. The preaching they heard from Sunday to Sunday gave them no suspicion of any resignation, nor was there any note of depression in the sixteen sermons preached at this time and published under the title, *The Full-Orbed Gospel.* In accordance with its title, the book shows AGB was riding no hobby-horse. One of the sermons however leads us into a subject which clearly exercised him at this date. As he reminded the church in the sermon, 'A Sound from Heaven', the year 1909 brought them to an important anniversary:

> The sound from heaven came in 1859; that sound was maintained, in 1860, and indeed all through the 60s, the days were days of wonder and joy in the mighty working of God. I am very glad that revival is going to have its jubilee, and be remembered. Perhaps it will enable some of the Churches today to see how far we have fallen . . . All honour to dear Charles Haddon Spurgeon—we love his memory—but let it be remembered that Charles Haddon Spurgeon was living in that revival age. When was this building reared? It was reared when the flames of revival were sweeping through London.

The church upon which there came 'a sound from heaven' (*Acts* 2:2), he preached, was a complete congregation ('they were all in one place'); they were all in unity ('with one accord'); and a people 'steeped in prayer'. What was needed, as he repeatedly said at this period, was that 'the whole membership will join in devout and constant supplication for an outpouring of the Holy Spirit's reviving power'. In a sermon on 'The Supply, Fellowship and Worship of the Spirit', he went over the relationship between the giving of the Spirit and prayer, as stated in Paul's words, 'through your prayer, and the supply of the Spirit of Jesus Christ' (*Phil.* 1:19). Beginning with the axiom, 'All Christians are not equally filled with the Spirit', he urged that it is through prayer that other Christians receive a fuller supply of the Holy Spirit, and that it is fellowship with the Holy Spirit that is at the heart of a living church. Adhering to a tradition, and belonging to a denomination, he warned, was no substitute. Not that he believed the division of the church into denominations was necessarily detrimental to spiritual health: 'I believe it is a good thing, for one denomination looks after some doctrine that would be neglected if it were not made her speciality; but the moment one denomination interferes with Spirit-sharing and fellowship in the Holy Ghost, it becomes a curse and not a blessing.'

Building on an illustration used by James Hamilton, he contrasted churches without the anointing of the Spirit with those enjoying his favour: the first are like little isolated pools between the rocks on the sea shore when the tide is out:

> The little shrimp in this pool knows nothing about the little shrimp in the other pool, although only separated from it by a small ridge of rock. Every little shrimp is living in its own world. But by-and-by the tide begins to flow in, and it fills up all the separate pools until all the little pools become lost in the mighty ocean, and the little shrimps are no longer in their isolated pools, they are all in the great fullness of the ocean. So it is with us: when the religious life is low and ebbing, how big our little pools look! How little fellowship there is with others round about us! . . . You will never have fellowship with anyone so delightful as fellowship in the Spirit. That is the charm of the prayer-meeting . . . Did we not realise at our

prayer-meeting last Monday how really the Holy Ghost just came in and took possession of the meeting? . . .

I was so glad to hear that somehow the Spirit of God had laid hold of the teachers in the school this morning, and they said, 'Let us have a quarter of an hour's prayer before we begin teaching.' That is the right thing—the supply of the Spirit through prayer. Then let us ask God to give us the fellowship of the Spirit. Oh, dear little shrimp, do come out of that little puddle of your own! Do not be so small; do not live in a clique; ask God to let you know what it is in the power of the Holy Ghost to allow you to have fellowship with all those in whom the Spirit dwells.[4]

As already mentioned, Brown was now a Vice-President of the Pastors' College, and at the annual College Conference in 1908 he had pressed the need of the Holy Spirit in their midst. The Principal, Dr McCaig, reported in *The Sword and the Trowel*, that after other proceedings, 'Mr Brown gave his address on "How to Secure a Revival". Our brother spoke with great power and feeling, and brought his subject home to the hearts of the brotherhood in a very forceful way.' In that address he laid down six principles:

1. As ministers we must be right ourselves with God.

2. There must be absolute separation from the world in all the methods adopted.

3. We are not to accept the help of hell to cast out demons.

4. Strict limitation to the divinely provided means, *viz.*, 'The Book and the Holy Ghost'.

5. Freedom from all complicity with error.

6. Wait on God until he send the atmosphere of revival, that will produce the desired results without any 'forcing' on our part.

---

[4] *God's Full-Orbed Gospel*, pp. 138-45.

Brown clearly believed that confidence in their spiritual health was not warranted. While evangelism and missions were in vogue in many Baptist churches, and the immediate announcement of 'converts' was becoming more common, the annual 'Statistics of the Churches' for 1907 were disquieting. The churches pastored by men from the Pastors' College showed an average increase of about 3 members per church, losses were heavy: 2,683 by dismission to other churches; 108 by exclusion; 2,360 by erasure for non-attendance. Compared with figures kept for earlier years, these showed a failure to retain those who became church members.[5]

'Arrested Progress' was a theme for the 1909 College conference. In the main address on that theme, the speaker, Pastor E. Roberts, had this to say:

> It is not wide of the mark to ask whether some of these modern methods do any more than capture emotional professions. The secretaries of our associations can tell us that one column in the statistical returns of our churches has grown in gigantic size, *viz.*, the erasures column. I believe I am right in saying that more than half of the net decrease last year can be found in the erasures column of the LBA. I believe from this cause alone the Baptist churches of London alone lost more members last year than the early church gained on the day of Pentecost . . . Is that evil to be looked for on the surface or must we not go far deeper? Does not such wholesale slipping away point to a large amount of superficial conversions? There must be something better than the measures which produce such transient results.[6]

---

[5] Annual Report of the Pastors' College, the number of pastors making returns for the year being 419. The number of pastors, missionaries, and evangelists, trained at the College, and at this date in service, stood at 689. This would include men overseas, whose statistics are not included. *S&T*, 1908, pp. 308-9.

[6] *S&T*, 1909, p. 326.

Whether or not Brown had a hand in asking Roberts to speak, there can be no doubt that the above words represented his own concerns. Outside the churches of the Pastors' College men the situation was worse. In 1908: 'The Free Churches report a decrease of 18,000, our own Baptist Church of 5,000. *The Methodist Recorder* describes the last annual census of Wesleyanism as "distressing in the extreme".'[7]

* * * * *

Despite the trials he felt, Brown's years at the Metropolitan Tabernacle were filled with endeavour, and were certainly not without conversions. James Ellis, who was a contemporary and an eye-witness, says, 'Mr Brown at the Tabernacle proved a great success.' In his three years to June 1910, the additions to the Tabernacle membership numbered 454. If this did not stop the declining membership it certainly arrested the pace of the fall.[8]

Brown's sermon record for 1910 shows he was often conscious of much help from God, and notes included in *The Sword and the Trowel* by its editor confirm this: 'The Pastor has been sustained and helped in the preparation and proclamation of the Truth in a very gracious manner, so that the Word has been pleasant and profitable to God's people; whilst many, who had hitherto remained outside the family circle, have become participators in the grace of our Lord Jesus Christ.'[9]

---

[7] *S&T*, 1908, p. 400.

[8] At the end of 1909 the church roll stood at 2,796, having been 2,893 the previous year. It should be remembered that membership figures on church rolls can differ considerably from attendance figures. At their meeting of June 7, 1909, the deacons recorded that numbers attending on Sunday mornings had not decreased compared with two years earlier, 'whilst the Sunday evening services had increased and were very good'.

[9] *S&T*, 1910, p. 567.

But his sermon record for 1910 also notes concerns. While entries such as 'Good gathering', and 'Large gathering', predominate, there are also notes of 'Poor gathering'; 'Sweet subject. Congregation slack'; and 'Poor gathering but joy in preaching.' On a mid-week service on August 25, when he preached on 'But if not', from Daniel 3:18, he noted, 'Largest Thursday gathering yet. Baptism. Good time.' Attendance was evidently prone to fluctuate.

By 1910 the question whether his health could sustain the ministry was again forcing its attention on him. The year did not begin well. He was absent from the deacons' meeting of January 3 on account of influenza, and at the meeting on the January 24 it was recorded 'that Pastor A. G. Brown was very unwell, and that his medical man had forbidden him to preach for a month.' When the summer came, his health required him to be absent on Sundays from June 26 to August 7. On returning he noted in his sermon record, 'Had a most delightful holiday and feel better for it.' But this improvement did not last and on October 6 he wrote a letter of resignation:

Beloved Brethren,

After many weeks of constant thought and prayer, I have been led to the definite decision of retiring from public life, so far as a stated pastorate is concerned.

You will, I am sure, remember that when I came into your midst as Pastor, it was simply to try and fill the gap until some younger man could be found. This I have tried to do to the best of my power and amid many difficulties, and I gratefully acknowledge the measure of blessing granted of the Lord. At the same time I am painfully conscious of much weakness and failure.

For all the kindness I have experienced, both from the Deacon's Court and also the Elders, I am more than grateful, and as I retire into private life I shall carry with me many a happy memory that will abide for my remaining days . . .

The difficulty he had in writing these words is probably indicated by the fact that it was not until seven days later, on Thursday, October 13, that his sermon record has this note, 'This evening I handed in my resignation having decided to retire into private life.' Against the previous Sunday evening, when he preached on 'Hadad died also' (*1 Chron.* 1:51), his sermon record had this entry, 'Striking theme. Great slump in congregation.'

His resignation letter went first to the deacons. Instead of proceeding to give it the church they asked (October 17) 'for time to make mature deliberation . . . the fact that his ministry had resulted in so much blessing to themselves and the Church generally made it difficult for them to approach the subject calmly.' Two days later they decided to ask Brown to meet with them and the elders on October 31, and queried what assistance could relieve him of some of his heavier duties. This invitation the pastor declined, convinced as he told William Olney (chairman) 'that his health and age precluded the possibility of the retention of the pastorate'. Regretfully, at the October 31 meeting, Olney counselled the letter of resignation should go before the church. No resolution for the church was drawn up, so 'that whatever action is taken at the meeting shall be the spontaneous action of the membership.'

On the Lord's Day, November 13, Brown noted in his sermon record, 'Taken ill in the reading, but returned to preach.' The evening service was taken by Edwards, his assistant. Yet, not surprisingly, when a church meeting met the next day, and the resignation letter read, there was resistance to its acceptance. It was the first time they had ever heard that the subject had ever been raised. A fine resolution was drawn up, enumerating the reasons why his ministry meant so much to them; recording their 'profound and loving sympathy'; asking for any suggestion how 'the strain and burden may be lightened' for him; and affirming, 'it would rejoice our hearts if it were possible for him to reconsider his decision'. They also noted, with gratitude, 'that if any period of our Pastor's Service has been more blessed and more evidently full of power than another, it has been during the last three months; so that although God has permitted physical suffering, he has also granted special spiritual power'.

Reconsideration of his resignation decision was out of the question, as he wrote to a special meeting of the church on November 25, 1910:

> I would gladly do anything you ask that is in my power, but your request in the closing paragraph, — 'to reconsider my decision'—is impossible. Had I arrived at it hastily, and with little, if any, seeking of God, it would be different. It is not the result of emotion, but conviction. It has been arrived at through no little heart-agony, and the arguments of advancing age and ill-health retain all their force. The suggestion of lightening the work is very kind, but does not meet the case. Whoever is pastor should, in my judgment, be really so, and do the work.[10]

Brown was able to resume Sunday services, but not the mid-week ones, till Sunday, December 4, when his sermon record read: 'At home ill.' But he was out to preach the following Thursday on 'Ye Have an Unction' (*1 John* 2:20, 'Very wet night. Poor gathering'). The next Sunday, he took, 'The Cup of Trembling in Gethsemane' in the morning ('Had

---

[10] *British Weekly*, December 1, 1910.

a remarkably good time'), and 'Peace, Perfect Peace', in the evening ('Made a glorious theme'). After one more Thursday evening, and this time, 'Large congregation', his ministry at the Tabernacle closed on Sunday, December 18, 1910, with the texts Ephesians 3:21, 'Unto Him Be Glory', and Acts 20:24, 'The Ministry Received'. The sermon record, kept during his three pastorates, closed with this note: 'The Tabernacle was crammed in every part. I felt the power of God. Thus ends my pastorate at the Met. Tab.'

14

APOSTASY AND CALVINISM

A precipitous drop. A road travelled by Spurgeon in the south of France. This picture was used to introduce 'The Down Grade' in *The Sword and the Trowel,* 1887: 'We look down into the abyss of error, and it almost makes our head to swim to think of the perilous descent; but the road of the gospel, to which we hope to keep by divine grace, is a safe and happy way.'

'The character of an age is determined by
the theology of that age.'

CHS, quoting the *Princeton Review*,
in *The Sword and the Trowel*.

TO most men, looking back on a lifetime, it is a surprise how much change they have seen take place. Towards the end of his life Spurgeon was to say, 'Things are not now as in our early ministry',[1] and we have noted Brown saying the same. Such words are common to all generations, but in the case of these two men they saw a decline in progress in the churches that would affect generations to come. Their belief that they were at a turning point in history was not mistaken, and without a closer look at this subject a biography of Brown would be incomplete.

In 1890 Brown expressed this conviction on the direction of events in the churches:

> God forbid I should judge the motives of those who are trying some of these 'new departures'. I believe that many are honestly actuated by a deep desire to do good. They see the unconcerned masses, absolutely indifferent to the gospel; and they argue, would it not be well to try 'something else', that may, perhaps, lead on to God? That 'something else' is generally a lowering or breaking down of the wall of 'separation' which Christ prayed might ever be maintained . . . the awful and vital difference between being saved or unsaved

[1] *S&T*, 1888, p. 265.

disappears in a general pleasantness. Spiritual power in the church declines. Meetings for prayer grow miserably small. Fiery zeal for the glory of God burns low. Pleasing takes the place of saving. Questions of time 'crowd out' the certainties of Eternity. The 'spirit of the age' is satisfied, and the Holy Spirit is grieved. The church of God is nothing if not supernatural.[2]

These words expressed no passing mood. Two years later we have noted Brown telling young people they would see a day 'when a faithful man will be so scarce that you will have to hunt for him, and there shall be an apostasy on the right hand and apostasy on the left'.[3]

The thinking that led him to this conclusion was straightforward. The truth of Christianity as revelation from God rests upon Scripture as the Word of God. Once the authenticity of all Scripture is questioned, no definite doctrine can be grounded on it. When the foundation is gone, an uncertain message has to be the result. It might be supposed that this would have been clear, at least to professing evangelicals, but it was not. Brown speaks of a discussion with a minister who professed to believe in the deity of Christ, and yet who thought it had to be conceded that Christ's belief that Moses wrote the Pentateuch, and that 'the scripture cannot be broken' (*John* 10:35), was mistaken. 'He so emptied himself', Brown was told, 'that he was really liable to make the same mistakes as other people. He was speaking up to the best of

---

[2] *The Devil's Mission of Amusement, A Sequel* (London: Marshall & Scott, n.d.), pp. 27-28. Quoting this paragraph, Dominic Erdozain has written, 'These words were almost prophetic in their rendering of the issues. They describe very accurately the tone and tenor of congregational life in the following two or three decades—the period in which the great momentum of Victorian Christianity seemed to dissipate.' *The Problem of Pleasure: Sport, Recreation and the Crisis of Victorian Religion* (Woodbridge, Suffolk: Boydell Press, 2010), pp. 246-7.

[3] Psalm 7:3, May 15, 1892.

his knowledge, but he was not infallible.' On hearing this, Brown asked the man, 'Did Christ's knowledge remain "limited" after his resurrection?' On being assured that it did not, he asked for an explanation of the words of the risen Saviour, 'O fools, and slow of heart to believe all that the prophets have spoken . . . And beginning at Moses and all the prophets, he expounded unto them in all the scriptures the things concerning himself' (*Luke* 24:25, 27). 'Dear me', said the man who had sought to put Brown right, 'I had not noticed that before. Good morning. Good morning.' Like many others he had surrendered far more than he recognized. A generation of men were coming into pulpits who had been taught that the making of concessions to contemporary 'scholarship' was the best way to retain 'the essence' of the Christian faith.

From this kind of thinking a form of 'Christianity' was being popularised which lacked almost any definite teaching. 'There seems to be a dead-set made today against all doctrine', Brown said about 1905. 'Let any man dare to say that he does believe clear-cut, defined doctrine—"dogma" is the word—something that he believes God has revealed, well, he is counted far behind the age.'[4]

In the course of time, the advocates of liberal theology would openly rejoice that 'Christianity' no longer meant the acceptance of all Scripture. By the 1930s belief in the verbal inspiration of Scripture was attacked from almost all sides. Dr T. R. Glover, for example, President of the Baptist Union in 1935, believed that 'verbal inspiration is a monstrous belief', that 'Paul was driven to think out a Christology—lots of Christologies, one after another.' The Bible believers of former times were all 'obscurantists'. Asked to contribute an article

---

[4] *'Selah' Or Think of That* (London: Lovejoy, 1906), p. 78.

for *The Times* on the Free Churches, it came out on March 11, 1932, under the heading, 'The Defeat of Spurgeon'. He believed it was for the happiness of all that Spurgeon had 'lost' the Down-Grade controversy. 'Today', he wrote, 'if you want a real old obscurantist college, you have to found one.'

Few thought to ask whether there was any other explanation for this changed view of Scripture. For the large majority the claim that it was simply a matter of recognizing the advance in human knowledge was enough; scholarship had made the older belief untenable. But there was another explanation and it is the one given by Christ and the Scriptures themselves. Man by nature is not only ignorant of saving truth but he is hostile to it. The fall of man has made him the member of a realm in which he loves darkness rather than light, prefers error to truth, and hates anything that would challenge his right to live as he chooses: 'Why do ye not understand my speech?' Christ asked the learned unbelievers of his day. 'Even because ye cannot hear my word. Ye are of your father the devil . . . Because I tell you the truth, ye believe me not . . . He that is of God heareth God's words: ye therefore hear them not, because ye are not of God' (*John* 8: 43-47).

Here is a fundamental truth of Christianity. The dislike of Scripture springs from a hatred of God himself: 'I know you, that ye have not the love of God in you' (*John* 5:42); 'The carnal mind is enmity against God' (*Rom.* 8:7); 'The natural man receiveth not the things of the Spirit of God: for they are foolishness unto him: neither can he know them' (*1 Cor.* 2:14).

It follows that when unbelief becomes wedded with religion then God is no longer supreme. This change was already apparent in 1880 when R. W. Dale wrote, 'In our very religion

God has a secondary place. We have made ourselves the centre of our religious thought.'[5]

If there is one revealed truth about God to which man by nature is especially antagonistic it is his sovereignty. If God truly reigns, if he controls and governs all, then the natural man conceives his own will to be threatened and he rises up in opposition. Far from avoiding this humbling truth about human nature, Brown preached it plainly:

> If it pleases Jehovah to say anything, no matter how stern, how terrible, how searching, I contend there is only one position for man: that is to bow his head and say, 'Amen'. 'Oh', says someone, in the spirit of this proud nineteenth century, 'you are making a bold bid for your God this morning.' I am. The Sovereignty of God needs to be brought to the front. There has been too much trifling with Jehovah. Man needs to have the peacock's feathers plucked out of his cap and be taught that he is a poor little nothing, and that for God to speak to him at all is infinite condescension, and for him to say anything else than 'Amen' is boundless impudence. Shall I take the word of Jehovah my Maker and weigh it in my scales, and bring up his thoughts to the paltry bar of my fallen reason?[6]

Hostility to divine sovereignty enters into the way it has been caricatured. It is not some kind of blind caprice, to be accepted in fatalistic submission. Nor is it one attribute of the divine nature that can be separated from others, 'but a prerogative arising out of the perfections of the Supreme Being'. God in all his attributes, is the absolute sovereign, of right disposing all things for his own glory. 'Our God is in the

---

[5] *The Evangelical Revival and Other Sermons* (1880), quoted by Dominic Erdozain, *The Problem of Pleasure.*
[6] Jeremiah 11:5, December 2, 1894.

heavens; he hath done whatsoever he pleased' (*Psa.* 115:3); 'For of him, and through him, and to him are all things; to whom be glory forever. Amen' (*Rom.* 11:36).

Further, Scripture teaches that it is from God's sovereignty that salvation comes. The salvation of individuals is not on account of some present decision being made in the on-going course of history; rather it is 'according to his own purpose and grace, which was given us in Christ Jesus before the world began' (2 *Tim.* 1:9). Christ gives eternal life 'to as many as thou hast given him' (*John* 17:2). 'All that the Father giveth me shall come to me' (*John* 6:37). All who believe in Christ were elected to do so (*Acts* 13:48; *Rom.* 8:30). There is no explanation for grace apart from sovereignty. 'Even so, Father: for so it seemed good in thy sight' (*Matt.* 11:26).[7] Referring to this truth, Brown preached:

> The tendency of the present day seems to be to represent the emporium of God's Salvation as standing on the great highway, and God in great measure dependent on chance customers. There are no chance customers—there are no chance Christians; every Christian is the product of a Divine call.

That 'call', he showed from his text, is no general invitation but the sovereign action of God according to Romans 8:30, 'Whom he did predestinate, them he also called: and whom he called them he also justified.' To hearers who did

---

[7] The clarity of Puritan authors on this subject is one main reason for the opposition they incur. Thomas Manton on Titus 2:11 wrote: 'Grace doth all *gratis*, freely, and without any merit or precedent obligation or debt. Note then—That the original and first moving cause of all blessings we have from God is grace . . . God saw nothing lovely in us, but yet calleth us with a holy calling according to his purpose and grace. That same gracious purpose that distinguished them from others before all time, doth in time make an actual choice and distinction between them and others by effectual calling.' *Works of Manton* (London: Nisbet, 1874), vol. 16, pp. 39-40.

not understand this he recommended reading 'an old book we used to study years back—I do not know whether it is found in the homes of any of you now—Elisha Coles on *Divine Sovereignty*. Dear me! How that has gone out of fashion today, and yet I think it would serve as a remarkably good tonic to a great many.[8]

* * * * *

If these truths are identified with a man's name, as though he was the author of them, and the sovereignty of God was his teaching, then their rejection is made the more easy. This was done on a grand scale at this period. The controversy following Spurgeon's Down-Grade protest was blamed on his 'Calvinism'. 'John Calvin is supposed to ride us like a nightmare', Spurgeon commented, 'and we lead dogs' lives under his lash. Brethren it is far otherwise.'[9] In Joseph Parker's 'Open Letter' to Spurgeon in 1890 he wrote, 'The kind of Calvinism' which he 'occasionally represents I simply hate, as I hate selfishness and blasphemy.' Another contemporary wrote, 'If any such terrible being as Mr Spurgeon's God existed, I would not worship him.'[10] The *Christian World* (May 15, 1890) commended the former students of the Pastors' College who did not join the re-constituted annual Conference, as those who preferred 'liberty of conscience, to the Calvinistic yoke which it was sought to impose on them'. The same paper pitied 'the faithful few' who supported the Confession of the 'Whitey-Brown' fraternal in which 'The electing love of God

---

[8] Sermon preached on 1 Corinthians 1:9, November 18, 1906.
[9] C. H. Spurgeon, *An All-Round Ministry* (Edinburgh: Banner of Truth, 2003), pp. 268-9.
[10] A newspaper cutting in a scrapbook kept by Spurgeon and now in the archives of Spurgeon's College, London.

the Father', came first in their summary of 'the doctrines of grace'. Labelling it 'Mr Spurgeon's Manifesto', it protested, 'All must be wrong except the few who can pronounce this Shibboleth.' The *Echo* called it 'A Voice from Dark Ages'.[11] Whatever compliments Spurgeon and Brown were still sometimes paid, it was with the exclusion of their 'sour creed' of the 'old Calvinism'. At that point they were 'benighted Puritans'.

How far this rancour had gone by the time of the fourth centenary of John Calvin's birth in 1909 was noted by Principal McCaig, of Spurgeon's College, at that date: 'A well-known Baptist minister in London recently declared that "Calvinism was as dead as Queen Anne". The fashion of the day is all in favour of Arminianism . . . Man is exalted. The royal will of man is made the great ruler.'[12]

As the old Protestant confessions of faith and catechisms were nearly all Calvinistic it is not surprising that they had almost universally fallen out of use in England by 1909, and even where you might least expect it. In 1908, an article by Pastor Ernest Baker, one of Spurgeon's men, found its way into *The Sword and the Trowel,* expressing the belief that, unlike most denominations which have a Catechism or Confession of Faith, 'we have no such book'. Baker spoke of his 'creed' as 'Baptism and the Lord's Supper'.[13]

This was too much for McCaig to allow to pass without comment. He appended a footnote to the article, under his initials, saying: 'There have been in former days Baptist Confessions of Faith and Catechisms and "A Catechism with Proofs" compiled from the [Westminster] Assembly's

---

[11] *S&T*, 1891, pp. 447-8, where the fraternal's Confession is printed on p. 446.
[12] *S&T*, 1909, p. 336.
[13] *S&T*, 1908, p. 570.

Shorter Catechism, and the "Baptist Catechism" is still on sale by Messrs Passmore & Alabaster, price 1d, which we recommend our young readers to obtain and read.' This was followed up in the March 1909 issue of the magazine, with a reprint of 'Creed or No Creed' by George Rogers.[14]

But by this date doctrinal teaching was at a discount even among evangelicals. Thomas Spurgeon, scarcely a doctrinal preacher himself, spoke of the old truths as being given the treatment accorded to some of the apostles—they were being 'put in prison': 'There are certain doctrines that have been cast into the innermost dungeon—the doctrine of God's absolute sovereignty, the doctrine of election according to grace, the doctrine of the substitutionary sacrifice of the Lord Jesus.'[15]

The objection to the teaching of divine sovereignty in salvation is that it attributes partiality or favouritism to God and therefore cannot be true. But this objection rests on an assumption that is false. There is no obligation on the part of God to save any from the consequences of sin. All deserve condemnation. If all should perish it would be no reflection on the character of God. Such is the truth about human nature that there is nothing in anyone to merit or to induce the saving love of God. Scripture teaches that salvation comes from grace alone; it is love and favour for the altogether unworthy and the undeserving. Grace is salvation 'freely' bestowed, apart from anything in those to whom it comes: 'We have obtained an inheritance, being predestinated according to the

---

[14] Rogers took the same position as C. H. Spurgeon who, in recommending a commentary on the *Westminster Confession of Faith,* said: 'We are afraid that modern Christianity knows but little even about the existence of this "Confession", much less its doctrinal teachings. Anything that will secure for it revived interest and renewed study we heartily welcome.' *S&T,* 1882, p. 88, 'We regard the Shorter Catechism as one of the strongest bulwarks of the faith . . . It has been the backbone of Scottish Calvinism.' *S&T,* 1889, p. 576.

[15] *S&T,* 1910, p. 208.

purpose of him who worketh all things after the counsel of his own will' (*Eph.* 1:11).

Men challenge the grace of God because they do not know what sin deserves. In reflecting on how opponents misrepresent the truth, Spurgeon said:

> One said the other day, 'I hate that text which says, "Jacob have I loved, but Esau have I hated."' 'Why?' said a friend; 'what is the difficulty in your mind?' The reply was, 'I cannot see why God should hate Esau.' 'Nay', said our friend, 'I am not at all surprised that God should hate Esau, but I am greatly amazed that God should love Jacob.' That is indeed a marvel of grace, the other is one of the common-places of justice.[16]

When the biblical teaching is not understood it comes as a surprise to people that a man such as Brown could be the evangelist that he was, giving a universal invitation to sinners to come to Christ, and pressing for their immediate conversion. Those Calvinists who did this were accused of contradicting themselves. But Brown did this because Scripture authorises it. The summons to faith and repentance comes from the God who is not willing that any should perish, and to those whose own sin is the cause of their not obeying the gospel. At the same time, along with the preaching of the gospel there comes a call to the chosen, which implants new life, new birth, and repentance and faith are the consequence. A general call of the gospel comes to all, but the 'call' that joins predestination with final glorification (*Rom.* 8:30), is something more. In Brown's words,

> It is not God's world-wide mercy to a fallen race. The call that is intended here is, as Archbishop Leighton beautifully puts it, that call which goes deeper than the ear, touches the

[16] *S&T*, 1888, pp. 260-1.

heart within, throws open the door, and admits Christ. And consequently you find that the word 'called' becomes the title of the true Christian. In Romans 8:28 we read, 'All things work together for good to them that love God.' Who are they? 'The called according to his purpose.'[17]

It is a false theology which in any way does away with the universal call to repentance and faith. Unrepentant gospel hearers are responsible for their unbelief. The invitations of the gospel are real, and truly represent the compassion of Christ towards those who hear them.[18]

At the same time, it is also a false theology which would explain away the sovereignty of God in salvation. Arminianism says that God has foreseen those who will make the right decision and they become 'the elect'. But according to Scripture it is election that leads to faith, not vice versa, and that, necessarily because 'there is none that understandeth, there is none that seeketh after God' (*Rom.* 3:11). It is the person who is renewed by the Holy Spirit who 'sees' and enters the kingdom of God (*John* 3:3). Arminianism blurs the meaning of the grace of God. It fails to say, 'Even so, Father: for so it seemed good in thy sight', and ignores the words, 'I will have mercy on whom I will have mercy, and I will have compassion on whom I will have compassion' (*Matt.* 11:26; *Rom.* 9:15).

Brown's response to the mystery of divine sovereignty and human responsibility is that God has given us no explanation. There are many great truths in Scripture higher than our

---

[17] 'A Blaze of Diamonds', 1 Peter 5:10-11, 1893.

[18] For Brown and Spurgeon's convictions on this point, see my book, *Spurgeon v. Hyper-Calvinism* (Edinburgh: Banner of Truth, 1995). Man's natural inability to believe does not hinder the gospel preacher whose confidence is in the grace of God.

comprehension, and every Christian is called to believe more than he understands.[19] Brown asked his congregation,

> Is there a man in this place who can explain the permission of sin at all—what sin is—where the accursed thing came from—how sin was allowed to find its way first into heaven and then into the fair world that God had made, blighting, blasting, and withering creation, and ruining the soul made in the Maker's likeness? Can you explain it? Rather stand awe-struck at the contemplation of a fearful fact. And then, more mysterious still, out of that very sin God makes his own glory to redound.
>
> I never can understand the man who refuses to worship a God he cannot fully comprehend. I love to think that my God's ways surpass all human explanation and often defy all analysis.[20]

Is it not by the same approach that Paul answers the objection, how can anyone be held responsible if the will of God always prevails? (*Rom.* 9:19-20).

But if the sovereignty of God, and what is called 'Calvinism', rouses such constant objections might it not be the part of wisdom for such truths, if held at all, to be kept in the background? Brown differed from many of his contemporaries in not so believing. Despite the increasing censure of his age he did not swerve from what we have already noted him saying in 1865: 'In our experience we have found that God has blessed the preached gospel most when presented in Calvinistic form.' When the first volume of his sermons was published in 1870, he wrote in the Preface:

---

[19] 'Those who will only believe what they can reconcile will necessarily disbelieve much of divine revelation. They are, without knowing it, following the lead of the rationalists.' CHS, *S&T*, 1872, p. 256.

[20] 'A Sermon on the Sea', Psalm 77:19, June 11, 1876.

The doctrine contained in the sermons is what is generally called Calvinistic, a term which we believe to be synonymous with Biblical—we are among those who bow to the sovereignty of God in salvation, and love it whilst we reverence. The sermon on Redemption sets forth our views on the atonement of Christ, which we hold was made with special reference to his chosen ones. The necessity of the Spirit's work in order to salvation, and the perfect security of the saint in Christ will, we trust, always find a place in our preaching and printing.[21]

Again, at the time Brown became the pastor of the Metropolitan Tabernacle in 1907, he had no hesitation in affirming, 'I am a Calvinist.'

I conclude this chapter by summarising reasons why Brown, like Spurgeon, believed that these truths are too important to be kept out of sight.

1. Brown did not doubt that a person might be a believer with an imperfect understanding of what it means to be saved by grace alone. He did not believe anyone had to become a Calvinist to be a Christian. Indeed, for all Christians 'the ages to come' are needed for the better understanding what 'the exceeding riches of his grace' mean (*Eph.* 1:7). Even so, for strength and assurance of faith this truth is needed by the believer now. Speaking of his own experience, Brown, in a sermon on the words of Zechariah 3:1-5, 'The Lord that has chosen Zion rebuke thee', said,

> There are times when I would not for all the world be without the doctrine of God's electing love. Oh, if you have never done business on the great waters of soul depression, I can understand some of you sneering at it; but if you have known

---

[21] *Sermons Preached at Stepney Green Tabernacle*, Preface (London: Francis, 1870).

what it is to be wiped right out, and to feel what an unutterable sinner you are, you will thank God that, when he loves, he finds the reason of his love in himself and not in you. [22]

Again, in preaching on Isaiah 43:22-25, he said: 'I have often wondered that men kick so at the doctrine of sovereign grace, for they are kicking at that which is their only hope. Turn away from that and you turn away from the only possible way in which God can save anyone.'

For Brown it was grace that enabled him to praise God while still being a sinner. But additional to the believer's own comfort, there is a greater reason for the truth to be known. Salvation is for 'the praise of the glory of his grace, wherein he hath made us accepted in the beloved' (*Eph.* 1:6). In the words of one of his favourite authors, R. M. M'Cheyne:

> Chosen not for good in me,
> Wakened up from wrath to flee,
> Hidden in the Saviour's side,
> By the Spirit sanctified,
> Teach me Lord, on earth to show,
> By my love, how much I owe.

To keep truth in the background that redounds to the praise of God would be to act contrary to the programme which he has determined. In the words of Spurgeon, 'The Lord will take care that, in the transactions of his grace, his sovereignty as well as his goodness shall be conspicuous.'[23]

2. Opposition to 'Calvinism' needs to be countered because history shows that decline in the church commonly begins when the sovereignty of grace is put to one side. This

---

[22] 'The Angel of the Lord Stood By', preached at East London Tabernacle.
[23] Spurgeon, *Commentary on Matthew* (repr. Edinburgh: Banner of Truth, 2010), p. 287.

was the point that Robert Shindler made clearly in his first article entitled 'The Down Grade', from which the subsequent controversy took its name. Examining the period of English church history after the Great Ejection of 1662, Shindler argued: 'In proportion as the ministers seceded from the old Puritan godliness of life, and the old Calvinistic form of doctrine, they commonly became less earnest and less simple in their preaching, more speculative and less spiritual.'[24] Critics who read this article saw the intended application before they read at the end, 'These facts furnish a lesson for the present time.'

Spurgeon protested that the Down-Grade controversy was not about Calvinism, but about the very heart of the gospel,[25] and yet he also said that the inroad of error in the 1880s had for its starting point the attack on Calvinism: 'At first, Calvinism was too harsh, then evangelical doctrines became too antiquated, and now the Scriptures themselves must bow to man's alteration and improvement.'[26] Again, 'Sooner or later, those who rage against sovereignty resist justice also.' As John Owen stated so clearly in his *Nature and Causes of Apostasy from the Gospel,* acceptance of the claim that the truths of Scripture must submit to the corrupt reason of fallen men leads, in its final stage to 'downright atheism'. What Owen saw happening in the late seventeenth century was being repeated two centuries later:

[24] *S&T*, 1887, p. 122. A second article argued, from the same example in history, 'that where ministers and churches have held fast to the truth that the Holy Scriptures have been given by God as an authoritative and infallible rule of faith and practice, they have never wandered very seriously out of the right way. If this be a fact, then there is great peril very near to all, whoever they be, who call in question the divine inspiration of the Word of God' (p. 170).

[25] *S&T*, 1887, p. 642. 'We do not conceal our own Calvinism in the least; but this conflict is for truths which are common to all believers.'

[26] *S&T*, 1885, p. 514.

All those doctrines of the gospel which have anything of spiritual mystery in them, are by many so laden with contempt and scorn that it is sufficient to expose any man unto the contumelies of 'ignorant, irrational, and foolish', who dares to avow them. Such are the doctrines of eternal predestination, of the total corruption of the nature of man as unto spiritual things by the fall, of the power and efficacy of the grace of God in the conversion of sinners.[27]

In 1888, when the Down-Grade controversy was at its height, an extract from *Princetoniana* was put in *The Sword and the Trowel* under the heading 'The Final Conflict of the Systems'. It began: 'The last issue must be between Atheism in its countless forms and Calvinism. The other systems will be crushed as the half-rotten ice between two great bergs . . . you won't get rid of the difficulties of Calvinism by turning Arminian.'[28]

3. The truth that God is sovereign, rightly believed, leads to prayerful dependence and greater care to honour him. In the words of Spurgeon: 'If all the power to create faith must come of the Holy Spirit, those who would propagate truth must be careful to go to work in his way.'[29] In practice that had led the Protestant churches to present the gospel according to the directions of Scripture. But in the Victorian period, such priority came to be given to successful evangelism that whatever methods promised results came to be regarded as legitimate. Will it be 'successful' was the primary consideration, and in

---

[27] *Works of John Owen*, ed. W. H. Goold (repr. Edinburgh: Banner of Truth, 2009), vol. 7, p. 132. It is hard to think of a Puritan work more important and relevant at the present time than Owen on the *Causes of Apostasy* which is to be found in this volume 7. It is also available in an abridged and easy to read Puritan Paperback edition as *Apostasy from the Gospel*, ed. R. J. K. Law (Edinburgh: Banner of Truth, 2003).

[28] *S&T*, 1888, p. 288.

[29] *S&T*, 1886, p. 154.

some circles 'soul-winning' was almost treated as the exclusive Christian duty.

This change has a relationship with the missions of D. L. Moody in 1875. Moody and Sankey were first heard of by some readers of *The Sword and the Trowel* through a commendation of their work in the north of England written by 'an esteemed friend' of Spurgeon's. The words of support from this friend had only one proviso: 'I do not, of course, commit myself to every method our brethren use; but the men are worthy of all confidence and love.'[30] The problem was that the Americans were followed by a generation of lesser and younger men for whom the methods became a necessary part of evangelism, especially the 'enquiry room' to speed up conversions. Spurgeon and Brown were friends of Moody and he had their support, but of the 'Moodyism' that came into the churches in the aftermath of the Moody missions they were by no means uncritical. 'Conversion' made easy was their particular concern. By 1882 Spurgeon was writing: 'Sometimes we are inclined to think that a very great portion of modern revivalism has been more a curse than a blessing, because it has led thousands to a kind of peace before they have known their misery.'[31]

As ever, the situation was mixed. That good was being done by increased numbers of Christian workers was not to be doubted, and agencies for evangelism multiplied. But for Brown there was a deepening concern that a 'machinery' of methods and organisations was taking the place of

[30] *S&T*, 1875, p. 190.
[31] *S&T*, 1882, p. 545. His warnings were heard as early as January 1876, when he reflected on the previous year as 'a year of revival which did not revive the churches, and of mass meetings which have left the masses very much as they were'. *S&T*, 1876, p. 1.

dependence on the Holy Spirit. He feared 'the bringing of the supernatural into one's life work' was being left out. 'One may take a mundane, worldly, merely businesslike view of God's work until the supernatural becomes all but eliminated.' Yet this may happen alongside a lot of evangelistic effort: 'I am inclined to think that in the present day there is an unholy lust after mere visible success . . . we are responsible, as workers, not for success, but for faithfulness.'[32] 'There is such a thing as even desiring conversion work from wrong motives. Have you never had the temptation, "Pray to God to send revival because it will make the church look conspicuous in the eye of the world." You and I must get above all this, and learn to say, "Lord ornament the church and do it for thine own sake! Oh, church of God, if conversion work is going on in our midst, it is the Lord's doing. If round her neck young converts are seen like glittering pendants, remember the bridegroom has put them there. She has no income apart from her Lord.'[33]

Among the new things now being popularised was the use of music and of musical instruments. Both Brown and Spurgeon were concerned at the change. The services at the Tabernacles, both in East London and at the Elephant and Castle, throughout their ministries, had no instrumental accompaniment of any kind. Praise consisted only of the human voice, this being a practice that was recovered at the time of the Reformation. But additional music appeals to human nature, so why not use it to win a larger hearing from the world? The answer that the New Testament church used no such instrumentality was not heard by those who put

---

[32] 2 Corinthians 2:14-16, 1894.
[33] 'The Bride's Ornaments', Isaiah 49:18, April 20, 1873. This sermon pre-dates Moody's coming, a reminder that the main danger ever lies in human nature.

success first. Brown seemed to be speaking for a bygone age when he said:

> God, in his sovereignty, has been pleased to make preaching his greatest power for the ingathering of souls. I do not read that they went forth lecturing, or band playing,[34] or amusement providing; but they went forth preaching. The church has in great measure lost her faith in this mighty weapon, I do not wonder at it, for the church today is losing faith in her Lord, and it follows that she should lose faith also in the Lord's selected instrumentality . . . We are living in grievous times. The church of God is not staking her all upon the power of spiritual weapons. Gymnastics take the place of prayer meetings, concerts in the place of testimony, laughter the place of pleading, and the spirit of the age the place of the Holy Ghost. Pricking of the heart is being changed for tickling the ear.[35]

As Calvinistic belief lost ground, so changes in the life and worship of the church increased.

4. Upholding the sovereignty of God is necessary to a true understanding of revival. It is significant that a major change in thinking on revival took place simultaneously with the passing of faith in divine sovereignty. An idea, promoted by anti-Calvinist teachers, gained wide acceptance. It was argued that just as individual conversions were to be secured by prayer and the use of right methods, so the same means used on a large scale must bring revival. This was the thinking that gave rise to a new class of preachers spoken of as 'revivalists'. To clinch this argument it was asked whether or not God has promised blessing to an obedient people, and therefore if there is no 'revival' the fault must lie with the church.

---

[34] See also Appendix 3 below.
[35] 'Signs Following—What?' Mark 16:19-20, April 1, 1888.

Does not Scripture say, 'No good thing will he withhold from them that walk uprightly' (*Psa.* 84:11)?

The effectiveness of this argument lies in part on a confusion in terminology. The 'reviving' of greater spiritual life within believers is a word referring to renewed devotion to Christ. If this is spoken of as a 'revival' then it belongs only to those already Christians, and it stands related to their obedience. But in the course of history the word became more generally identified with something else—with times of remarkable gospel success and large increase in the number added to the church. In other words, times when something like the Pentecost pattern of 120 becoming 3,000 is seen again, when thousands, awe-struck in the presence of God, attend on the Word of God in great seriousness, and the moral tone of whole communities is affected. Such periods have been like new starting points in church history, but they have never been planned or organised. Commonly they come as a surprise for both the church and the world. In days when Christian testimony has been small and feeble, suddenly there arise many bold witnesses for Jesus Christ.

Such times of revivals were understood in the words of Jonathan Edwards as 'remarkable communications of the Spirit of God'.[36] They were not seen as part of the normal life of the church, nor was their absence taken as evidence of divine judgment, but, to quote Edwards again, 'Though there be a more constant influence of God's Spirit always in some degree attending his ordinances; yet the way the greatest things have been done towards carrying on this work, always have been by remarkable effusions, at special seasons of mercy.'

---

[36] *Works of Jonathan Edwards* (Edinburgh: Banner of Truth, 2005), vol. 1, p. 539.

To make revival dependent upon human obedience—to say, 'If the right lessons are obeyed, revival will follow'—is seriously wrong.

It makes the number of conversions dependent upon men, contrary to the express teaching of Scripture (*1 Cor.* 3:5-7). The time and measure in which God saves sinners is determined by his will. 'It is not for you to know the times or the seasons, which the Father hath put in his own power' (*Acts* 1:7).[37] The extent of the numbers saved lies in the will of God (*Acts* 2:47). As Brown saw at the age of twenty-three, no one should be called a 'revivalist'.[38]

Further, where the use of means and methods is regarded as the sure means of obtaining revival it leads, sooner or later, to discrediting what claims to be the work of God. Where this teaching was accepted missions or campaigns were called 'revivals', even before they ever took place. And thereafter, to give weight to the claim, it was necessary to give speedy announcement on the numbers making 'decisions'. But the real thing cannot be duplicated at the will of man and these procedures ultimately lead to disillusion. When that happens the real thing itself is likely to be forgotten. This is not to deny that earnest evangelistic work is always necessary, but it is not the same as revival.

The error of making revival dependent on the consecration of Christians is inevitably depressing to pastors who think that revival ought to be normal, yet who sow and teach faithfully without seeing any great days of harvest.[39]

[37] This is not to deny that God fulfils his purposes through human instrumentality, and that prayer is a part of that instrumentality. But prayer is not a 'condition' that, once fulfilled, secures revival. I have addressed prayer and divine sovereignty in revival in *Pentecost Today? The Biblical Understanding of Revival* (Edinburgh: Banner of Truth, 1998), pp. 64-79.

[38] See above, p. 46.

[39] This is what happened to William McCulloch of Cambuslang, much used in

For Brown this consequence was bound to follow a misunderstanding of divine sovereignty in revivals. In a sermon on Pentecost, he said,

> The disciples had to learn what we have, that there is a sovereignty in revivals. Man has no power to command one. He can but cry and wait. The sovereignty displayed in the salvation of individual souls, is not more marked than in the revival of churches. In both cases 'one is taken and another left', and the only reason faith can give is 'even so Father, for it seemed good in thy sight'.[40]

The reader of Brown's life will understand that he is not saying the church plays no part in what may lead to revival; no pastor stressed the place of prayer more than he did. But true prayer itself is God-given; it is not human effort which determines the outcome. 'Revivalism' put the emphasis in the wrong place. In a later sermon, 'A Sound from Heaven', on the words, 'And suddenly there came a sound from heaven' (*Acts* 2:2), he began:

---

an awakening in 1742 but discouraged at not seeing the same in following years. Whitefield counselled him: 'I should be glad to hear of a revival at Cambuslang; but, dear Sir, you have already seen such things as are seldom seen above once in a century.' I will note below how Brown's son, Douglas, was the instrument in local revival in East Anglia in 1921. In 1929 he was President of the Baptist Union. But a lack of his earlier influence was noted in his later ministry, and he is reported to have said at a ministers' meeting, 'Pray for me. I have lost my power.' With respect to that petition, Stanley Griffin has queried: 'Was there some personal failure on the part of the preacher? Or had organisation and the denomination taken him over?' *A Forgotten Revival* (Bromley: Day One, 1992), p. 82. The truth may rather be that while he had something of his father's spirit and gifts, he did not have the same theological understanding and this affected his judgment on revival. At the Keswick Convention of 1922 he said: 'I believe that in a very short time we are going to see the greatest spiritual awakening that has ever taken place in the history of our land.'

[40] Acts 2:12, May 19, 1872. In Brown's early teaching on revival there may be a measure of inconsistency on this point. At that date the measure of C. G. Finney's departure from orthodox belief was not yet widely recognised. A discerning criticism of the American's Autobiography was printed in the *S&T* in 1876, pp. 213-18.

Instead of putting the emphasis on the word 'sound', let us put it on 'heaven'. 'There came a sound from heaven.' That is how all revivals come. Do you observe that nothing comes before this sentence? It is the very first record we have of the Pentecostal day of glory. There is no preface . . . We have heard so much of the clatter of machinery, and the noise of restless workers on earth, but what we need to hear, if there is to be a real revival of the Holy Ghost, is a sound, — not that rises up, but that comes down from heaven.

He went on to point out how conviction of sin was missing in the contemporary scene. Those who remembered the last great revival period, following 1859, saw something which men can never produce: 'I will defy any man to make another man feel his sin.' In a touch of autobiography he went on to speak of the difference which he and his friend Pastor Frank White experienced fifty years earlier. White, Brown said,

was one of the thousands of young men who were converted during that revival, and the preacher this morning was another one. I thank God that the sound came from heaven and picked up Frank White and Archibald Brown and put them in college together. Dear Frank White, talking about those days, said, 'I remember such a sense of unworthiness came over us; how it came about I do not know, but we found ourselves with our arms round each other's necks, just sobbing; none could speak and none could pray — there was such a sense of unworthiness and sin.' When the sound comes from earth it puts men up, but when the sound comes down from heaven it casts men down. There is the sense of sin.

May the Spirit of God return again in power to his church! But, brethren, do not be looking here and there for revival; do not say, 'Oh, if we could only get Mr So-and-so, we should be sure to get a blessing!' The only revival worth having is the revival inaugurated by a sound from heaven. May God give it to us all, for Christ's sake. Amen.[41]

5. A denial of the sovereignty of God removes confidence in the government and control of Christ over all history. God reigns in all days, whether of winter or of spring, whether of advancing faith or of growing apostasy. Without in any way being the author of sin, he determines all events: 'I form the light, and create darkness: I make peace, and create evil: I the Lord do all these things' (*Isa.* 45:7).[42] In times when floods of unbelief and wickedness 'have lifted up their voice' the message is the same, 'the Lord reigneth . . . thy throne is established of old' (*Psa.* 93:1, 2). So when the majority of Israel had rejected salvation, Paul remains certain that 'the election hath obtained it' (*Rom.* 11:7). So Brown preached that for the Christian there ought to be no 'gloomy forebodings about the future'. The God of yesterday is the God of tomorrow, and nothing can stop the fulfilment of his saving purposes. 'Nothing can shake the government of God. The election of God it standeth sure; and although the earth may quake the foundation of God's church can never tremble.'[43] As he says in another sermon, the progress of God's work is certain:

---

[41] *God's Full-Orbed Gospel*, pp. 160-1. A commemoration of the 1859 revival in Scotland, held in Aberdeen in 1909, noted how at that time 'the one deep dominant note was an overpowering sense of sin', and believed that the *British Weekly* had been right to say that in recent times, 'An agonizing sense of sin was dying out of English Christianity.' The writer added, 'We fear it is also rapidly dying out of Scottish Christianity, if it has not already done so.' *Reminiscences of the Revival of '59 and the Sixties* (Aberdeen: University Press, 1909), p. xii.

[42] Modern translations do not weaken the force of these words. The New American Standard, for example, reads, 'I am the Lord and there is no other, The One forming light and creating darkness, Causing well-being and creating calamity: I am the Lord who does all these.' Thus even the most dreadful act in human history was determined by God (*Acts* 2:23).

[43] 'Selah', p. 30.

The work of the Lord is continued steadily and surely, night and day, despite all drawbacks, and God knows we are having an awful slump in spiritual work for God everywhere just now, but in spite of all the church grows larger and purer. The walls of the temple will be higher tonight than they were when the day dawned.[44]

How can this be true unless God is sovereign?

The pre-eminent hope of the church is the second advent of Christ. This was central in Brown's ministry and he saw it bound up with the sovereignty of God. The present world will end at his decision. 'He hath appointed a day, in the which he will judge the world in righteousness' (*Acts* 17:31). Now the eye of faith sees Christ with all authority in heaven and on earth, but at his 'appearing', it will be seen by all, 'who is the blessed and only Potentate, the King of kings, and the Lord of lords' (*1 Tim.* 6:15). The original purpose of these words of Paul, as Patrick Fairbairn has written, was 'to fortify the mind of Timothy to a consistent and persevering adherence to the Christian faith and life amid the scorn or opposition of worldly powers of the stamp of Pontius Pilate, by placing distinctly before him the sole supremacy, the peerless eminence, and infinite sufficiency of him who has decreed the future manifestation of glory in Christ, as he had done that of his past humiliation.'[45]

Brown's closeness to the New Testament is not to be seen more clearly than in the place that he gave to the second advent. Consistently throughout his ministry it was a pole star in his thinking. In the 1880s, when the days of remarkable revival had recently passed at the East London Tabernacle,

---

[44] *Full-Orbed Gospel*, p. 235.
[45] Patrick Fairbairn, *Commenting on the Pastoral Epistles* (Grand Rapids: Zondervan, 1956), p. 245.

it was not to engagement in nostalgia, or to expectation of the next revival, that he called the people to fix their attention. When his church at Chatsworth Road was enjoying full pews—the building was redecorated, and a new building added—the message was not of present satisfaction. On the wall above the renovated pulpit platform he had the text placed, SURELY I COME QUICKLY (*Rev.* 22:20). On those words he preached at the re-opening of the church building, and told the people:

> I would not have the text on any of the side walls or at the back, but before you; and my prayer is that this truth may always be in front: not something that you only think of occasionally . . . My hope is that long after many of us have gone to rest, and when a fresh voice will be heard from this platform, it may be a reminder to the preacher who stands where I am standing this evening. It is under this truth we preach. We are waiting for his coming, and he says, 'Occupy till I come.'[46]

* * * * *

These five truths are reasons why Brown in his day stayed faithful to doctrines that so many were neglecting or despising. All five reasons are inter-related. Because the natural man's condition in sin was being under-estimated, the necessity of divine grace to change that condition was giving place to dependence on the human decision. With a sense of sin and of its guilt departing, salvation by grace alone ceased to have the attraction which it needs to have for sinners. And as the churches moved in a man-centred direction, the affairs of

---

[46] 'Selah', pp. 138-9.

this present world muted the biblical focus on the day when salvation will be truly seen to have been 'To the praise of the glory of his grace.' Archibald Brown was looking for the day when he would hear 'the voice of a great multitude' saying like thunder, 'Alleluia: for the Lord God omnipotent reigneth' (*Rev.* 19:6).

15

WORLD TRAVELLER

The last home, Rock Cottage, Easton on the Hill.

'When our friend has left our shores, the memory of his messages will still remain a permanent heritage for God's servants. As Pastors shall we ever forget those three rallying cries of the preacher:

Back to the Bible: The need of the day is Bible teaching.

Evangelical Preaching: This is the road back to greater spiritual power in our Churches.

Faith in the Holy Ghost: To give results to our teaching in saved and sanctified souls.

These words sum up some underlying principles in that great life, and in adopting them as the basis for our future work we shall continue to be blessed and to reap the harvest of labours, for which as a denomination we are unspeakably thankful.'

Thomas Chapman, Maritzburg,
in the *South African Baptist,* January 1913

ARCHIBALD Brown laid down the work at the Metropolitan Tabernacle with the prayer of the people expressed in the words 'that the sunset hours of his long day of service may be filled with abounding consolations'. Perhaps they thought he would be heading for the cliff-top cottage of which he had once spoken. In fact he remained in London in 1911, and was often to be seen, sometimes heard, at the Metropolitan Tabernacle where he remained a member.

The church had arranged a Valedictory service for him and Mrs Brown on January 30, 1911, at which Dr A. C. Dixon presided. Dixon, the pastor of Moody Church, Chicago, was supplying at the Tabernacle, and welcomed Brown with the remark that 'he looked so robust after his recent rest that he was tempted to change the valedictory meeting into a reception, and to welcome him back to the pulpit'. Among the speakers that night was the Rev. A. Douglas Brown. A cheque for £150 was presented to the former pastor from the church, and Mrs Brown was given a gold pendant set with pearls.

At meetings to mark the Jubilee of the opening of the Metropolitan Tabernacle, Brown was 'received with much applause' when he rose to speak at the Public Meeting on

March 16, 1911. The next Sunday morning 'he was in good form, and full of vigour' as he preached on 'Worthy' from Revelation 5:9. That same month Dixon was called to the pastorate. At his reception in June, Brown was one of the speakers, declaring the American 'would ever be remembered as Spurgeon's successor—all other names were merely interludes'.[1]

The Sword and the Trowel, on which I am dependent for the above information, gives what would be a last entry on Brown for some time, when it records:

> Pastor A. G. Brown, whose health has greatly improved lately, has started on a journey to South Africa. He will first visit his daughter Nellie, whose work amongst the Kaffirs he has greatly wished to see for years past.
>
> On Sunday, November 12th, Mr Brown was present at the evening service at the Tabernacle , and at the earnest solicitation of Dr Dixon preached the sermon. It was an exceedingly beautiful discourse from the Saviour's question to the disciples on board the sinking boat, 'Where is your faith?' On the following evening, at the Prayer Meeting, Pastor Brown in saying 'Farewell' to the Church, of which he is still a member, gave a choice address upon the words in the parable of the Prodigal Son, 'And shoes for his feet'.

The almost incidental reference to the Browns' departing for South Africa is not as surprising as it might sound. It marked the beginning of a new stage in his life, and one far-removed from 'sunset years'. Seeing the world from the angle

---

[1] Time would show the words to be over-generous. Although no incoming pastor had sounded just as Dixon did, the difference turned out to more than one of accent alone. 'Why should not every Christian Church double itself once a year?' Dixon asked at his reception, and in an article on 'Winning Souls' (*S&T,* June 1911) he had already shown what would be a great emphasis.

of a quiet retirement would never have been consistent with his make-up. He was now to be a world traveller.

The year 1911 was part of an age when sea-travel was always recommended for health. That was not, however, the reason for a voyage to South Africa. His daughter Nellie, who we last noted leaving for China in 1891, and was said to be so like her mother, was now at Grahamstown, South Africa, and working among the Kaffir people with her husband, the Rev. Ernest Eve, a Congregational minister. Her father was anxious to see her again.

The Browns arrived at Cape Town on the Blue Funnel line ship, *Ascanius,* on Saturday, December 9, 1911, 'both', it was reported, 'looked well. They had enjoyed and profited by the voyage.' He was ready for work, and plans were already in hand among the Baptist churches to use his ministry. On that first Sunday he preached morning and evening in the Wale Street Church. The *South African Baptist* reported: 'The evening congregation was an overflowing one, aisles and passages all being crowded with eager listeners. There is no need to describe Mr Brown's preaching to Baptists. It is full of teaching, illustration and unction. Mr Brown has always seemed to me the only successor to Mr Spurgeon.'

On the Monday the visitors had their first extended view of the scenery in a 'motor ride' around Table Mountain, a distance of 32 miles, before catching the mail train that evening for Grahamstown and the family welcome that awaited them. The news of Brown's arrival and preaching in Cape Town led to other Baptist churches enquiring from H. J. Batts, the Secretary of the Baptist Union of South Africa, whether the preacher could also visit them. Batts indicated in the *South African Baptist* that he was hopeful a programme of visits could be arranged, but he warned that his health would need to be considered, and 'Mr Brown does not undertake missions in different centres, but likes to help by taking the regular Sunday and week-night services.' To encourage churches wishing to invite Brown, Batts also published this letter from him:

> Baptist Manse, Grahamstown,
> December 14th, 1911

Mr dear Brother, Please accept my heart's warmest thanks for your kind telegram of welcome received on my landing at Cape Town. I stayed over the Sunday there with our good friend Mr Baker, and then came on here to visit my daughter, Mrs Eve. It is several years since I saw her.

We purpose going on to Tasmania, and then returning here after the hot season is over, when I hope to have the privilege of preaching in some of the South African Churches.

Again thanking you for your brotherly welcome. Believe me, yours affectionately in Christ,

> Archibald G. Brown.

From Grahamstown this news of Brown's visit was subsequently published:

For some years, during this season, the Baptist and Congregational Churches have united holding the services alternately in each church, the other being closed meanwhile—the two smaller congregations together not making a large one. Mr Brown who, like Paul, must needs preach the gospel, has been conducting most of the services, and many others have gathered with us to hear the Lord's message through his servant; some holiday-makers even returning to town for them.

The name of Archibald Brown is a household word among Baptists and well known, too, among all sections of the Christian church, some ministers of sister denominations being present at some of the services and gratefully acknowledging help. Needless to say it is not in 'wisdom of words' that our honoured and beloved brother preaches, but simply, straightforwardly, a direct message, and in language all can understand. As one said on coming away from a service: 'It is so simply put yet there is so much in it.' Long shall we remember this visit and are looking forward to Mr Brown's coming again, as we understand that after visiting his son in Tasmania, he purposes returning to South Africa, and then hopes to see more of our churches and work in this sub-continent.

We much regret that Mr Brown found the change of climate very trying, but coming as he did from the English winter to our summer the contrast was very great; and some of us inured to this climate have found this summer equally trying. We trust, however, that on his return in the cooler months he will enjoy physically his visit here much better.

The Browns returned from Grahamstown to the Baker's manse at Cape Town on January 24, 1912; then left by sea for Tasmania on January 28. Once again their destination was in the first instance determined by a family consideration. The youngest son of the family, Cecil, aged 23, was now settled in Hobart, after completing an apprenticeship as an electrical engineer in London. There is no record of what took him so far but he was not among strangers. Numbers of the Pastors' College men, known to his father, had joined in the emigration to Tasmania and were serving churches. In 1891, of the nine Baptist pastors who had formed a Baptist Union in that colony, seven were men from the Pastors' College. By 1912 their number had been augmented by Frank W. Boreham. Boreham had gone from London to the young Baptist church of Mosgiel, New Zealand, in 1895, and then moved on to the Baptist Church in Hobart, Tasmania, in 1906. One sunny summer morning, in February 1912, he entered his pulpit as usual, and glancing around the sea of people before him, writes his biographer,

> his eyes lighted on a strangely familiar face. His heart nearly stood still. Sure enough, sitting in the congregation was C. H. Spurgeon's successor at the Metropolitan Tabernacle, FWB's old hero of the East London Tabernacle, the Rev. Archibald Brown! The face was a little more wrinkled and the back a little bent, but there was no mistaking the Homeric figure on whom he had first cast admiring eyes twenty years before. There were sudden memories for FWB of the days when he had sat spell-bound listening to this famous preacher away in London. But what could AGB be doing in Hobart?[2]

If Boreham did not know the reason for Brown's arrival he would soon have learned it. Two years earlier the *Mercury,* Hobart, had published three columns of one of Brown's sermons,[3] and it was not slow to announce he 'arrived in Hobart on the *Ionic* and is staying with Mrs Brown at Old Beach' (February 23, 1912). The location was the place of Cecil's home.

Boreham must have seen a good deal of AGB in the next weeks, and welcomed him to his pulpit. The visit to the Antipodes lasted until April when the *Mercury* noted on Saturday 13, that the next day 'will be the last opportunity of hearing the Rev. Archibald Brown in Hobart'. From there the Browns moved on to mainland Australia. The *Sydney Morning Herald* reported on May 17 that he was spending a few days in

---

[2] T. Howard Crago, *The Story of F. W. Boreham* (London: Marshall, Morgan & Scott, 1961), p. 146. Brown sent an account of the services at Hobart Baptist Church that day to the *British Weekly.*

[3] 'Golden Lines', *Mercury,* September 3, 1910. This was by no means the first Australian paper to write of Brown. The *West Australian* (Perth), March 15, 1886, carried an account of his ministry at the East London Tabernacle ('a perfect network of beneficent agencies') and described him as 'a man of strong individuality'.

Sydney 'on the way to South Africa from Tasmania, where he has been visiting his youngest son. Mr Brown will preach in Bathurst Street Baptist Church this evening.'

En route to South Africa, the Browns stopped at Adelaide, on the south coast of Australia, where the *Advertiser* reported their arrival on May 25, 1912. After a summary of his ministry and close association with Spurgeon, the paper continued:

> While in Tasmania he delivered the Baptist Union sermon at Launceston, of which the following account was given:
>
> 'The great preacher has such a noble presence and delightful simplicity of manner, that before he begins to speak he has won all hearts. His voice has music, and astonishing carrying power. He compels the assent of every listener to everything he says and leaves him wondering he did not see it all before. There was something hypnotic in the ease and massive simplicity both of matter and manner.'
>
> Mr and Mrs Brown will remain in Adelaide till Wednesday when they sail by the *Aeneas* for the Cape, where Mr Brown will fulfil several engagements before returning to England.

'Several engagements' proved to be a considerable understatement. On arriving at Durban on the *Aeneas* on Sunday, June 16, 1912, Brown was in the pulpit that same evening. In the preceding months, H. J. Batts, the Secretary of the Union, had lost no time in arranging an itinerary for him, which he announced in the *South African Baptist,* with an introductory caution:

> We must be content with one Sunday and one week-night service in places where we have only one church. Our plan is rather a formidable one, even for a young man to fill, so that we must go carefully.
>
> The campaign opens at Cape Town on June 23rd and lasts over July 14th. Then the order will be as follows for Sunday

and week-day, unless otherwise expressed:—July 21st, Kimberley; July 28th, Cradock; August 4th, Queen Street, Port Elizabeth; August 11th, South End, Port Elizabeth; August 18th, Grahamstown; August 25th, Alice; September 1st, King William's Town; September 15th, Cambridge (Sunday only); September 22nd, East London; September 29th, Stutterheim (Sunday only); October 6th, Queenstown; October 13th, Union Sermon, Johannesburg; October 20th, Bloemfontein; October 27th and November 3rd, Johannesburg District; November 10th, Pretoria; November 17th Maritzburg; November 24th and December 1st, Durban.

In due course, with some changes, and still more additions the itinerary proceeded and from different corners of the land reports flowed into the columns of the *South African Baptist*. At Lovedale 'you could have heard a pin drop as he spoke to native people'. At Cradock, 'the capital of the Karoo', he preached two Sundays and held two 'united services' midweek, in the Dutch Reformed Church which, in 'a spirit of unity' had been made available. Of Mrs Brown it was said, 'Her bright and genial spirit added much to the pleasure of the visit.' In Kimberley the Presbyterian hall, used for a meeting, was 'fuller than ever before and nearly all the ministers of the Kimberley churches were present.'

The church at Grahamstown reported:

We have been again having a refreshing time with Mr and Mrs Archibald Brown, who have paid us a second visit. A breath of the English springtime seems to accompany them, invigorating and bracing, and their time with us seemed all too short. Long will the words of this uncompromising warrior of the Lord be treasured in our memory. On Sunday the message in the morning at Bathurst Street Church on Pleasing God, and in the evening in the Town Hall (which was packed) on Immortality, have left their mark on many minds.

On the Friday evening Mr Brown addressed a large gathering of Coloured and native people in the New Shaw Memorial Wesleyan Church in the Location. As one cart driver said next morning, with his face all aglow, 'Baas, I no speak much English, but I unnerstan. The big Baas speak very good last night, he make it plain. When Jesus call Zachee he want him here (pointing to his heart). Baas (very impressively), our Mr ____ is very good man, good preacher, but no speak like that. If all preachers speak good like the big Baas, all the Kaffirs come to God.'

King William's Town:

Rev. Archibald G. Brown was with us and our German sister churches. We had a most refreshing time. We had no counting of fruits, but I am sure the blessing of his ministry amongst us will abide. Mrs Brown addressed our Women's Christian Union. I was not there, at least not this half of me, the 'better half' was, and thoroughly enjoyed it.

Annual Assembly, Johannesburg, October 16th to 23rd:

The opening of our 34th Annual Assembly, held in the 'Golden City', took the form of a Reception on Wednesday evening, October 16th, in the Wanderers' Hall. There were some four to five hundred guests. The Rev A. G. Brown was greeted with loud and prolonged applause when he rose to address the audience by special request. In a few heart-inspiring words the keynote was given for all the after-gatherings. We were sent home with the conviction that the time is short and that life's only worthy aim is the winning of men for Christ.

On Thursday morning we assembled in the new and beautiful Troyeville Church for the Union Sermon, the preacher being the Rev A. G. Brown. It was a memorable occasion. The praise, the Scripture exposition, the discourse upon the text 'the goodwill of him that dwelt in the bush', together with the gathering at the Lord's Table, constitute a fragrant memory.

The gatherings in our churches were large, and 'Union Sunday' will long be remembered. The afternoon and evening services in the Orpheum Theatre conducted by the Rev. A. G. Brown were seasons of remarkable power, and were attended by great audiences. The afternoon address upon the words 'And shoes on his feet', was listened to with wrapt attention, as was also the message at night upon the text 'All have sinned'. These powerful theatre discourses were the outstanding feature of a memorable day. The Rand press on Monday morning aptly referred to 'the veteran preacher, whose white locks and confession to fifty years of devotion to the work of the church of Christ were somewhat out of harmony with his clear ringing voice, upright presence, and sturdy appearance.'

Pietermaritzburg:

We have been favoured with the long-looked for visit of the Rev. Archibald Brown, who arrived on Friday, the 15th, by the Transvaal mail. Notwithstanding the heavy rain that was falling there were quite a number of people at the railway station to welcome him. The Sunday was a perfect day as regards the weather. There was a large congregation in the morning, and at night the church was crowded, there being between six and seven hundred persons in the church. A meeting was held on the Monday night, when a most impressive address was given on 'The Lost Piece of Silver' to a large congregation, and these meetings are being continued until the Thursday.

Durban:

On the final night, Bulwer Road was again packed with a congregation of nearly 300, to whom Mr Brown spoke in his own inimitably simple way on the text 'And shoes on his feet'. At the close two verses of 'God be with you till we meet again' were sung, and Mr Brown thanked the friends and said the address that evening was his 152nd, and what a pleasure the whole tour had been to him. At the closing Sunday service in the Town Hall more than 2,000 persons were present, and the discourse on 'The Common Salvation' was listened to with the deepest interest.

As this long tour came to an end the Secretary of the Union wrote:

The itinerary of the Rev. Archibald G. Brown will have been almost completed by the time these lines appear. From all centres we hear of blessing received and the coming together of hundreds of people to listen to the message of the distinguished visitor, whose old-time presentation of the truth has been so greatly enjoyed.

That Mr and Mrs Brown have been able to endure and even to enjoy their long African journeyings is a cause for much thankfulness.

Many more services than were arranged for were readily taken by Mr Brown, and the total amounts to more than 150 different meetings; while Mrs Brown has done her part in addressing the Ladies' Associations in connection with the different churches, and they have been greatly appreciated. These have all been generously voluntary, and were not provided for in our programme.

It is difficult to say how great and blessed are the results following these services, so ungrudgingly carried out and beautifully rendered. Not in our history have we had such an uplift, or have our churches been so greatly helped.

The value of these six months was perhaps best summed up by Thomas Chapman, the pastor at Maritzburg, who wrote in the January 1913 issue of the *South African Baptist:*

The Rev. Archibald Brown has completed his tour among our South African Churches, and as one of the Pastors rejoicing in the blessing received I desire to write a word of thanks and expression of deepest appreciation for services he has rendered to our Denomination.

Every Baptist Church along the line of communication has been visited. He has travelled over the whole of our railway system in the four South African Provinces. No Church has received more favour than another. One Sunday and two or more week evening services, with afternoon services added at the request of local Churches, have been given to small and weak Churches, and to those having the largest membership in populous districts.

We have not been allowed to refer to Mr Brown as a Missioner nor to his services as a 'Mission'. The restriction was no doubt a wise one. The visit was not intended to add another to the list of highly organised and boomed missions. At the same time few missions have done more good than the visit of Mr Brown. We needed one to come into the centre of our Church life; to speak to us as a brother; to touch the source of our Church activity; to rally workers to the strenuous labours of our various organisations. This has resulted from the special services and conferences, and has shown us that in future we should as a Denomination encourage personal visitation of our Churches by men of similar character and spiritual power.

Another value is the larger evangelistic work these services made possible. Every Church has been gladdened to see its seating capacity being overtaxed, or has had to hire halls or theatres, or use the buildings of other Denominations.

These services have resulted in notable conversions and the reclaiming of many of the vast army of backsliders. What a demonstration we have had of the power of the gospel to draw; to compel attention; and arouse the conscience. It has been a manifestation to us all, that when set forth in its simplicity and in the power of the Holy Ghost, the gospel is God's power unto salvation. South Africa needs this, is drawn by it, and in the face of all other attractions when preached by such a preacher there is no greater power than the gospel.

There has been a deep work of refreshing grace in God's people. We can all recall some outstanding services when spiritual sources were laid bare, and we drank deeply of the waters of life. Such a time was that in the Troyeville Baptist Church, when Mr Brown preached the Union sermon. How God stirred our hearts as we listened to that wonderful exposition of 'A Flame of Fire in a Bush'. Moses was revealed in new aspects of life and character. In his life we saw many of the explanations for our own failures, and saw too the pathway, narrow and steep, leading to success and power. Another occasion of refreshing was during the series of services at Maritzburgh, when the message was 'I have need to be baptized of thee'. Of the last sermon, when the subject was 'Jesus as King of kings and Lord of lords',—many have testified they did not know whether they were 'in the body or out of the body'. Some impressions of these times may fade away, but the vision of the Lord high and lifted up abides for ever. He has been set before us in his glory, dominion, and majesty as Christ our Lord.

Coming to other aspects of the visit, probably I am not the only one overwhelmed by the graciousness of our visitor, his humility and brotherliness. We knew of him by name; some of us had seen and heard him; few probably were not without fears lest arrangements were not of the best, whether our friend would in all things be happy among us. How quickly our fears were removed! His eye saw everything that was good; he spoke to encourage the despondent. He has left no wounded heart behind him. His sentences revealed a wise and deep insight into character and need. He has not faltered to show faults, and has enhanced the value of his coming by directing attention to weaknesses, but all has been done in a spirit of winsome love and inspired counsel.

Shall we not all learn, too, the meaning of sacrifice? How ungrudgingly the veteran soldier has given himself to the battle of the Lord. A full programme was his delight. Evening meetings, afternoon Bible Readings with a temperature 100 degrees in the shade, were conducted with the glee of a young man. To speak a word for the Master is his greatest delight.

We have had a distinguished preacher, and do not hesitate to say that he has done a work which alone would make him most distinguished among the preachers and leaders of our day.

* * * * *

After spending the Christmas of 1912 in Cape Town the Browns returned to England early in the following year. What they did in the early part of that year is not recorded, but by July 1913 we know that he was supplying the Baptist Church at Sandown, Isle of Wight. An article by the Rev. H. H. Turner of Ryde in the October 1913 edition of *The Sword and the Trowel,* says that the former pastor at Sandown had been a friend of Brown, and that Brown was now coming to the end of three month's service to that church during its vacancy. Turner reported:

The Church, Sunday by Sunday, has been crowded to excess. The blessing of this brief ministry will be a very great stimulus for months to come. And now it will soon end, and not only the Island but England will bid farewell to this preacher of renown, as he again sets sail to take up a period of service in Jamaica. The selfish thought arises in my mind, cannot we retain his services in England? A course of Bible study under him, a few months of his evangelistic services in any town, would leave a lasting impression.

Turner was of the opinion 'that no man of modern times, of his school of thought, can command a more respectful hearing, or larger audiences'. 'Of his school of thought' is a significant expression. It was a school of dwindling numbers. Brown evidently referred to his 'closing days' while speaking to Turner in private, on which the latter commented: 'Mr Brown is giving his closing days, and thinks it a great privilege, to helping small, struggling churches in this and other lands, in Africa, Australia, Jamaica, and in different parts of our own country.'

We have seen no account of how long Brown stayed in Jamaica, or of what happened while he was there. He was back in England by 1914 as the following letter shows, and perhaps the letter also indicates that he had over-taxed his health while in the West Indies. From the Steyne Hotel, Worthing, Brown wrote to one of his friends at the East London Tabernacle on February 16, 1914:

My dear Friend,

I am slowly picking up but it is very slowly. I was quite unable to go up to East London yesterday, but am looking forward with great interest to next Sunday, it being the exact date on which the late CHS opened the building 45 years ago.

Many thanks for kind gift for which I enclose receipt. It is quite beyond my power to say anything as against Mr Wickes and the Thanksgiving. The distribution will be entirely in the hands of the church officers but first of all the hare has to be caught and from all I can see this will entail no little work.

Enclosed cutting proves my point, that the Thank-offering movement has to be raised from the mire, into which it has fallen. It was never intended to be a mere dodge for the benefit of the church making it.

In March 1914 the Browns again left England for South Africa, and this time would be away for five years. That same month Ernest Baker, the Baptist minister in Cape Town, had returned to England and his church had written to ask for Brown's aid for six months. The Browns arrived in Cape Town on April 4, but he stipulated he took a break before supplying the vacant pastorate. Accordingly it was not until May 8 that a welcome meeting was held. The *South African Baptist* reported:

> The Rev. Archibald Brown, who was enthusiastically received, spoke of the pleasure he felt in returning to South Africa, which was for him one of the most charming countries, and one which had fascinated him. He dwelled at some length on the dangers of a man becoming used to preaching and of the need of rising above mere denominationalism.

In June, the same paper reported that Brown was now fully employed in conducting services at the Wale Street Church and the Alhambra. It was added: 'We hope he will continue to find strength for each day's demands, and be the means of doing much good in this country. Let us all remember to pray for him, and the work.' There was good cause for prayer and not only locally, for while Brown was in the midst of this work the 'Great War' began between Britain and Germany in August 1914. South Africa, as part of the British Empire, was

immediately involved. A history of the Wale Street Baptist
Church records that, after the commencement of the war, for
reasons unstated, 'The Alhambra services were discontinued,
and the whole work concentrated in the Wale Street building.
Pastor Brown's forceful preaching had its due effect upon the
membership, which was added to considerably as the result
of his ministry.'[4]

While the Baptist Union churches of South Africa were
ignorant of the Browns' future plans, a note in the June issue
of the denominational paper indicated what was their hope:
'All the Churches join in the welcome to the Rev A. G. Brown
and Mrs Brown, and sincerely hope they will find a permanent home among us.' However, on concluding the Cape
Town ministry, they sailed for Tasmania on January 3, 1915,
and the *South African Baptist* reported:

> We wish him and Mrs Brown a pleasant and prosperous voy-
> age. Wonderful service was rendered by Mr Brown in Cape
> Town, the preaching of the gospel being the power of God
> unto salvation. We believe that during his stay of six or seven
> months he baptised about 60 who had become obedient to
> the faith. May he go on from strength to strength.

How far Brown was preaching in the months after his
return to his son's home near Hobart is not on record; it must
have been limited as one source indicated that he 'suffered
from poisoning, the results of the drought having contami-
nated the water supply'. He was certainly better by May 11,
1915, when the *Argos*, of Melbourne, reported that 'The Rev.
Archibald Brown, the distinguished Baptist preacher, late of
the Metropolitan Tabernacle, London, will preach at the Collins Street Baptist Church tonight and on the two following

[4] The *South African Baptist,* January 1915.

Tuesday evenings.' He was now on a tour of the Australian mainland and from Victoria travelled north to Queensland, where, for two months, he served the City Tabernacle, Brisbane, the date coinciding with the 60th anniversary of that church. Other churches also benefited. The *Brisbane Courier*, Saturday, July 24, 1915, reported:

> Last Monday evening the Rev. Archibald G. Brown conducted an evangelistic service in the Sandgate Baptist Church. He took as his subject, 'Not I, but Christ', and from there delivered a powerful address. The congregation was large, the seating accommodation being fully utilised.

The *Australian Baptist* gave a lengthy report of one of his sermons at this time, introduced by these words:

> It does not take long to learn the secret of Mr Brown's influence as a preacher. He has ever with him a deep sense of his high calling; every sentence proclaims the deep spiritual life that is behind his speaking is but an overflowing of himself. It is the very lovableness of the man that is irresistible. Surely it was true of himself what he spoke when he said last Sunday, 'It is not what is said that counts, but the one that says it.' One can listen long to Mr Brown, because of the ring in the message he utters. Perhaps, this is why he appeals to so many. The one who can feel and sympathise cannot speak to unheeding ears. It is a splendid thing to compel respect, to compel admiration; but to compel love, this is surely the greatest power God has put into man's hands.

* * * * *

From Australia they sailed to New Zealand, to be in Auckland in time for the annual conference of the Baptist churches which began on October 6, 1915. On the Thursday of the

Conference he was the chief speaker in discussion on the work of God, and again at the 'Home Mission demonstration' the same evening. The War was the headline news at this period. New Zealand was much occupied with raising help, but with one means of help the Auckland conference had no sympathy: the churches should not be involved in 'the holding of carnivals and lotteries for the purpose of raising funds for patriotic purposes'. Brown would certainly have been in agreement.

From Auckland the Browns proceeded by rail to Wellington, where the newspapers announced he was to fill the vacancy at the Vivian Street Baptist Church for the next two months. The *Evening Post* announced their arrival in that city on September 8, and after a summary of his London ministry, continued:

> During recent years he has visited Switzerland, South Africa (twice), Tasmania, and the Commonwealth States of Victoria and Queensland, and he has been 'supplying' a Brisbane church for the past two months. Mr Brown has the distinction of being able to say that he is the only English Baptist minister to have visited all the South African churches. Those of his readers who remember the controversy in England some years ago upon the 'Down Grade' will be interested to know that Mr Brown closely identified himself with the attitude that Rev. C. H. Spurgeon took up in the matter. Mr Brown, who is now past seventy years of age, still preaches with great force and fire.

The same paper the next week reported a Welcome meeting for Mr Brown at the Vivian Street Church, describing it as 'a very pleasing function'. The people of the church evidently concurred with the paper's initial report of Brown's preaching. On October 5 the *Evening Post* noted: 'The Rev. Archibald

G. Brown has accepted an invitation to continue his ministry at Vivian Street Baptist until the end of the year.'

With the New Year, 1916, the Browns re-crossed the Tasman Sea to Hobart, for a further period with his son Cecil and daughter-in-law, Gladys. He was to find, however, that the circumstances of the Hobart Baptist Church were not as they had been a year earlier. The pastor, Frank Boreham, had broken his leg a few months earlier and a long illness followed. The consequence for Brown was inevitable and it was announced by the *Mercury* on January 29, 1916:

> The Rev. Archibald Brown is at present on a visit to his son at Old Beach. He has consented to take the duties of the Rev. F. Boreham, who has not yet recovered from his accident.

In his autobiography, Boreham attributes to Brown a critical decision he took this year. It was probably in March 1916 that Boreham received a call to the influential Baptist Church at Armadale, an attractive suburb of Melbourne. The prospect of leaving Hobart, he would later record,

> seemed unthinkable. How could I tear myself away from Hobart? How could I leave the people who were doing everything in their power to nurse me back to health? I was actually drafting a telegram declining the call when the Rev. Archibald G. Brown intervened. Mr Brown had been living for some months in Hobart and we had all become very fond of him. He strongly urged me to take my time. 'Do not reply in a hurry', he pleaded. 'It is by no means clear that your health will permit you to resume the burden of your work here. A change might work wonders. And if you are to have a change, what could be better than Armadale? It is splendidly officered and highly organized; you would be relieved of all

administrative duties . . . make quite sure you are acting in harmony with the will of God before you finally decline!'⁵

Boreham listened and accepted the call to the suburb of Melbourne in April 1916.

The last notice we have of Brown preaching in Hobart was at a Christian Endeavour Union meeting on September 14, 1916. His address, reported by the *Mercury,* was on the word 'endeavour'. He dealt with the word in relation to 'duty' and traced the meaning wherever it is used in the New Testament.

'Duty' was a word of added significance as war raged in Europe and beyond. Australia and New Zealand had led the way in sending their men to the aid of the home country. That fact had implications for the peaceful home of Ravensbourne, Old Beach, where there must have been discussion about the cost that duty may bring. The next year, Cecil Brown, at the age of twenty-nine, filled up enlistment papers for the Australian Imperial Force and by 1918 he was with the AIF in Europe.

For Cecil Brown's now-elderly parents the discussion in 1916 seems to have been whether they would sail east for Canada and home, or west again to South Africa. The latter route was decided on, in part because his daughter Nellie and her husband, Ernest Eve, had now moved to the Cape Town area, and also because the Wale Street Church had invited him to take the pulpit through November 1916. The November issue of the *South African Baptist* welcomed him back, and said, he 'was reported to have come back here for a rest'.

---

⁵ F. W. Boreham, *My Pilgrimage* (London: Epworth, 1954), p. 206.

If 'rest' was in view it had to be postponed until December when his help at the Wale Street Church concluded. But December 3, found him in the pulpit of the Wynberg Church, in a suburb of Cape Town on the Cape Peninsula, meeting an engagement termed a Sunday School Anniversary. The church recorded: 'The Rev. Ernest Eve preached an excellent sermon to the children in the morning, and kept the attention of young and old throughout. Curiously enough, Pastor Archibald Brown, who preached in the evening, took the same text as Mr Eve.'

What happened next was almost inevitable. The Wynberg Church was without a pastor, and what could be better than having Mr Brown as 'temporary pastor'. So it was that in this small cause Brown happily undertook his last pastoral charge as he served Wynberg from December 1916 to April 1917, with an interruption early in March as he recovered from influenza.

The news of this ministry in the Wynberg Church was reported by them in the May 1917 copy of the denominational paper:

> From December to April, Pastor Archibald G. Brown occupied the Wynberg pulpit on Sundays and on Wednesday evenings. Although Mr Brown's age—he is 74—is beginning to make itself felt on the natural man, in spirit he is as young as ever, and we in Wynberg consider ourselves greatly privileged to have had five months of the preaching of one whom Sir Robertson Nicoll, in the *British Weekly* of 1st March last, referred to as 'the foremost of the "unrecognized orators" of Britain'. Whilst we have found that he loves to have his Master's message received with favour, he himself does not seek applause or public recognition. We part from him with deep regret, and trust that at some future time he will again be able to 'come over and help us'.

From this date it seems that the time for rest had now come at last, or at least there is only one record of his speaking again, at a 'Thanksgiving Day' Sunday at the Wale Street Church, August 12, 1917. He was not at the Bloemfontein Assembly of the Baptist Union in October, and a wire of greeting was sent to 'Pastor and Mrs Archibald G. Brown'.

Not until February 1919 is there another reference to him in the *South African Baptist*. In January of that year he assisted at the burial service of Mrs George Williams, wife of the Secretary of the Cape Town Baptist Church at Wale Street.

The War now being over, the call was for England where they had not been for five years. The Browns last evening with the friends they had come to love at Wale Street was on Wednesday, June 11, 1919, at a public meeting held to bid them farewell. In the columns of the *South African Baptist* the church reported:

> The meeting was presided over by our Pastor, the Rev A. B. Jack, who spoke of the seal of God's blessing having been seen upon the ministry of Mr Brown during the time when, five years ago, he was the temporary pastor of that Church. He was now returning, after a long absence, to his friends in the Homeland, and they had met that evening to wish him and Mrs Brown a pleasant voyage, God's-speed, and every blessing.
>
> Messrs G. McDougall and A. Durston having given expression to the regret at Mr Brown leaving South Africa from the Observatory and Wynberg Churches respectively, Mr Brown, who was heartily received, said he thanked them from the depths of his heart for the many kindnesses they had received from time to time, and for the Christian fellowship they had enjoyed with the Cape Town friends. He was, he said, pleased to be with those who stood by the old evangel.

[Two days later] The Pastor and many of the friends of the Cape Town Church and the Rev. T. Aitken, Secretary of the South African Baptist Union, met on board the *USS Saxon* to have a final handshake with our aged friend, who was one of the most distinguished preachers of the last generation. We pray that God may accompany our friends, and at the eventide of their lives they may continue to experience the joy of the Lord arising from the assurance that God is still their Sun and Shield.

The joy at home-coming and reunion with family must have been mixed with sorrows. The shadow of bereavements lay on many homes. His former charge at Chatsworth Road, South Norwood, had lost forty-one men in the War; similar figures being repeated all over the nation. Many once familiar scenes were changed. The Metropolitan Tabernacle was again in a vacancy period, Dixon having resigned on March 1, 1919. Thomas Spurgeon had died two years earlier at the age of sixty-one. Cecil Brown, serving in the Australian army in France, had survived the War only to be laid low by the influenza epidemic of 1918-19 which took the lives of thousands. He had been invalided to England in March 1919, but had embarked for Australia the month before his father left Cape Town.[6]

It is doubtful if the Browns' return was mentioned in the British press. 'Church news' was now receiving less attention, and the world where AGB had been known, and which he knew, was passing away.

How the location of their last home came to be chosen is not recorded but it harmonised with desires expressed long before. At Easton on the Hill, a small and scenic village in

---

[6] Cecil Brown was discharged from the armed services at Hobart as 'medically unfit' on August 7, 1919.

Northamptonshire, two and a half miles south west of Stamford, a former wish to be in 'the countryside' was perfectly fulfilled. Although far from the sea, the location even had a similarity with the desire for a 'cliff-top cottage'. Built in 1761, the new home was indeed a cottage, and almost immediately behind it was something of a cliff falling away into a quarry. By this date, and perhaps long before, the latter was disused and overgrown with greenery, but it had given a name for the dwelling above, Rock Cottage, or sometimes simply, 'The Rock'. In this peaceful setting Archibald and Hannah Brown were now cared for by his eldest daughter, Annie.

AGB had once said: 'Some of us find the waters do not get smoother as we get nearer the harbour, and life does not always get easier as we get older.' This was true of his closing years but he knew how to face them. We can be sure he remembered the past with thankfulness, and he was thankful for the present also. In the twelve months before he died, his son Douglas was preaching in Lowestoft, and then at Yarmouth, where there was a remarkable work of the Spirit of God. Sixty years later there were numbers who would recall this revival on the coast of East Anglia.[7] The evidence for its genuineness was to be seen at the other end of Britain, for the places where Douglas Brown preached were ports crowded with 'fisherfolk' from the north of Scotland during the herring season (their boats distinguished by the fact that they did not sail on Sundays). Many of these Scots were converted and went home 'preaching the Lord Jesus'. Suspicion about superficial evangelism was common in the north of Scotland at this date. In the General Assembly of the Free Church of Scotland in 1923, one of the denomination's leading preachers, George

---

[7] See Griffin, *A Forgotten Revival.*

Mackay of Fearn, warned that the absence of conviction of sin and true repentance was too common among professed converts in the country. Then he went on, as reads a report of his address,

> To quote a dictum of that greatly-blessed servant of the Lord, the Rev. A. Douglas Brown, whose name is a household word in all our fishing villages on the north-east of Scotland—'Revival', says he, 'is not going down the street with a big drum, it is going back to Calvary with a big sob.'[8]

Two years after his father's death, Douglas Brown dedicated a volume of his sermons to 'My dear father, whose life and example were a constant and sacred example to me, not only in my early life, but also through the later years, until he fell asleep in Jesus. Whatever blessing has come to other lives through my ministry and revival work I owe, under God, to the inspiration of one who, by his fidelity to the truth and loyalty to Christ, awakened in my own heart the Calvary passion for souls.'[9]

The revival in Suffolk in 1921 was what an earlier generation of Scots called 'a sun blink'; but if it did not have any national impact it surely brought gladness into the Brown home in Northamptonshire. 'Kept by the power of God unto salvation', Hannah Brown died suddenly in March 1922. Nine days later Archibald Brown entered into rest on the evening of Sunday, April 2, at the age of 77, 'after many months of weakness and suffering'. We do not know whether he was able to sing that Lord's Day, but certain it is that

---

[8] Quoted in G. N. M. Collins, *The Diary of James Morrison* (Edinburgh: G. N. M. Collins, 1984), p. 65.

[9] Griffin, *Forgotten Revival*, p. 19. The Douglas Brown quotation is from the dedication of his book, *The Great Harvester* (Stanley Martin, 1923); he died April 27, 1940, aged sixty-six.

before the day was over he had entered into song which would be forever. We can well believe that, near the end, his thoughts went back to earlier years and included the friend whose ministry had been so closely bound up with his own. Once, speaking on the words 'Thy Praise' and 'My Praise', and referring to Spurgeon, he said:

> I see that departed one. Oh, how he sings it now, 'Thou art my praise!' He believed it, and he preached it when he was upon earth, and with radiant face and seraphic tongue, he sings more sweetly than ever, 'Thou art my praise.' And in a little while, brethren and sisters, one after another of us, as we pass away resting on the fact, shall enter into the eternal experience and the undying song. God says, 'He is thy praise.' There is the doctrine. My heart says, 'Thou art my praise.' There is the experience. Soon I shall sing it, and that will be my heaven.[10]

A few years after that April Sunday, in the little history entitled, *Chatsworth Road Baptist Church,* the death of their much-loved pastor was noted in the words,

> There, in God's Acre, in the secluded village of Easton, rest the mortal remains of this beloved sister in Christ, and of the Pastor and friend whose memory will be revered as long as time endures.[11]

In the parish graveyard, there is a stone beyond the church on which is inscribed the words:

---

[10] Deuteronomy 10:21 and Jeremiah 17:14, February 5, 1893.
[11] *Chatsworth Road Baptist Church,* p. 18. *The East London Advertiser,* of May 13, 1922, recorded that 'Rev. Archibald Brown, a leading Baptist minister, left £4,222.'

IN

LOVING MEMORY OF

ARCHIBALD GEIKIE BROWN

BORN 18 JULY 1844, DIED 2 APRIL 1922

AGED 77 YEARS

A Servant of Jesus Christ
And God's Messenger to multitudes of People

PASTOR AT BROMLEY, KENT 1862-66

STEPNEY GREEN AND BOW, EAST LONDON, 1867-96

WEST NORWOOD, 1897-1907 AND

OF THE METROPOLITAN TABERNACLE, 1907-10

ALSO OF

HANNAH GEARING BROWN

HIS DEVOTED WIFE

WHO PREDECEASED HIM BY 9 DAYS

24 MARCH 1922 AGED 72 YEARS

16

THE MAN AND THE PREACHER

Rev. Archibald G. Brown.

'The passing of Archibald Geikie Brown recalls a commanding personality. Tall, and erect, with military bearing, this veteran preacher reminded one more of the army than the ministry. He was a born fighter and protagonist for the faith once delivered to the saints. To hear his challenging voice, to note the fire in his eye, to watch his methods and gestures, one was impressed instinctively with the fact that he would have fulfilled Morley Punshon's ideal of a "commanding ministry". With nearly sixty years of such ministry behind him, exercised largely in the Metropolis of the world, with wonderful experiences of blessing in the past, linked to the fact that no man of modern times of his peculiar school of thought, could command a more respectful hearing or larger audiences, gave him the right to be heard by all sections of the church of God, and to be designated in the obituary notices of the Press as "a Baptist Leader". He was a leader. He had initiative. He was original, and in certain ways had a touch of genius all his own. If personality counts at all in preaching, Brown made a great impact not merely upon the senses but upon the human mind by the sheer force of his own great soul.'

H. H. Turner, *The Sword and the Trowel*, 1922.

PUBLIC notices of Brown's death appear to have been few and short compared with the practice of the press in earlier years. *The Times* gave a short column of four paragraphs to him as a 'Leading Nonconformist Preacher'. It was a tribute by someone who never knew him, containing mild praise and major inaccuracies. He was said to be 'pastor for fifteen years' at East London Tabernacle, and 'married five times.' The *Evening Post* of New Zealand, gave a fuller but still impersonal account communicated by a London correspondent. The East End of London was perhaps still the part of the world where he was remembered with the greatest affection, and it was fitting that the *East London Advertiser* should carry the fullest press accounts of his life and ministry. Under the heading 'More Stories of Archibald Brown', articles on his life continued through several weeks in June and July 1922, and provided us with material already used in these pages. They also gave the following first-hand insight into his character:

> In his dealing with men and things, Archibald Brown displayed many rare qualities. No one had a more tender heart than he when listening to the recital of real need; no one enjoyed a good joke with keener humour than he; no one

337

could utter a plain truth in clearer language or with more irresistible force than he; no one could offer thoughts, and words of brotherly and sisterly helpfulness, uplifting, sympathy and encouragement than he; and no one could be more frank and outspoken whenever occasion demanded it than he. Even his friends, if they sought counsel of him, knew that they must expect 'the truth, and nothing but the truth'.

While the preceding pages will have given the reader an impression of Brown, it is to be wished that we had a fuller description from more of his friends. The features which stand out for all to see were his ability to lead, and his capacity to get close to people. As a leader, both in physique and temperament, he was fitted for what might have been a military career: he could command and inspire others. It is said that on one occasion he entered a tailor's shop and, being mistaken for a well-known army officer, was greeted with the words, 'Colonel Grey, I believe.' 'No', said the preacher, 'I'm Private Brown.' And so he was. At a time when birth and parentage commonly divided society, Brown was at home with all. 'Your father was a gentleman,' a man once said to him as he sat at his bedside in an East End home. The speaker must have heard it from others for that was not how Brown presented himself. The days of riding in a carriage belonged to his boyhood.

Many of his traits belonged to him by birth. He would have led in any calling, and had the geniality that thrives in being among people. But if grace had not been added to his natural gifts, there would be no explanation of his life. From the time Archibald Brown became a Christian he was a new man, set in a new direction. Without the Saviour, he would never have known what it means to 'be servant of all' (*Mark* 10:44). Without Christ, whether among believers in the East

End, or on the karoo of South Africa, he would never have lived the words, 'One is your Master, even Christ; and all ye are brethren' (*Matt.* 23:8). Only a source higher than nature can explain his life.

What Brown thought of himself is clear enough from personal references. He would tell his people, 'If God only forgives sins committed before conversion, I am an undone man. Every hour of every day there is need of pardon.' He never professed as a Christian to have attained to 'higher life,' and he hoped that none of his hearers supposed they had advanced to it. For him, the graces of being 'poor in spirit', and of being among those that 'mourn', were not preliminary to the spiritual life, to be left behind as the result of progress. Rather, while fully pardoned, he did not cease to be a sinner, and his sense of unworthiness only grew with his experience. 'Our own unworthiness will appear great in proportion as we have communion with Christ.' Thirty years after he first knew the Saviour, he said, 'If God says to me, "What is thy name?" I have to say from the very depth of my heart, "My sinful name is Archibald Brown."' So Paul, many years an apostle, says that of sinners 'I am chief'. Not, 'I was'. It is such self-knowledge that finds rest in the sovereign and eternal love of God.

It was this realistic conviction about sin remaining in all believers that kept Brown from supporting the 'Higher Life' movement that gained much popularity in the 1870s. Seven thousand, including his friend Arthur Blackwood, attended a Convention at Brighton in 1875, where Hannah Pearsall Smith 'was a herald of the evangel'.[1] At the heart of her

---

[1] The phrase is that of Evan Hopkins in Alexander Smellie, *Evan Hopkins, A Memoir* (London: Marshall, 1920), p. 64.

message and that of her husband was a consecration that would take the Christian 'out of Romans 7'. This became a key-note at the Keswick Convention which followed Brighton, and the idea spread far in Mrs Pearsall Smith's book, *The Christian's Secret of a Happy Life*. Christians, it was said, by a simple step of faith could leave the 'defeat' of Romans 7 for all 'the joy and victory of Romans 8'. On the contrary, Brown believed that at regeneration the Christian already knew the greatest change and thereafter there is no one experience necessary to take the believer to new heights. He warned his people: 'I am afraid lest some of you should be drifting into this heighty-flighty balloonism that is getting so wonderfully popular at the present day—the frothy spiritual life that has not any deep sense of personal sin about it.'[2] *'Living in a state of ecstasy is not all the good that we imagine it to be.* I think that at the present time there are many indications abroad of the subtle evil of mistaking an experience for Christ himself. It is said perhaps, "Oh, if you could only go to a certain little town in the north of England, you will get such a blessing." Ay, but if I am going to allow "Keswick" to enter into partnership with Jesus Christ himself, or if I am going to allow any delightful feeling that I may have here and there to take the place of the ordinary Jesus Christ who walks with me day by day, I am, I believe on the brink of a very terrible precipice . . . May God give you many a season of ecstasy; but *ecstasy is not good everyday diet.* Jesus Christ himself, the everyday Saviour, is the simple diet of life.'[3]

[2] Psalm 51, September 10, 1893.

[3] Mark 9:8, c.1893. The later lives of Robert and Hannah Pearsall Smith would show that the reference to 'precipice' was not too strong. See *A Religious Rebel: the Letters of 'H.W.S'*, ed. Logan Pearsall Smith (London: Nisbet, 1949). J. C. Ryle's book *Holiness* (1877) was a response to the 'holiness by faith' teaching. In modified form, the 'Keswick teaching' would continue for some eighty years. Brown

'The more holy a saint becomes, the more he will loathe and mourn over the remains of indwelling sin.'[4] The words are Spurgeon's and they were AGB's experience. Humility is the consequence of right belief about God and self.

But humility did not mean for Brown that a Christian should have no assessment of gifts that God has given. In assessing those gifts, in his own case, he gave no high place to his intelligence. That gift in Spurgeon was such that Brown used to say it made him feel 'unutterably small'. Yet no man could publish sermons, as Brown did, for over forty years without mental powers. That he was a constant student is beyond question. In the interview given to a reporter from the *British Weekly* in 1896, he said: 'I am afraid I get the credit for not reading anything myself, but this is a great mistake. I believe in reading, and I think that if a minister is going to do a good work he must spend much time in study.' He went on to speak of the help he found in Godet and Delitzsch for exegesis. In a sermon on 'The Bible My Critic' in 1907, he interjected, 'I think I may say that I am second to none here in love of books. I am never happier than when alone in the study, with my volumes.'

A reflection of his assessment of himself comes from a conversation he had with the captain of a boat on which he was crossing to Ireland. Although, as Brown learned, the captain had been a hearer at the East London Tabernacle on a few occasions, he did not recognize his passenger as the preacher.

---

maintained friendship with some of the leaders, believing with Ryle that 'to exhibit bitterness and coldness toward those who cannot conscientiously work with us is to prove ourselves very ignorant of holiness.' Peter Toon and Michael Smout, *John Charles Ryle, Evangelical Bishop* (Swengel, PA: Reiner, 1976), p. 70.

[4] *Metropolitan Tabernacle Pulpit*, 1878, p. 436. '"Oh, wretched man that I am", said the Apostle Paul, "who shall deliver me from the body of this death?" He said this, not because he was not a saint, but because he was so far advanced in the way of holiness.'

Thus, on hearing that Brown came from London's East End, he proceeded to ask him, 'Did you ever hear Brown at the East London Tabernacle?' 'Oh, several times', was the reply, 'in fact I question if he has preached half a dozen sermons that I have not heard.' 'Well, what do you think of him?' was the next question. 'In what way do you mean?' Brown quizzed. 'Well, he's a very clever man, don't you think?' 'No, I don't think he is. I shouldn't say he is at all.' 'Well', the captain said again after a pause, 'Don't you think that he means what he says?' 'Yes', says Brown, 'I can answer for that.' Before they parted Brown gave him his card and invited him to visit the church again!

Honesty, earnestness, imagination and humour Brown did possess. He also abounded in physical energy. The reader who has any acquaintance with London, has to be surprised to learn that when, as a pastor in the East End, he had to preach at the Metropolitan Tabernacle, he would walk there on a Sunday morning. His physique was no small gift. When at times, as we have seen, his health broke down, the failure was in nervous rather than in physical energy. Martyn Lloyd-Jones, who knew what it was to pastor a large congregation, used to distinguish between these two forms of energy, believing he had plenty of the former but little of the latter. Brown had both, but situations of acute stress might be too much for him. This seems to be the explanation why, with the stress of public office at the Metropolitan Tabernacle removed by 1911, he could go on to do so much in South Africa.

Brown believed that the Holy Spirit is given to believers in different measures, and that receiving more from him is essential to spiritual progress. Among the Spirit's gifts he gave love the first place, as does the Scripture. To know more of the love of Christ was his steady desire, and few knew him without recognising that love in him. Non-Christians might see only compassion and sympathy; believers saw the love of God, and, by a contagion that only the Holy Spirit can give, they sought a similar life and usefulness. His teaching was that love is the element that determines the health and unity of churches: 'Services, prayer meetings, reading of the Word, all these lose their sweetness and charm when unity is wanting.' What James Ellis said of AGB's ministry at Chatsworth Road Chapel was true in all his pastorates, 'The secret of it all had been the atmosphere of love; there could be no blessing without love.'[5]

Often in church history Christians have not found it easy to maintain the love which Christ commands towards others, while opposing errors for which they are blameworthy. Strife arising from contending for the faith can too easily negate peace-making and brotherly love. Brown's example in this respect is noteworthy. In a world where prejudices, even hostility between Christians, have too often marred the churches, Brown constantly sought to maintain friendship with those with whom he had differences. This was the case, for example, in his relationship with Fuller Gooch, his predecessor at Chatsworth Road Baptist Chapel. Gooch, it will be remembered, greatly depleted that congregation by his removal to a new cause in the same neighbourhood. Yet Brown's friendship with him never faltered, and went to the extent of asking Gooch to lay one of the foundation stones, with his name on it, for the new building opened in 1900.

His relationship to Dr Joseph Parker, the eminent preacher of the City Temple, London, showed the same trait. It is hard to classify Parker's theology. In 1877 Spurgeon strongly

5 *God's Full-Orbed Gospel*, p. 25.

343

criticised what he wrote on Christ's priesthood.[6] In 1883 Spurgeon and Parker drew temporarily closer, but private correspondence between them in 1887 shows Spurgeon declining co-operation in a proposed evangelical conference: 'Your conduct puzzles me', he explained. 'I can understand a consistent course of action, either for the faith or against it, and yours does not seem to exhibit that quality.'[7]

A response from Parker came in the 'Open Letter to Spurgeon', published in the *British Weekly* (April 10, 1890). Its content was a blot both on that paper, and on the writer who accused Spurgeon of 'the worst kind of spiritual ignorance'. Parker instanced 'cases' where he believed the preaching at the Metropolitan Tabernacle did 'infinite harm'.[8] John MacLeod, a future Principal of the Free Church College, Edinburgh, but at this date a young man, was so disgusted with Parker's 'Open Letter', and its attack on a man 'to whom he owed so much,' that he never read the *British Weekly* again. MacLeod's great library would never include any of Parker's many writings. Yet, by way of contrast, Archibald Brown, although so close to Spurgeon, maintained a public appreciation of Parker. No doubt he saw the man's inconsistency and weakness, but he viewed him with the love that 'hopeth all things', and, not without reason, valued much that he wrote.[9] Thomas Spurgeon was present to stand at Parker's grave in 1902, and probably Brown was also there. In the light of eternity they

---

[6] *S&T*, 1877, p. 42.

[7] W. Y. Fullerton, *C. H. Spurgeon, A Biography* (London: Williams and Norgate, 1920), p. 298.

[8] The letter is printed in full in Lewis Drummond, *Spurgeon, Prince of Preachers* (Grand Rapids: Kregel, 1992), pp. 733-6.

[9] For example, in a sermon on 'He wrote of me', he quotes Parker at length on the divine authority of Old Testament Scripture. On Spurgeon's death, in the *British Weekly,* Parker wrote one of the finest tributes published anywhere. He was indeed an inconsistent man.

were practising the forgiveness and forbearance that becomes those who have themselves been forgiven much. To harbour an unforgiving spirit was alien to Brown's Christianity.

We think Brown's readiness to allow the Baptist Union the use of the Metropolitan Tabernacle for the Presidential Address in 1908 has a similar explanation. As we have noted, Thomas Spurgeon saw a principle involved and opposed the suggestion. On Brown's behalf, let it be understood, he favoured no soft approach to unfaithful preachers. He spoke plainly on the case of such men, and believed they should not be tolerated in churches built for a different message. His warnings of apostasy were never muted. Why then a willingness to appear friendly to an association which contained such teachers as Dr Clifford? And was such friendliness consistent with Spurgeon's stand in the Down-Grade controversy?

Some of Spurgeon's statements in 1887 were certainly critical of 'professedly orthodox Christians publicly avowing their union with those who deny the faith' but stayed in the Baptist Union or the LBA.[10] But there were later statements by him which touched on another aspect of the problem. In 1890, in the next to last volume of *The Sword and the Trowel* published in his lifetime, he spoke in this way of men who had left the Pastors' College Association and remained in the Union:

> Over those who left our Association two years ago, we sorrow not as those that are without hope. The larger part left under a misapprehension, and are as personally loyal to the old faith as those who remain with us. When they see that

---

[10] *S&T,* 1887, p. 558. At the same time he could say, 'With deep regret we abstain from assembling with those whom we dearly love and heartily respect, since it would involve us in a confederacy with those with whom we can have no communion in the Lord' (p. 515).

they mistook us, they will probably return to their place in the brotherhood, and be heartily welcomed; but if they do not so return, so long as they remain faithful to the Word of God, we shall not reckon them as a loss, but as a gain. It was natural some should think us too severe in our censures, though in this we fell short of all that was deserved; and it was equally natural that more should cling to denominational institutions, in the belief that rising evil could be cured. May the hopes of those who can hope be more than fulfilled! We are glad that they are able to be sanguine . . . If they preach the gospel, though they follow not with us, we herein do rejoice; yea, and will rejoice.[11]

On the last evening of 1891, a month before his death, Spurgeon said: 'During the past year I have been made to see that there is more love and unity among God's people than is generally believed . . . There is more love in the hearts of Christian people than they know of themselves. We mistake our divergences of judgment for differences of heart . . . For my part, I believe that all spiritual persons are already one.'[12]

At the Memorial Meetings at the Metropolitan Tabernacle, held the week of Spurgeon's funeral, one of the finest addresses was given by Colonel Griffin, President of the Baptist Union.[13] That event, and Spurgeon's words just quoted, would have been fully in accord with Brown's thinking. Not prepared to re-join the Union himself, he wanted to help those who remained—probably a majority—who still held the gospel.

---

[11] *S&T*, 1890, p. 314.

[12] *From the Pulpit to the Palm Branch*, pp. 25-6. These quotations, of course, are not to be understood as any correction of earlier statements. Contending for the faith and being a peacemaker are not antithetical.

[13] *Ibid.*, pp. 170-2. 'Generation after generation', said Colonel Griffin, 'the tradition will be handed down of him who laboured here, and whom God enabled to be a minister of his eternal truth.'

In 1896, according to the *British Weekly* interview, when asked about the future of the Baptist cause in London, AGB replied: 'There is every reason for hopefulness. The Down-Grade controversy has, in my opinion, done immense good. Quite a different tone is now heard at Baptist Union meetings. The pendulum has swung round. Although I left the Baptist Union there was never the slightest bitterness between me and my brethren.'

These words, if accurately reported, may throw light on why Brown acted as he did in the difference that occurred at the Metropolitan Tabernacle in December 1907. There was no doubt that Charles Brown (who, it seems, would have spoken if the meeting had taken place at the Tabernacle) was an evangelical; [14]he was the concluding preacher at the Tabernacle in a week of Jubilee Celebration in March 1911. Brown was clearly concerned that belonging to, or not belonging to the Union, should not constitute the test for fellowship among Christians.

It has long been a matter of difference between Christians whether they should belong to associations or denominations in which there can be no exercise of the discipline warranted by Scripture. By his example Brown did not favour such belonging, but he was determined that disagreement with those who disagreed should not nullify the command, 'that you love one another as I have loved you' (*John* 15:12). He saw no reason to believe that allowing the Union to use the Tabernacle should be interpreted as any lessening of opposition to the teaching of a minority within the Union. While

---

[14] Born in 1855, he was minister at Ferme Park, N. London, 1890-1925. He seems to have followed the unscriptural practice of dealing only in the 'positive' not the 'negative', and thus retained relationships with men responsible for the decline in faith.

he certainly did not believe in putting unity before truth, he may well have thought that the Union, hopefully recovered in time from the influence of a minority, represented the long-term prospect of holding Baptist fellow-believers together. Time was to show that his hopes were too sanguine. If he was wrong in this, it was because of fallible human judgment, not because of any clear denial of biblical truth.[15]

Some may wonder whether Brown's emphasis on love sometimes took him too far as a peacemaker. If it did it was a noble fault, and he would be the first man to tell us that no Christian is to be followed in everything.

* * * * *

From Archibald Brown as a man I turn to the subject on which he speaks so clearly to us today. It is what he was as a preacher that leads us to the abiding lesson of his life. This was the note struck at the time of his death by those who knew him best.

By that date there was a new pastor at the Metropolitan Tabernacle, H. Tydeman Chilvers (1920-1935). He

---

[15] While Scripture is very definite on the discipline of both members and teachers in a local church—it is not equally clear that an association of believers or churches must end as soon as some of the participants are found unfaithful. Baptists were to be more resistant to apostasy than most denominations in the 20th century, but the toleration and assertions of such men as T. R. Glover, quoted earlier, were to confirm what Spurgeon feared for the future. Alarmed at the temporary disquiet that Dr Glover caused in the 1930s, the Union leaders (as those in 1887-8) made 'unity' their priority, and asked Percy Evans, the Principal of Spurgeon's College, to present 'a more traditional view' of the atonement than Glover's. See Mike Nicholls, *Lights to the World: A History of Spurgeon's College, 1856-1992* (Harpenden: Nuprint, 1993), p. 149. Following the Down-Grade Controversy, Spurgeon saw greater hope for evangelical unity in the Evangelical Alliance, but the toleration of teachers of error within denominations came to be one of the issues which divided the Alliance in 1966.

understood what Brown had been, and spoke of him as a 'love, blood, and power preacher . . . There are thousands of souls in London and in different parts of the country who bless God for what grace made his servant.'[16] There followed in the June 1922 issue of *The Sword and the Trowel* a short tribute from H. H. Turner which included the words:

> He preached the old, old gospel. He delivered his message, presented his case with an advocate's skill and then pressed for a verdict on the spot. He was old-fashioned enough to denounce 'Entertainments' and cheap-jack methods of reaching the masses. Cinema stunts and palace picture services would not appeal to him. He scorned the new-fangled ideas of the new order. The energies of the Spirit of God charged the entire man. He was a diligent student of the Word. The Holy Ghost, he used to tell us, never worked apart from the Book; 'Faith cometh by hearing, and hearing by the word of God.' If we dishonour the Word, the Spirit must be grieved and may be grieved away. The low standard of spiritual religion, the laxity of Sabbath observance, the growing indifference to religious worship in its simpler form, these, and many other evils, are undoubtedly traceable to neglect of the Bible.

Probably the first newspaper in the Empire to speak of Brown's death was the *South African Baptist*. After a cable from the home country, this paper was in print by April 25, 1922 with an article by John Russell of the Queenstown church which saw Brown in his God-given role:

> So 'Archibald Brown is gone.' Precious memories rush in. We are back in the eighties and see his erect figure in the Metropolitan Tabernacle pulpit. He is taking the great pastor's

---

[16] *S&T*, 1922, pp. 355-6.

place, and his intense, powerful delivery holds the vast congregation spellbound. He was verily a 'master of assemblies'.
Again we hear him preaching the opening sermon of Peckham
Rye Tabernacle, his theme being, 'But Christ as a son over
his own house'. Can we ever forget it? Now it is Spurgeon's
birthday at Stockwell Orphanage, and the beloved President
always spent that afternoon among the boys and girls. We see
two men strolling in earnest conversation, and it is easy to see
their hearts are knit in bonds of affection; the one the massive suffering form of 'CHS', the other the tall military figure
of 'AGB'. Again the scene shifts and we are in the Pastors'
College Conference Hall. In the midst of a great gathering of
ministers Mr Brown is reading the Word in his own inimi-
table way, and as he reads expounds the work of the Holy
Spirit as Christ's Expositor. His was ever a Christ-honouring
ministry. Now we are down at Barking Tabernacle. He is
preaching a Monday afternoon church anniversary sermon
upon the text, 'We have redemption', the emphasis being
upon the second word. Said he, 'Could we but pierce these
leaden London clouds we should see him as our intercessor
before the throne this very afternoon.' Deep was the assurance that our cause was in safe hands and the joy bells were
ringing in our hearts. In the vestry we helped him into his
overcoat for the day was biting cold, and then we tramped to
the station . . . At the time of the 1859 revival Archibald G.
Brown was well on in his teens. To tell of those days of the
crowds coming to Jesus was heaven to him. In the days of our
youth Archibald Brown was toiling and triumphing in the
East End of London, and his name was a household word.

What, then, accounts for the effectiveness of Brown's ministry? For some it was just that he was at the end of an era
when a certain type of preaching had been popular. They
were confident that it could not be duplicated in the future

for tastes were changing. Progress was in the air. 'Preaching an obsolete creed' and a 'dying theology', they supposed, would never again attract the masses.[17] A new idea of preaching was coming into vogue, which Spurgeon had described in the words, 'If you listen, not only for twelve months, but for twelve years, to the common run of preachers, you will not arrive at anything like an idea of their system of theology.'

But for all that was said in praise of a new approach to preaching, the question arose whether preaching of any type should remain at the centre of the church's mission. The emphasis on new methods, with interest given to music, choirs and religious theatre—were all part of doubt on that point, as was the thinking that wanted to see changing social conditions as the church's main mission. For many it seemed to be axiomatic that in a new age, a new approach to building the kingdom of God was a necessity.

At one point this departure from the old was correct. The message preached by such men as Brown and Spurgeon had no natural appeal. Teaching on the universality of human guilt and depravity, necessitating the condemnation of the Son of God as the sinner's substitute, was as contrary to modern thought as anything could be. It was 'an offence to man's intelligence'. To recognize this is to see the real difference between the old and the new approach to preaching. Brown preached not what he thought might be acceptable, but what he believed is truth which the Holy Spirit will honour. To suppose that a sermon only succeeds if it 'appeals' to people is to miss the real explanation of effective preaching. It was because Christ's disciples once entertained the wrong idea that they were alarmed when Jesus 'offended' his hearers by

[17] See above, p. 158.

speaking on the corruption of the human heart (*Matt.* 15:12). Many of Brown's contemporaries were thinking in that same way, like a famous clergyman of whom it was said, 'He made people feel good.' In contrast, it was said, 'Archibald Brown made them feel bad, and in sore need of a Saviour.'[18] He could do that because he knew it is not speech which pleases men that leads them to enter the kingdom of God: 'With men it is impossible, but not with God' (*Mark* 10:27).

The gospel of God has never been popular to the natural man, anywhere or at any time. An attraction to Christ is no part of our fallen nature: 'When we shall see him there is no beauty that we should desire him' (*Isa.* 53:2). Salvation by grace, without our works, has always been contrary to human pride. But there is another Person besides the preacher, and without him all preaching is in vain. 'How shall they preach except they be sent?' 'We preach Christ crucified, unto the Jews a stumbling block, and unto the Greeks foolishness; but unto them that are called, both Jews and Greeks, Christ the power of God, and the wisdom of God' (*Rom.* 10:15; *1 Cor.* 1:23-24).

But lest this be misunderstood, it should be added that where there is offence it ought to be from the gospel itself and not from its presentation. In speech a Christian is to be 'gentle, shewing all meekness unto all men' (*Titus* 3:2). Give 'none offence, neither to the Jews, nor to the Gentiles' (*1 Cor.* 10:32).

For Brown, recognition of the place of the Holy Spirit is foundational to all true preaching:

---

[18] *East London Tabernacle: A Brief History*, p. 7.

He is the sole administrator of the Church of Christ. Everything is subject to his will. 'All these'—the gifts, workings, and ministries—'worketh that one and the self-same Spirit, dividing to every man severally as he will' . . . In too many of our churches he is but little known even by name, and in all our churches too little known in person. My deep conviction is that our churches today are suffering in a hundred different ways, all because the Gracious Spirit is practically ousted from the position that is his by right. The spirit of the age is the practical ruler, while the Spirit of God is the nominal Lord. A Holy Ghost church will consult him before doing anything. She will not draw up her plans, pass her resolutions, transact her business, and then ask that his gracious influence 'may follow all that she has done'. No; the Holy Ghost church will ask him for the plans and will lowly wait on him to know his resolves, and seek to be allowed to do his business.[19]

I will seek to summarise what this meant for Brown's preaching in a number of principles:

1. *In the church the Word of God must have 'the highest possible position of honour'.* A preacher has to be soaked in Scripture. In Brown's study, the Bible stood apart from every other book: 'Other books may have a measure of power about them, but this book has an indescribable vitality—it lives. Oh, it talks to me; it communes with me; it smites me often; sometimes it kisses me; it rebukes me. God's life is in it from beginning to end.'[20]

There are some who would argue that Brown's method of preaching from individual texts is inconsistent with his high view of Scripture. In their view, the best understanding of

---

[19] Sermon, 'A Holy Ghost Church'.
[20] Sermon on Hebrews 4:12; March 24, 1907.

Scripture is given to hearers when the preacher follows a purpose and programme, working consecutively through a book or passage over a period of time. This is a point that requires comment if Brown's preaching is not to be passed over as second best. For the sake of clarification I will distinguish the difference involved in this issue by the terms 'textual preaching' and 'expository preaching'. These terms are imperfect for discriminating between the two, for all true preaching must have Scripture for its text and all true preaching is exposition. But the two terms point to what is the well-recognized difference between preaching which takes unrelated texts, Sunday by Sunday, and preaching that continues consecutively in a series. The latter has come to be regarded by numbers of preachers as the only true 'expository preaching'. Without this, it is argued, hearers gain only a piecemeal understanding of Scripture, and no coherent view of the whole.

The prevalence of this understanding of preaching in contemporary churches of reformed persuasion is comparatively new in the history of the church. It is true that at various periods an 'expository lecture' has been given by preachers, but not on the assumption that it was the *only* right way to preach.[21] Now, of course, the form of the sermon—whether in a consecutive series or on individual texts—is secondary to its content. But I believe that if the form adopted by such men as Brown and Spurgeon had been excluded in times past the churches would have been without many of their richest ministries. While exposition of a book or a section

---

[21] See, for example, the Westminster divines 'Of the Preaching of the Word', in *The Directory for the Public Worship of God* (1645). The point is discussed by yet another John Brown in *Puritan Preaching in England* (*Beecher Lectures for 1899*); on 'continuous expository preaching' he comments, 'One can only say that it depends how a man does it as to whether it is desirable or not.'

of Scripture—if well done—is valuable, preaching which concentrates on pressing home a single text has the longest history of usefulness.[22] And when it comes to specifically evangelistic preaching the single-text sermon, using 'a capital text', has the greatest record of effectiveness.[23] A leading nineteenth-century preacher judged right when he said: 'We must have great preachers, who shall give great sermons on great themes, or the time is not distant when no preaching will be popular.'[24]

The argument for consecutive 'expository preaching' often proceeds on the assumption that the sermon is the congregation's one means of gaining knowledge of the Bible. That is not so. Where preaching moves minds and hearts, people will not wait another seven days to learn more from the pulpit; they will have received a stimulus that will set them reading themselves. In former times Christians commonly used commentaries on Scripture in their homes, such as those of Matthew Henry, John Brown of Haddington, and Thomas

[22] Both forms of preaching have their dangers. The one-text procedure may deal with a text artificially, without regard to the primary sense and context as did the preacher who took the words, 'Can you speak Greek' (*Acts* 21:37), to enforce study of the original language! But the 'expository' can range so widely over verses that nothing is easily remembered, and exegesis can take the place of preaching (which ought to proceed on the basis of exegesis). Commentating on a passage is not preaching, and is calculated to make preaching unpopular. David Breed observed a phenomenon not unknown today: 'A preacher may occupy half the winter, or even more, in discoursing, let us say, upon the Gospel of Matthew, or the Epistle to the Romans. Unless he is very highly gifted, and a man of unusual spiritual power, this will become intolerably wearisome.' *Preparing to Preach* (New York: Hodder & Stoughton, 1911), p. 397.

[23] It is a serious mistake to think all texts are equally likely to be used for the conversion of men and women. Spurgeon is right in saying, 'God the Holy Spirit can convert a soul by any text of Scripture . . . but there are certain Scripture passages, as you know, that are the best to bring before the minds of sinners.' *The Soul-Winner* (London: Passmore & Alabaster, 1895), p. 92.

[24] Austin Phelps, *The Theory of Preaching, Lectures on Homiletics* (New York: Scribner's, 1882), p. 394.

Scott. Good preaching will always ignite hunger for Scripture. As Lloyd-Jones has written:

> The main function of the preacher is inspirational. It is not merely to dole out information, or lecture on the books of the Bible, or lecture on doctrine. He can tell people where they can read this. He does so up to a point of course, but his supreme task is to inspire the people, to bring the Bible alive to them.[25]

It was also the case, as has been noticed earlier, that apart from the sermon, Scripture—not merely a few verses—was read and always with a short comment. When a deacon of the Metropolitan Tabernacle called on Brown one Saturday, and apologised for intruding on his 'sermon time', he received the reply, 'Oh no, my sermons were done during the week, and I make a practice of giving the whole of Saturday to study for the purpose of commenting upon the chapters I intend to read on the Lord's Day.' George Page went as far as writing, 'Several thousand people believed that it would be worthwhile to come for the Scripture reading, even if there were no sermon.'[26]

It would be a bold person who would argue that the congregations of those days were less well instructed in the Bible than those of today where the consecutive series of sermons prevails. Brown was describing something not unknown in his congregation when he said in a 'Holy Ghost church',

> The only sermon enjoyed will be one that opens up, not hangs up the Word. The preacher's sermon will be accompanied throughout with the musical rustle of Bible leaves, as

[25] *Knowing the Times: Addresses Delivered on Various Occasions* (Edinburgh: Banner of Truth, 1989), p. 362.
[26] Page, *AGB*, p. 12.

passage is quoted to illustrate passage . . . every member will come to learn more of the Word. He wants no political reference or magazine article. He has come to hear the Book talk, or rather to hear God talk to him out of the Book. No church where the Bible is not enthroned in the hearts of the members is a Holy Ghost one. It may be a church impregnated with the spirit of the age, but not a church saturated by the Spirit of God. Where he reigns, Scripture is supreme.

2. *The preacher must know the Holy Spirit in his personal life.* We have noted Brown's belief in an on-going giving of the Holy Spirit in answer to prayer. That being so, prayer is primary for preaching, as Augustine said long ago.[27] With a characteristic use of illustration, Brown argued that for a preacher, 'the secret of power with others is heart elevation'. He told how recently on the sea front in Hastings, he had watched workmen driving massive piles of wood, bound in iron, into the shingle for a breakwater. For this procedure a hammer of herculean size and weight was slowly pulled up to a considerable height, then allowed to fall on the top of a pile. Supposing, he said, an onlooker had suggested that the use of a child's spade would have made for faster work—needing no time to be hauled up and able to deliver a hundred taps to one blow of the hammer. Such a proposal the workmen would have laughed to scorn, and the onlooker who made it would have been told,

> that one of their blows would do more than a whole century of his tapping; that there was no waste of time in raising the iron thunderbolt, for the power of its blow was in proportion to the height from which it fell. So believer, your power and mine to affect men is in exact proportion to the elevation of

---

[27] 'The Christian teacher will succeed more by prayer than by gifts of oratory.'

our soul and life, and this elevation can only be obtained by secret communion with God, and abstinence from all that panders to the flesh and hinders the Spirit's fellowship.[28]

Brown sought to practise this in his personal life. His son, Douglas, recorded how at the age of ten he would cautiously creep near his father's study door on a Friday night, the night of sermon preparation. What he heard was prayer, and he wrote in later years, it was 'more wonderful than what I heard from the platform on Sunday morning. I could not understand it all as a little boy, but it gripped me. I feel the aftermath of it today.'[29]

Has this not been true of all preaching significantly used of God? Prayer has to go before the ministry of the Word of God (*Acts* 6:4; *Eph.* 6:19), indeed take priority over it:

> As an agency in promoting the kingdom of God on earth, prayer is to be put, not side by side with the preaching of the Word and ordinances, but above them. They are nothing except a divine influence vitalizes them, and that divine influence the power of the Spirit of God, that comes only along the channels opened by prayer.[30]

In history this priority has commonly been found with a Calvinistic understanding of the work of God. It was exemplified, for instance, by the school of Welsh preachers used to transform their nation in the eighteenth and nineteenth centuries. One of them, Henry Rees, is described in words equally applicable to Archibald Brown:

> Praying and preaching were with him indissolubly connected. He besought aid in the choosing of his texts and in

[28] 'The Secret of Failure', Matthew 17:19, 20, March 30, 1873.
[29] Quoted in Griffin, *Forgotten Revival*, pp. 18-19.
[30] James Murray on 'Christ as a Man of Prayer', *Princeton Sermons* (New York: Fleming Revell, 1893, p. 208.

the treating of them . . . I heard him tell several times how one moment of expansion of soul in God helped him more than anything else to make darkness light before him and to open his eyes to the wonder of the subject he had in hand . . . The consciousness that he had mastered his sermon was not enough to satisfy him, he desired also that his sermon in its turn should completely master him. [He counselled a candidate for the ministry] 'You will overcome all difficulties if you but give yourself to prayer. Praying! Praying! Praying! How dimly do we discern even a thousandth part of the power of praying upon preaching!'[31]

3. *The preacher needs the Holy Spirit in both the preparation and delivery of sermons.* It is on this subject that Brown's thinking differs with that of many preachers who would not disagree with his message. The objection is raised, 'If Brown's practice of preaching from different places in Scripture every week, with no set programme, is followed, then what is to stop the preacher from being governed by the mood and the impulses of the moment in his selection of his text?'[32] It is true such a danger exists and that the 'textual' preacher who discounts it may be governed by his feelings. But to think that the only alternative to the danger of the subjective is to work consecutively through passages is to miss what Brown regarded as vitally significant: the Holy Spirit prompts the

---

[31] A. M. Davies, *Life and Letters of Henry Rees* (Bangor: Jarvis & Foster, 1904), pp. 286-9. The literature of the Calvinistic Methodists of Wales is rich in this material. See, for example, John Elias, *Life, Letters and Essays* (repr. Edinburgh: Banner of Truth, 2004), and Thomas Charles, *Spiritual Counsels,* ed. Edward Morgan (repr. Edinburgh: Banner of Truth, 1993), pp. 441-3.

[32] Phillips Brooks underlined the danger in the words: 'There is no consecutive purpose in your teaching. You float over the whole sea of truth, and plunge here and there, like a gull, on any subject that either suits your mood, or that some casual and superficial intercourse with your people makes you conceive to be required by a popular need.' *Lectures on Preaching, Delivered at Yale Divinity School 1877* (London: Allenson, n.d.), p. 90.

birth of sermons. The fact that all Scripture is given by inspiration of God, and is profitable, for him did not mean he could preach from any text at any place or time. He did not regard it enough that a sermon be scriptural; he wanted the message intended for his hearers at a particular hour. He believed in a difference between his people hearing a message from Scripture, and hearing a message from God through Scripture. It was the latter that he wanted to give them and for which prayer was indispensable.

'Get your texts from God', M'Cheyne counselled. That means the preacher is to take to others what is first laid on his own heart. In Brown's words, 'I am always obliged to preach what presses upon me.'[33] 'My usual practice is passing on to you everything that proves of profit to me.' 'How often we have learnt by experience that when we have had the greatest trouble in finding a subject, it has been a theme that has been the most blessed by God. For our texts we shall have to be dependent upon Jehovah-Jireh.'

The awareness of being arrested by the truth in settling on the text of a sermon will make a major difference in its delivery. The man who has been, in Rees's phrase, completely 'mastered' by the message he delivers, is going to bear the resemblance of a witness. He knows it is not his message. He persuades others because he is himself persuaded. This element was very prominent in Brown as it is in all true preaching. So speaking on the text, 'From henceforth let no man trouble me; for I bear in my body the marks of the Lord Jesus' (*Gal.* 6:17), he could say:

[33] 'What is the right text? How do you know it? We know it by the signs of a friend. When a verse gives your mind a hearty grip, from which you cannot release yourself, you will need no further direction as to your proper theme. When the text gets a hold of us, we may be sure we have a hold of it.' Spurgeon, *Lectures to My Students*, p. 94.

Oh, brethren and sisters, I would to God I could speak to you this morning as I would. I only wish I could make this text blaze away before your eyes as it has before my own. I would that its tremendous force might be realised by you, as it has been felt in my own heart before coming here. Oh, how it would shake some of you out of your selfishness, out of your worldliness, out of your pandering to the maxims of this world.

There is a compulsion for hearers to listen to a man who speaks in this manner.

Something more also is involved here. Brown belonged to a school of preachers who did not regard it as a matter of personal choice whether or not a sermon should be read off paper. It should not be read at all.[34] If a man is truly gripped by his message, if it has a unity to it, and its divisions are natural and easily remembered, then there is no need to stick to a manuscript. All excuses to the contrary, boldness and authority in preaching are rarely to be found in those who only repeat what they have written beforehand.

A preacher cannot have his eye both on his paper and on the people. Brown was certain that to hold attention one needs to speak straight to hearers and to be able to read their faces while speaking. The preacher dependent on his notes is not likely to say, as Brown could do, 'The application of this subject is so very evident that I can tell from your countenances that you have already worked it out.' 'How often', he recalled on another occasion, 'have I sat in positive misery in a chapel listening to a man who I felt never looked at me

---

[34] This is not to say sermons should not be written beforehand. Although, like Brown, Spurgeon only used an outline of notes, he commended the writing of sermons. Lloyd-Jones wrote a sermon in full every week for the first ten years of his ministry. It should also be noted that he was some 20 years in the ministry before, for some services, he took up the consecutive exposition of books of Scripture.

or anyone else. I felt that the pulpit was entirely separated from the pews, and that there was no mysterious chord of sympathy linking them both together. The want of attention in an audience is nine hundred and ninety-nine times out of a thousand the fault of the preacher or speaker.'

But the necessity of eye-contact is not the only reason why the preacher needs freedom from a manuscript The man who is limited to saying only what he has prepared beforehand is not open to the Spirit prompting words that may occur at the moment of speaking. Of course, the preacher should know where he is going beforehand, but many of the most thrilling passages in Brown's sermons could never have been framed at a study desk. It would have been impossible for him to read from paper such words as, 'I would that I could take the whole of this congregation in my arms, and never drop one until all of you were safely carried to the kingdom.' Speaking freely, under the anointing of the Holy Spirit, gives birth to the feeling necessary for true eloquence. Brown would have agreed with the words of William Jay, 'All eloquence which does not arise from feeling, and produce it, is as sounding brass and tinkling cymbal.'

The objection that this way of preaching is difficult is indeed true. Immensely difficult, and that is precisely why preaching has to be more than the work of the human messenger. The arguments against the school of preachers that Brown represented—that it is too subjective, and unsuitable for most men—comes close to questioning what Scripture says about preaching. Christ is directly involved in preaching. The Holy Spirit is the author of effective preaching. That a counterfeit and fanatical preaching may claim the authority of the Spirit is only proof of the desire of Satan to corrupt the agency God has appointed for the establishing of truth in the earth.

I am not saying that authority and boldness in preaching is only true of such preachers as find their texts, and form their sermons, in the same manner as Brown, yet I believe that the preachers and evangelists who get closest to the hearts of their hearers are usually men of this school. Some who preach consecutively through a passage or book of Scripture, Sunday to Sunday, may make the text 'blaze'; but history seems to show that gripping, persuasive, converting preaching, is more usually found to be of another type.

4. *Good preaching is the product of hard work.* This needs to be underscored because there have been those who have spoken of preaching as though reliance on the supernatural makes human effort unnecessary; the preacher may simply wait for the sermon to be 'given him', and the more spontaneously thoughts occur to him, the more sure he is that they are of God. This is thinking akin to the way Brown, as a child, once thought he might be given Euclid. Preachers have not been unknown who have boasted how quickly their sermons 'came' to them; some have even thought it spiritual to begin a sermon without even knowing what they were going to say when they stood up. Fanaticism of this kind sees no need for careful preparation. But the Holy Spirit works through and with the individual, not apart from him. Thus Lloyd-Jones could say, 'The Spirit generally uses a man's best preparation.'[35] We can be sure that all which makes men proud, and offers relief from hard work, is counterfeit. A man led by the Spirit will use his mind and think more rather than less.

To ignore the human element would be to miss much that made Brown's preaching what it was. Because the unregenerate

---

[35] Iain H. Murray, *Lloyd-Jones, Messenger of Grace* (Edinburgh: Banner of Truth, 2008), p. 87. There is much on the subject of preaching in that book.

mind is contrary to the gospel it did not mean that the manner of its communication is insignificant. The 'form' in which a sermon is delivered—its arrangement, argument, illustration and application—has a vital relation to its influence.[36] The preacher cannot change the heart but he ought to be able to awaken interest and hold attention. It was not without much mental toil that Brown was able to interest, and often enthral, his hearers. Simplicity, accuracy, and a logical division of the subject, are no easy things to arrive at; and to succeed in doing this, in one congregation through thirty years, with freshness and without predictability, was the consequence of determined and wise labour. An enduring popularity can be attained in no other way. In the words of W. E. Sangster, 'It is only constant and fresh work in sermon preparation which keeps the life in preaching.'[37] There is nothing mysterious about why ordinary people in the East End of London crowded to hear AGB and long remembered him. 'The words of the wise are as goads and as nails fastened by the masters of assemblies' (*Eccles.* 12:11).

It is the mark of a good division of a text that, once heard, the sense is clear and obvious. Take these examples from Brown. On John 11:11, 'Our friend Lazarus sleepeth.' His threefold division was:

---

[36] By 'illustration' I am not referring the story-telling which became so common in late Victorian preaching. Brown used anecdotes only sparingly, but he regularly sought to present truths as pictures, following the example of our Lord who would say, 'the kingdom of heaven is like . . .' One book on preaching quotes the following needs for a sermon. The preacher: (1) should throw his material into such a shape that it will be easily remembered; (2) must stimulate the imagination; (3) should convey sympathy; (4) should take up such topics as move himself deeply. Breed, *Preparing to Preach*, p. 164.

[37] *The Craft of Sermon Construction* (London: Epworth Press, 1949), p. 195.

1. A sweet relationship declared, 'Our friend'.
2. A solemn fact suggested, Christ's friends die.
3. A cheering description given, 'Our friend sleepeth'.

On Jeremiah 15:16, 'Thy words were found, and I did eat them; and thy word was unto me the joy and rejoicing of my heart', his 'heads' were similarly natural:

There is first of all, the finding of the food: 'Thy words were found'. Then, secondly, there is eating the food: 'Thy words were found and I did eat them.' Thirdly, we have the result of the food eaten, that word which, being found and inwardly received, becomes the joy and rejoicing of the heart.[38]

Whatever Brown's hearers thought of his message, few could ever complain that they could not follow it. As with Spurgeon, his treatment of texts has been criticised, and considered too infantile by some preachers, but the words of J. C. Ryle on Spurgeon are relevant: 'I am not a bit ashamed to say I often read Spurgeon . . . We ought always to examine and analyse sermons which draw people together.'[39]

* * * * *

The challenge to the church today is the same that it has always been. It is the challenge to believe that faith in God,

---

[38] In these instances a 'text' meant a single verse. It did not necessarily mean that for Brown. Essential to a text is a unity of truth, or a few related truths. It may involve a passage of Scripture, but if that is the case it does not mean (as expository preaching often means) attempting to cover every truth in the passage. 'He needeth not always to prosecute every doctrine which lies in his text' but what is 'most needful and seasonable' (*Directory for Public Worship*).

[39] 'Simplicity in Preaching', in *The Upper Room* (repr. Edinburgh: Banner of Truth, 2006; also published as a separate booklet by the Trust, 2010), p. 42. The subject of how Brown divided texts is far too large for further consideration here but it warrants study by students for the ministry today. I would not argue that he was always true to the context, although that was his general aim, as it ought to be.

and in the means he has appointed to build the church, are sufficient for all times. This entails resistance to any idea that a changing world requires priorities different from those of the apostolic or any other age. A failure to overcome that temptation has repeatedly led to periods in the life of the churches when attention to preaching wanes, both in pulpit and pew. The temptation is subtle because it does not appear as a temptation at all, a false confidence giving assurance that something else is able to fill the place of preaching.[40]

As we have seen, Archibald Brown had only limited success in opposing the change which took place in his lifetime, but he knew there is such a thing as preaching 'with the Holy Spirit sent down from heaven,' and was content to leave the future of the church in the hands of God.

It is true that the office of the minister and pastor has sometimes been wrongly exalted. It is also certain that witness to Christ belongs to the whole number of his people. Yet, because the strength of the church comes through Scripture, it is also true that the recovery and revival of the church after periods of declension always begins in the ministry of the Word.

Brown gave no assurance to his contemporaries that the apostasy of his later years would pass, and there would be a brighter day for the churches in Britain. For one thing, he believed that apostasy would mark the age closest to the second coming of Christ, and he did not know whether the

---

[40] This mode of thinking was prominent again in the 1960s, often countered by Martyn Lloyd-Jones: 'These proposals that we should preach less, and do various other things more, are of course not new at all. People seem to think all this is quite new, and that it is the hallmark of modernity to decry or to depreciate preaching, and to put your emphasis on these other things. The simple answer is that there is nothing new about it.' Lloyd-Jones, *Preaching and Preachers* (London: Hodder & Stoughton, 1971), p. 33.

apostasy he witnessed would be the last before that day. But he did not hold that understanding as a man who believed the work of God might be defeated. 'Is the down grade going to continue forever? Is scepticism to increase? Are the churches to get increasingly cold? Oh, what painful questions these are. But the Lord will see to it. God has never been hard up for a workman yet, and He never will be.'

Whether times to us are bright or dark, the promises of Christ are the same, and the Holy Spirit's purpose to glorify Christ is immutable. So, while scorning new ways for the recovery of Christian influence, Brown believed that if God sent a new generation of messengers, baptized with love, compassion, and boldness, a change for the better would not be in doubt.

Such God-sent men all have a remarkable likeness. While they differ in gifts and personality, they share the common ambition to see Christ honoured and believed on in the world. The work of such men does not change. In Brown's words, 'First, a living Christ is the warrant for preaching; next, that an ascended Christ is the inspiration for preaching; next that the gospel must be the matter for preaching; then that the Lord co-working is the power of preaching.'

Preaching on 'Suddenly there came a sound from heaven' (*Acts* 2:2), during the decline which marked the early 1900s, he said:

> When the sound is heard from heaven, and the next revival comes, there will be nothing said from the pulpit or platform about 'up-to-date' or 'social subject', or the clap-trap that is popular today; it will be Bible! Bible! Bible! And the people clamouring, 'Let us have the Word of God.' The gospel was preached [at Pentecost], and what followed? Conviction! 'They were pricked in their heart.' They said to Peter, 'Men

and brethren, what shall we do.' 'But', says someone, 'do you imagine such a thing could ever happen today?' Yes, indeed I do. I have seen it! Every week for years, men and women coming and saying, 'What shall we do?'

After my heavens and my earth have perished he remaineth, and he ever will. My Saviour is the eternal God. My Christ, the I AM, he who died on the cross for me, liveth evermore, throughout eternity 'the same'. In spirit I look far down those endless ages. Aeon follows aeon, and still the song rises and swells, filling heaven with its melody, 'Thou remainest; thou remainest; the same Eternal, Immutable, Lord Jesus!'[41]

[41] The last paragraph is from 'Thou Remainest', an undated sermon on Hebrews 1:10-11.

APPENDIX I

SERMONS OF
ARCHIBALD G. BROWN

A sermon of Brown's was published monthly from October 1868 until 1896, the end of his ministry at the East London Tabernacle. Thereafter further sermons were published at regular intervals until 1910, often as single items in booklet format. Numbers of publishers were engaged in their publication and we are not able to give a definitive listing. In this book I have quoted sermons by their text and date, rather than by reference to the published source, in part because the early published volumes of his sermons are very rare, and in part because numbers of the same sermons were reprinted and by different publishers. The sermons were originally mainly sold separately, or in packets of six. Some were published in hardback volumes, others in paperback. The reader who does have access to the titles listed below may be able to trace a number of the sermons I quote by comparing their dates with the dates when the volumes below were published.

The majority of Brown's early sermons were taken down shorthand and printed, it seems, without any revision by the preacher; nor did he earn royalties from their publication. Later sermons were edited by him and the difference is apparent. The numbers of publishers involved, and the different formats in which the sermons appeared, is indicative of their popularity.

Pre-1900

(1) *Sermons Preached At Stepney Green Tabernacle, 1868-9* (London: Francis, 1870). Currently reprinted by Kessinger Publishing, ISBN: 978 0 21787 161 7.

(2) *East London Tabernacle Pulpit* (London: Francis/Morgan & Scott, 1873), 408 pp. Contains fifty sermons including the twelve in (1).

(3) Title page of our copy missing, contains all in (1) and (2), with an additional 175 pp. of sermons from 1872-74, 584 pp.

The Penny Pulpit: A Collection of Accurately-Reported Sermons by the most eminent Ministers of Various Denominations, Vol. XIII (London: Davis, 1875). Contains eight Brown sermons. Later it appears that Charles Higham took over *The Penny Pulpit* series, and continued to include Brown sermons. From that publisher came the following:

Forty Sermons Preached by the Rev Archibald Brown in the East London Tabernacle (London: Higham, 1886). These were sermons already printed in the *Penny Pulpit* series.

The People's Pulpit, Selected Volume (London: Higham, 1899), contains eighteen sermons of Brown from late 1880s and early 1890s, together with those of other preachers.

Twenty Sermons by Archibald G. Brown, Volume 1, New Series (London: Banks, n.d.), sermons from the period 1891-93.

Twenty-Five Sermons by Archibald Brown, Volume II, New Series (London: Banks, n.d.), sermons from the period 1893-95.

Sermons by Archibald G. Brown, Volume III, New Series (London: Banks, n.d.), sermons from years 1895-97.

A Song About Redemption (London: Banks, n.d. [c.1898]). A reprint of ten sermons.

Post-1900

'*Thou Remainest*', *and Other Sermons, Archibald G. Brown* (London: Stockwell, 1902), 162 pp. These are earlier sermons republished as Volume XXII of *The Baptist Pulpit* series.

In the Valley of Decision, Archibald G. Brown (London: Simpkin, Marshall, Hamilton, 1903), 185 pp. This is a reprint of sermons already published by others.

'*Selah*', *or Think of That, Archibald G. Brown* (London: Lovejoy, 1906), 139 pp. Contains fresh material and reprints.

The Four Evangelists, Character Sketches by Rev. Archibald G. Brown, Metropolitan Tabernacle (London: Lovejoy, 1909).

Twelve Assorted Sermons by Archibald Brown (London: Lovejoy, n.d.)

Sermons preached at Chatsworth Road and the Metropolitan Tabernacle, 1906-09.

God's Full-Orbed Gospel, and Other Sermons Preached at the Metropolitan Tabernacle, Archibald G. Brown (London: Allenson, n.d.), 242 pp.

APPENDIX 2

FAMILY TREE OF
ARCHIBALD G. BROWN

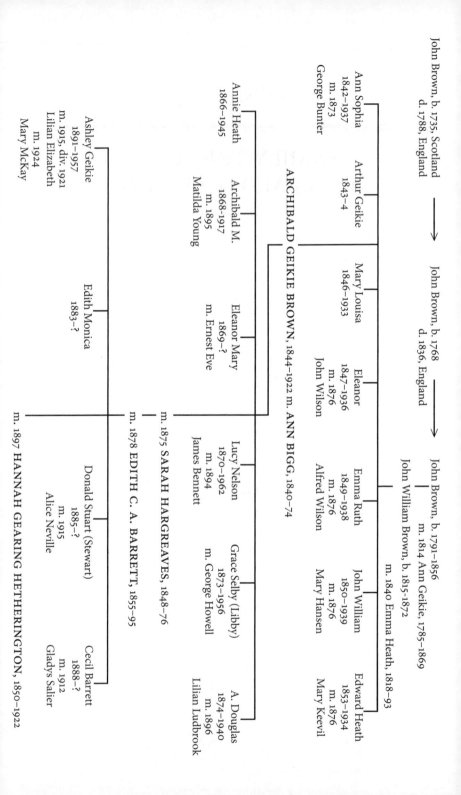

APPENDIX 3

MUSICAL INSTRUMENTS
IN WORSHIP

THE gift of music is part of the wonder of life and musical instruments are almost as old as the creation. Spurgeon and Brown never doubted that fact. Spurgeon's wife, Susannah, was an accomplished pianist, and music would have been familiar in both homes. Yet neither man advocated the use of a musical instrument in public worship. In the words of one of his friends, 'Pastor Brown was no enthusiast for the employment of musical instruments in the Sanctuary.'[1] Was this simply the survival of a fading tradition, or did it rest on grounds which remain relevant today? The answer to the question may seem too obvious for it to be asked. Surely Scripture makes it abundantly clear that the use of many musical instruments has divine approval. The Book of Psalms gives repeated endorsements in such words as those of Psalm 98:4-6, 'Make a joyful noise unto the Lord, all the earth . . . sing unto the Lord with the harp . . . with trumpets and sound of cornet.' The same Book closes with a call that praise be accompanied by a great crescendo of instruments (*Psa.* 150:3-6).

But the very clarity of such verses ought to give cause for pause. Brown and Spurgeon were far from unaware of their

---

[1] *Chatsworth Road Baptist Church*, p. 17.

teaching, indeed Spurgeon spent more than twenty years commenting on every verse in the Psalms in his work *The Treasury of David*. A serious examination of the reasons why they did not regard the continual use of musical instruments as warranted by Scripture will show that the issue is not as simple as is often thought. The following considerations need to be taken into account:

1. Praise is the duty of the whole creation, and in a 'poetical apostrophe' the Psalms sometimes call upon all things to worship God, not only all musical instruments, but as Psalm 98 goes on to say, 'Let the sea roar, and the fullness thereof . . . Let the floods clap their hands' (verses 7, 8) Fields and woods, hills and valleys—all are to rejoice in God. The world of nature makes up one song. But while this teaches us that all creation is to render praise, when it comes to the use of musical instruments Scripture gives us more detail.

From ancient times musical instruments were used on occasions of thanksgiving. Psalm 81:2 refers to such an event, when Miriam 'took a timbrel' and sang at the deliverance of Israel from the Egyptians and the Red Sea (*Exod.* 15:20). We read of the same instrument being played by other women in times of joyful procession (*Judg.* 11:34; *1 Sam.* 18:6). About such instances there is no controversy.

2. The specific direction of the Old Testament for musical instruments in public worship has to do with the assembling of the people of God. When this development came in the history of Israel two things became standard:

(1) The tribe of Levi was appointed by God for all that concerned worship. At the centre of what was commanded was the offering of morning and evening sacrifice: 'In the day of your gladness, and in your solemn days, and in the beginnings of your months, ye shall blow with the trumpets over

your burnt offerings' (*Num.* 10:10). This was the practice in the Tabernacle and then in the Temple where the number of instruments was increased. Of that latter period we read: 'And the Levites stood with the instruments of David, and the priests with the trumpets . . . And when the burnt-offering began, the song of the Lord began also with the trumpets, and with the instruments ordained by David king of Israel. And all the congregation worshipped, and the singers sang, and the trumpeters sounded: and all this continued until the burnt-offering was finished' (2 *Chron.* 29:26-28).

The trumpet sound accompanying the sacrifice was 'the song of the Lord'. For Israel it was 'the joyful sound'; the sound indicated that God himself took pleasure in what the sacrifice typified.

(2) Music in worship was a responsibility within the Levites' office. No one else shared that responsibility and there are now no references to women (*1 Chron.* 6:31, 32; 15:16). Over fifty psalms directed 'To the chief Musician', are reminders to us of the centrality of the Temple in the worship of God under the old dispensation.

3. It appears to be universally agreed that while Jewish worshippers met regularly in the smaller assemblies of synagogues, no musical instruments were heard there. The only obvious reason for this is that the instruments played in the Temple had typical significance. Where there was no sacrifice, as in synagogues, there were no musical instruments. It was to the Temple worship alone that the whole priestly arrangement of sacrifices, incense, vestments, and lamps belonged. While there were over 300 synagogues in Jerusalem in the time of Christ, in none of them were musical instruments used.[2] As

---

[2] The Jewish Talmud says there were 394 synagogues in Jerusalem in AD 70.

in the upper room at the last supper, it was customary for psalms to be sung without any accompaniment.

From this it is argued that musical instruments in temple worship were part of a dispensation in which all had God-given typical and symbolic meaning. Therefore when that era came to an end, and to fulfilment in the gospel era, the musical accompaniment ceased along with much else that had been part of worship in the temple. Such was Spurgeon's understanding. On the words, 'Praise the Lord with the harp', he wrote:

> Men need all the help they can get to stir them up to praise. This is the lesson to be gathered from the use of musical instruments under the old dispensation. Israel was at school, and used childish things to help them to learn; but in these days, when Jesus gives us spiritual manhood, we can make melody without strings and pipes. We do not believe these things to be expedient in worship, lest they should mar its simplicity.[3]

In this belief, Spurgeon was following leaders in the Protestant Reformation. The opinion, however, did not originate in the sixteenth century. The non-use of musical instruments by Christians goes right back to the first century. Despite the popularity of all types of music in the Greek and Roman world, and the availability of portable instruments, the early Christian churches did not employ them. In this they followed the synagogues, but for a reason unrecognised by unbelieving Jews. There was no need now for musicians, trumpets, and singers to give a joyful sound. Christ's sacrifice had been accomplished once and for ever. The gift of the Holy Spirit

---

[3] On Psalm 33:2 in *The Treasury of David* (repr. London: Marshall, Morgan & Scott, 1950), vol. 2, p. 104.

raised worship to a higher realm. There was no place for
the shadows of external symbols where the kingdom of God
existed in power. The praise from the hearts of the redeemed
was now led by the risen Saviour himself (*Psa.* 22:22; *John*
17:26). What Old Testament Scripture prophesied had
become a reality, 'From the uttermost part of the earth have
we heard songs, even glory to the righteous' (*Isa.* 24:16).
No more temple or priests, no more need for the type. The
hour had come when 'the true worshippers shall worship
the Father in spirit and in truth' (*John* 4:23). The great rule
for worship was now, 'Be filled with the Spirit; speaking to
yourselves in psalms and hymns and spiritual songs, singing
and making melody in your heart to the Lord' (*Eph.* 5:18-
19). 'The gods of Greece and Rome may be worshipped well
enough with classical music', wrote Spurgeon, 'but Jehovah
can only be adored with the heart, and that music is best for
his service which gives the heart most play.'[4]

It has been said that 'Not long after the destruction of the
Temple [AD 70] instrumental music fell into disuse and for
some reason or other was never revived.'[5] But the reason for
the disuse need be no mystery. For the Jews, when sacrifice
ended, the Levitical worship ended. In the case of Christians
the reason for the disuse is clearly stated by a whole succession of the Early Church leaders, Justin Martyr (AD 150),
Clemens of Alexandria (AD 190), Cyprian (AD 240), and
Theodoret (AD 390). The words of Chrysostom (AD 396)
provide a summary of their united opinion:

> It [instrumental music] was permitted to the Jews, as sacri-
> fice was, for the heaviness and grossness of their souls. God

---

[4] On Psalm 81:1 in *Treasury of David*, vol 3, pp. 399-400.
[5] *Zondervan Pictorial Encyclopedia of the Bible* (Grand Rapids: 1978), vol. 4, p. 315.

condescended to their weakness, because they were lately drawn off from idols; but now, instead of instruments we may use our bodies to praise him withal. Again, let no man deceive you, these [instruments] appertain not to Christians; these are alien to the Catholic Church; all these things do the nations of the world seek after.[6]

This was precisely the reason recovered at the time of the Reformation. John Calvin, for instance, had no objection to musical instruments *per se*. He wrote, 'If believers choose to cheer themselves with musical instruments, they should, I think, make it their object not to dissever their cheerfulness from the praises of God.' Music belongs to the realm of common grace. 'But', he goes on,

> when they frequent their sacred assemblies, musical instruments in celebrating the praises of God would be no more suitable than the burning of incense, the lighting up of lamps, and the restoration of other shadows of the law. The Papists, therefore, have foolishly borrowed this, as well as many other things from the Jews. Men who are fond of outward pomp may delight in that noise; but the simplicity which God recommends to us by the apostle is far more pleasing to him.[7]

* * * * *

From all this it can be seen that the views of Brown and Spurgeon were no personal idiosyncrasies. But another question now arises. If it is granted that the apostolic church,

---

[6] Quoted in James Kerr's booklet, *Consensus of Opinions against Instrumental Music in Worship* (Greenock: Black, n.d.), pp. 1-2. Also in *Treasury of David*, vol. 4, p. 123.

[7] Quoted on Psalm 98:5-6 in *Treasury of David*, vol. 4, p. 218. See also Calvin, *Sermons on 2 Samuel*, translated by Douglas F. Kelly (Edinburgh: Banner of Truth, 1992), pp. 241-2.

and others following, laid aside instrumental music in worship, does that prove it is forbidden? Why cannot they be employed today, not as a type of anything, but as an aid to worship? Apart from any scriptural principle for their continued use, may they not be employed on the grounds of expediency? Cannot their use be considered an advantage as an aid to worship?

On this question there has clearly been disagreement among evangelical Christians. Spurgeon did not make the disuse of musical instruments a matter of strict principle. He wrote: 'We do not affirm them to be unlawful, and if any George Herbert or Martin Luther can worship God better by the aid of well-tuned instruments, who shall gainsay their right . . . As a help to singing the instrument is alone to be tolerated.'[8] Brown allowed the same liberty. He faced the issue at Chatsworth Road Baptist Church where an organ was in use when he went there, and he did not insist on its removal.[9] If an instrument is considered only as an aid, and no more a part of it than a pulpit or platform, then it is not a major issue. So understood, an instrument only gives notes to guide the singing. It does no more, for, in Spurgeon's words, 'keys and strings do not praise the Lord'.

But if the case was put for an instrument in terms of its advantage in worship, the two men argued the negative. They were sure that praise would not have been improved at the

---

[8] On Psalm 33:2 in *Treasury of David*, vol. 2, p. 104.

[9] A privately published work, *Chatsworth Centenary 1878-1978*, gives us this information on the restoration of the building during Brown's ministry: 'Only one change was controversial. Mr Brown disliked anything that he called "entertainments" in the service and like his mentor, Mr Spurgeon, he did not approve of organs in the church. However, the original 'box of whistles' finally collapsed, and in 1905 the church decided to replace it with a nobler instrument, but in deference to the pastor, it was put at the back of the gallery, where it could only be heard and not seen.'

Metropolitan Tabernacle, or the East London Tabernacle, by the adoption of an instrument. Many who attended these churches were of the same judgment. One visitor to London has written:

> I once attended service at a week day afternoon at St Paul's, where there were both an organ and a choir, with solo singers employed in the service of praise. The audience were listening as mutes while the musical performance was going on, and it was utterly impossible, if one yielded to the impression which the service was intended to make, to rise above the feeling which he might have at a concert. From this specimen of formal sensuous worship I passed to the Metropolitan Tabernacle, and what a contrast to the heartless melody of the Cathedral was the burst of song which warm hearts gave out from the lips of thousands who joined in the service of praise.[10]

Similar testimony comes from those who, unlike the man just quoted, had no objection to instrumental music. A book written by J. Spencer Curwen, which Spurgeon refers to as 'of considerable interest and importance', was published early in the 1880s, with the title, *Studies in Worship-Music, chiefly as regards Congregational Singing*. Included in it was a description of the music in the principal places of worship in London in 1881. In his review of the book, Spurgeon noted:

> Mr Curwen says, 'The beauty of the Tabernacle singing is religious and spiritual'; and when he speaks of the singing at the Presbyterian Church, Regent Square, he says, 'I have always been in favour of organs, but a Sunday at Regent Square is enough to shake one's faith in them. The organ

---

[10] John Kennedy, *The Introduction of Instrumental Music into the Free Church Unscriptural, Unconstitutional and Inexpedient* (Edinburgh: Gemmell, 1883), p. 13.

gives a great deal of pleasure, but after all it is sensuous pleasure. We worship when we send up aspirations and feelings of
adoration, prayer and joy in God.'[11]

The idea that the best singing in churches will be found
where there is instrumental aid is not endorsed by history.
There was much singing in the Puritan period, not only in
churches but in homes and even on battlefields, and it was with
the human voice alone. When the Methodist revival began in
the eighteenth century it was with vibrant song which needed
no instruments. 'If there be such a thing as heavenly music
upon earth, I heard it there', reported a Nonconformist minister at a Methodist meeting in 1739.[12] Certainly organs were
to be found in some church buildings and meeting houses
in John Wesley's time, and we read of one such at Louth in
Lincolnshire. When Wesley took a service at Louth, the organ
so annoyed him in the singing of the hymn, 'I thirst, Thou
wounded Lamb of God', that he ordered, 'Let the organ stop,
and let the women take their parts.' In response he was told,
'They cannot sing without, sir.' 'Then how did they do before
they got one?' was Wesley's end to the supposed problem.[13]
This was in 1788, long after the beginning of the revival.

Of course, neither Brown nor Spurgeon thought of song
in worship in isolation from the other parts of a service. If
preaching was dull, if a congregation cold and joyless, then
unaccompanied singing would be equally unattractive. They
did not argue for singing without an instrument as a solution where there is little life. Where such a situation exists, to

---

[11] *S&T*, 1881, p. 86.
[12] *Life and Times of John Wesley*, L. Tyerman, vol. 1 (London: Hodder &
Stoughton, 1890), p. 253.
[13] *The Journal of John Wesley*, Nehemiah Curnock, vol. 7 (London: Kelly, n.d.),
p. 411.

exchange one external practice for another would make no difference. But the enthusiasm for musical accompaniment that came in during the later nineteenth century regarded it as of more importance than a mere aid. If an instrument did not commend the worship to God, at least it commended the service to a congregation. And if one instrument had this effect, would it not be all the greater if others were added? In this reasoning the improvement of the singing was not seen as the main advantage; the main advantage was the supposed greater appeal to a public in which church-going was beginning to decline.

In a lecture, 'How to Attract a Congregation', Spurgeon introduced a comment on this trend with these words:

> I am so anxious that men should hear the gospel and be saved that I would rather commend than censure the originalities and eccentricities of sincere soul winners. So far as I know my own heart, I am prepared to rejoice in the success of any man living who sincerely serves the cause of Christ, and I am ready to put up with a world of things which I could not myself endorse; and yet at this time I must speak, even if I be charged with bitterness.

He proceeded:

> If you want to know how to distract a congregation, you have only to go to the great drum-thumping establishments, and hear for yourself how noise can be glorified. Outside of those emporiums instruments of brass are in full blast. The other day we read in an official report, 'Brass bands better than ever: thirteen blowing salvation through their instruments.' . . . Supposing the big drum and the tambourine should cease to charm, what next? Will you stand on your head? . . . An American friend has admirably sketched the method too often followed in the United States, with their quartettes of

operatic performers. I sincerely wish that we had nothing in Great Britain to correspond therewith: we have the beginnings and may soon have the full-blown mischief.[14]

This trend was set to increase. Three years later, Spurgeon wrote again:

All the denominations seem to be alike in practising all manner of novelties, musical and horticultural. It only needs the fashion to be set, and the performance or display to have anything striking about it, and the game of follow-my-leader is played at once, both by Conformist and Nonconformist.[15]

But supposing (what Brown and Spurgeon would deny) that the change had the advantage of attracting numbers and building larger churches, wherein lay the harm? Simply that to look for a spiritual advance by dependence on the natural appeal of music is to employ a method unknown to the New Testament. Without question, human nature is so constituted that strong impressions can be made on the senses by music. Music has power to create atmosphere, and power to affect the non-Christian as well as the Christian. This has always been true, and it leads to the question why Paul did not insist on 'the use of music as a power source in the overwhelming task of witness and persuasion which the church took on itself'? After all, music has the same appeal in the first century as it has today. The writer who puts the question is surely correct in his answer: 'It seems obvious that Paul intended to keep clear of anything which to the presuppositions of the unsaved, would have a power of its own and by virtue of this, tincture the primary, essential power of the gospel.'[16] In

---

[14] *S&T*, 1883, pp. 418-20.
[15] *S&T*, 1886, pp. 90-91. 'Horticultural' is presumably a reference to the decoration of churches with flowers, *etc.*
[16] *Zondervan Pictorial Encyclopedia*, vol. 4, p. 319.

other words, to adopt such means of influence would blur the difference between divine power and natural means (*1 Cor.* 2:4-5).

This Pauline conviction continued right down to the time of Chrysostom and beyond. Not until the seventh century, it seems, did musical instruments find entrance into church worship, and it was centuries later before the change became widespread. It came in with the apostasy under the papacy. Now a form of Christianity was introduced designed to impress by priestly vestments, incense, and candles. Explaining this change John Owen wrote:

> To maintain some appearance of spiritual affections, men introduced carnal incitations [stimulants] into evangelical worship, such as singing with music and pompous ceremonies.[17]

This policy of strengthening the church by an appeal to the natural senses of sight and sound was, in reality, an attempt to find a substitute for the loss of spiritual power.

The eventual outcome was the darkness of the Medieval period when churches were given music instead of the Word of God. By the fifteenth century, believers in Scripture could be denounced by the professing church for teaching what the early church had never doubted. One such instance occurred at the trial of a priest and follower of Wycliffe, William Thorpe, for heresy in 1407. In his examination before Archbishop Arundel, Thorpe referred to the current abuse of music. When Arundel argued that 'David, in his last psalm, teaches men to have divers instruments of music, for to praise therewith God', the prisoner replied, that the words were to

---

[17] *Works*, vol. 7, p. 424. Owen's note from Augustine on the curtailment of music in the church at Alexandria by Athanasius, lest 'the minds of men' be diverted, is related to the same point (p. 425).

be understood spiritually or else they also gave warrant for worshippers to take a sword and slay men literally (as *Psa.* 149: 6). Thorpe's account of this exchange has survived:

> And the archbishop said to me: Lewd losel! Is it not lawful for us to have organs in the church, for to worship there-withall God? and I said: Ye Sir, by man's ordinance; but by the ordinance of God a good sermon to the people's understanding were mikle more pleasant to God. And the archbishop said that organs and good delectable songs, quickened and sharpened more men's wits than should any sermon. But I said; Sir, lusty men and worldly lovers, delight and covet and travail to have all their wits quickened and sharpened with divers and sensible solaces; but all the faithful lovers and followers of Christ have all their delight to hear God's Word, and to understand it truly.[18]

These were not words calculated to avoid the sufferings imposed on him. By the time of the Reformation, except for a remnant, it was Arundel's view of religion which prevailed. Erasmus could write:

> We have brought into our churches a certain operose and theatrical music . . . as I think was ever heard in any the Grecian or Roman theatres. The church rings with the noise of trumpets, pipes and dulcimers; and human voices strive to bear their part with them . . . Men run to church as to a theatre, to have their ears tickled.[19]

---

[18] *The Acts and Monuments of John Foxe*, vol. 3 (London: Seeley, 1854), p. 269. Thorpe referred the archbishop to 'divers doctors' who took the words of Psalms 149 and 150 spiritually. The understanding of the Early Church had not altogether disappeared in Medieval times for Thomas Aquinas (1260) taught: 'In the old law, God was praised both with musical instruments and human voices. But the Church does not use musical instruments least she should seem to Judaise.'

[19] Quoted by John L. Girardeau, *Instrumental Music in the Public Worship of the Church* (Richmond, VA; 1888), p. 162. The reformer, Peter Martyr, in his *Common-Places*, observed that services were 'so filled with chanting and piping that there

This was not a return to Judaism, it was plain unbelief. As Calvin wrote from personal experience:

> Now that Christ has appeared, and the church has reached full age, it were only to bury the light of the gospel, should we introduce the shadows of a departed dispensation.[20]

This history can only be regarded as irrelevant to modern time when the unchanging character of human nature is ignored. There are other powers apart from the power of the Holy Spirit, and they work at the natural, 'sensuous' level. 'This age of novelties would seem to have discovered spiritual power in brass bands and tambourines', Spurgeon commented in 1882.[21] The attempt to produce emotion and more 'life' by music was not new. Speaking of high emotion as no test of spirituality, Archibald Brown warned his people:

> It is comparatively easy to surrender one's self to enthusiasm. Let there be a mighty shout of praise such as would fill this building, and he would be a strangely stolid soul who remained unmoved. Let there be a multitude of people brought together, and one thought filling all minds, and, in all probability, 'animal magnetism' will be quite sufficient to account for a good deal of thrilling emotion. But oh, brothers and sisters, to bend the will, to bow myself—this is no easy achievement. For me to sing ecstatically about the greatness, the glory, and the majesty of God, and yet not be surrendered to him, is not worship.[22]

---

is no time left for preaching, whereby it cometh to pass that the people depart out of church full of music and harmony; but, touching heavenly doctrine, fasting and hungry starved.' Quoted in *The Signal, A magazine devoted to the maintenance of sound doctrine and pure worship*, 1883, p. 199. Hugh Latimer, the English martyr warned, 'When candles go up, preaching comes down.'

[20] Quoted by C. H. Spurgeon on Psalm 92:3, *Treasury of David*, vol. 4, p. 123.

[21] *Metropolitan Tabernacle Pulpit*, 1882, p. 377.

[22] On John 4:24, preached at the Metropolitan Tabernacle while he was still pastor in East London.

Spurgeon was speaking of the same danger when he wrote:

> Those of us who are of the conservative order are not carried off our feet by the amazing success of any sensuous methods of attraction which we have seen in operation up to the present.[23]

It was not only Nonconformists that spoke in this way. The Church of England evangelical leader, W. H. Griffith Thomas, was addressing the same subject when he wrote of 'spiritual worship':

> It is only too possible for worship to be occupied with the senses, and to come short of reaching the spirit or of proceeding from the spirit. Sensuous emotion may often be mistaken for spiritual emotion, and it is well to remember that music in worship is liable sometimes to be confused with the worship of music. A religion of the senses may be awe-inspiring without necessarily leading to spiritual worship. It is the universal experience of Christian people that the more the senses are attracted, fascinated, and occupied, the less room there is for the action of the soul. The teaching of Christian History points very clearly to the fact that simplicity of outward ceremonial has been usually accompanied by the reality of the inward spirit of worship.[24]

* * * * *

---

[23] *S&T*, 1883, p. 421.

[24] W. H. Griffith Thomas, *The Catholic Faith, a Manual of Instruction for Members of the Church of England* (London: Church Book Room Press, 1953; first published 1904), p. 147. A hundred years earlier, R. L. Dabney made the same point: 'Blinded men are ever prone to imagine that they have religious feelings, because they have sensuous, animal feelings, in accidental juxtaposition with religious places, words, or sights. This is the pernicious mistake which has sealed up millions of self-deceived souls in hell.' *Dr Girardeau's Instrumental Music in Public Worship, A Review* (Richmond, VA: 1889), p. 8.

For reasons such as these, Brown and Spurgeon held that the case for instrumental music cannot be settled by claims for its supposed advantage. They were sure churches may enjoy strong spiritual life while remaining with the simplicity of the New Testament. Where this is not recognised, where an instrument ceases to be a simple aid and is multiplied along with others, there is strong probability that spiritual decline will follow. The more services begin to resemble a concert, and the more they set out to be congenial to the unregenerate, the closer they are to apostasy.

In our own time there has been a renewal of the very thing against which these men spoke. A fashion began in the 1960s, with the claim that it was 'a new thing', and that more music would lead to more life. It entered Roman Catholic circles as well as Protestant, where it blended readily with existing ritual. Richard Bennett, a priest in a parish in Trinidad has recently given this testimony:

> The marvellous style, symbolism, music, and artistic taste of the Roman Church were all very captivating. Incense not only smells pungent, but to the mind it spells mystery. One day, a woman challenged me (the only Christian ever to challenge me in all my twenty-two years as a priest), 'You Roman Catholics have a form of godliness, but you deny its power.' Those words bothered me for some time because the lights, banners, folk music, guitars and drums were dear to me. Clearly I was unable to apply the Scripture to my life where it mattered most.[25]

This led to Bennett's conversion to Christ. The contemporary resurgence of musical instruments in the churches, far from being new, comes from the old theory, 'Music can

[25] Richard Bennett, *Catholicism: East of Eden* (Edinburgh: Banner of Truth, 2010), pp. 9-10.

make people happy, and when people feel happy they will find Christianity more acceptable.' When an older generation protested at the changes which this was bringing into public worship, they were told not to put their wishes before those of the outsiders whom the church needed to win. Martyn Lloyd-Jones was one of the few who pinpointed the danger. The impression made by music on natural feelings was being confused with spiritual truth:

> Because it [music] is performed in connection with a religious service or by Christians, people imagine and persuade themselves that they are feeling the truth. But they are not. This feeling has no direct connection with what they have believed. If you start clapping your hands or stamping your feet or moving them in a rhythmatic manner, you are the whole time dealing with this realm of the emotions. And there is a great deal of that today. Some even deliberately employ psychological methods—different coloured lights, for instance, to prey upon the emotions.[26]

The witness of these faithful men needs to be heard again in our day. We know of nothing to challenge Spurgeon's conclusion:

> The human voice is so transcendently superior to all that wind or strings can accomplish, that it is a shame to degrade its harmonies. We cannot see any connection between the glory of God and sounds produced by machinery. One broken note from a grateful heart must have more real acceptable praise in it than all the wind which swept through whistling pipes. We might as well pray by machinery as praise by it.[27]

[26] *Living Water, Studies in John 4* (Wheaton: Crossway, 2009), pp. 365-6.
[27] Spurgeon, quoted by James Kerr, *Instrumental Music.*

APPENDIX 4

NOTES FROM WHICH AGB PREACHED ON 'ASHAMED OF CHRIST', OCTOBER 28, 1906[1]

Luke 9:26

This is linked with Christ's personality ver. 20.

The sin. The folly & the shame is because of who Xt is.

Shame is the evidence of a middle character. Neither consecrated nor abandoned. Between two forces & mastered by neither.

It is not a Xtian failing. But failure to be a Xtian.

It is a proof of lack of knowledge of Xt's person and work.

I. The wonder of shame.

Can understand how men were ashamed of Him as He moved about villages in Galilee. Nothing to show. Living in obscurity in Nazareth—then claiming to be Messiah—Running counter to their hopes—Rejected by religious leaders—talking of cross, before resurrection. Difficult to understand it now. Enthroned on high. If believe in the resurrection shame a marvel. Believe He conquered death—Ascended & coming again yet ashamed!

---

[1] The sermon in full will be found in the forthcoming Banner of Truth publication, *The Face of Jesus Christ.*

II. How this shame manifests itself.

1. By secrecy or concealment. Con-cellar-ment. Hiding away. Dislike to be seen with anyone in public. Not mind in private or in a crowd. Ashamed to be seen in broad daylight walking in street. We may be ashamed though in private we pray and in public come to worship. It is walking the streets of daily life that is test. If we honour Xt we shall show friendship, if ashamed try to conceal.

2. By silence. Close tie between the two. Shame always seals lip. Child will be silent about what ashamed—disciples this way. Not suggest that all silence is this but in every Christian life there are hours when confession is imperative. Silence is stamp of shame.

3. By being ashamed of Him in the person of His friends. Ashamed to be seen with known Xtian. 'Who was that you were walking with?' 'O, I only happened to meet him.' Ashamed of being associated with a poor, humble, despised lot.

4. By being ashamed of Him in His book. 'My words'. His words concerning Old Testament. Xt and higher critics absolutely opposed. Intellectual pride. Would you be embarrassed if caught reading a novel [yet] flustered if seen with Bible?

5. By being afraid of the society that surrounds us. Peter's company cause of Peter's fall. Afraid of men and women. Moody Stuart, 'Are you willing to be a fool for Christ?'

III How this shame may be overcome.

Realise who He is! Who are you! How absurd for you to be ashamed. Realise what He has done for you. Not ashamed of our home country, nor of woman who is my Mother. 'I am ashamed of myself, not ashamed of Christ.'

APPENDIX 5

LATER HISTORY OF THE EAST LONDON TABERNACLE AND THE METROPOLITAN TABERNACLE

FOR those readers unfamiliar with London in the twenty-first century I will add this information. All three of AGB's former London churches were so severely bombed in 1941 that none of the original buildings exist today, but their congregations continue.

The East London Tabernacle struggled through the first decades of the twentieth century, possessing a membership of 329 in 1934. In that year a gifted preacher, Geoffrey King, began his ministry, and carried it on unflinchingly through the War years. The building was burned out on March 19, 1941. When George Page's *AGB* was published in 1944, King appealed for aid: 'Archibald Brown's magnificent Tabernacle lies in ruins, one of the many victims of German bombs; but we hope to build again.' The distinctive Calvinistic theology of Brown was not evident at the Tabernacle at that date but Page concluded his short account of Brown's life with the words: 'It was a Calvinist who was moved to take the gospel to India, it was also a Calvinist who was touched with the needs of the poor in East London, and, like his Master, went about doing good.' Although King worked hard for the erection of a new building on the same site, this was not completed until 1956, two years after his removal to another charge. His successor was Paul Tucker (1955-72), a friend of Martyn Lloyd-Jones and of the present writer. He was succeeded by Steve Brady (1976-88). Kenneth Brownell became associate minister with Brady and succeeded him as senior minister two years later, a position in which he serves to the present day (2011). Brownell writes, 'Under Paul Tucker's ministry the church returned to its original Calvinism and has continued in it ever since.'

H. Tydeman Chilvers, pastor at the Metropolitan Tabernacle published a small book, *Is There a Future for Calvinism?*, in 1930. Few at that date would have given a positive answer, but he had received 1,650 into membership by the time his London ministry concluded in 1935. His successors, W. Graham Scroggie, W. G. Channon, Gerald Griffiths, Eric W. Hayden, and Dennis Pascoe, were all professing Calvinists but some leaned considerably to the 'fundamentalist' and Keswick stream of evangelicals. All but the front portico and the basement of the Metropolitan Tabernacle were destroyed in 1941 and it was not until October 1959 that a new building (the third Tabernacle) was opened, retaining the same front and part of the basement. In the intervening years the church met both in the basement and in a nearby Baptist Church.

Despite steep decline in the postwar years, the small remnant of elderly members had never lost the doctrines of Spurgeon and Brown, so when Peter Masters was called to the pastorate in 1970, a foundation for the future was in place. After forty years he continues in the pastorate, the building being well filled, and there is a strong website and weekly television ministry(see www.metropolitantabernacle.org).

INDEX

THE FACE OF JESUS CHRIST

Sermons on the Person and Work of Christ
by Archibald G. Brown

Named after the title of the sermon on 2 Corinthians 4:6, preached on the death of his wife in 1875, this book contains many of the preacher's outstanding sermons on the Person and Work of Christ. It takes the reader to the heart of Brown's ministry, with an attractiveness and relevance that will never dim.

'Christianity is all centred in a person. Conversion is not a mere change of human opinion; it is the devotion of heart to a person. A converted man is not a man who just changes his views concerning certain facts, or theories, or doctrines, but he is a man whose heart has become devoted to a living Christ. "He is altogether lovely." It is "he". Oh, may God take the impersonal pronoun out of our religion! All your religion, if it is worth anything, will just be centred in a living, personal Jesus. Your doctrines will all come from him—your motives will all be found in him, your joys in him, your acceptance in him, your completeness in him.'—ARCHIBALD G. BROWN

ISBN: 978 1 84871 147 1
Paperback

OTHER BANNER OF TRUTH PUBLICATIONS

PURITAN BOOKS

'Ministers never write or preach so well as when under the cross: the Spirit of Christ and of glory then rests upon them. It was this, no doubt, that made the Puritans such burning and shining lights. Though dead, by their writings they yet speak; a peculiar unction attends them to this very hour; and for these thirty years past I have remarked that the more true and vital religion has revived, the more the good old Puritanical writings have been called for.' GEORGE WHITEFIELD.

'Doctrine with them meant something, and we pray "God give the church in this respect a new race of Puritans."' A. G. BROWN.

* * * * *

Since the 17th century the effect of Puritan books has been felt at every period of evangelical recovery and missionary advance. At times forgotten, they have been repeatedly recovered, to speak with fresh power and to challenge superficial and lukewarm Christianity.

JOHN OWEN, the 16 volumes of his *Works* can be bought individually or as a set. For many preachers they have become the companions of a lifetime.

Owen on Hebrews, this is the only major Owen title not included in the above *Works.* It constitutes 7 volumes of outstanding exposition, illuminating not only the Epistle to the Hebrews but the whole Bible.

Works of John Flavel, **6 vols.** Flavel remains permanently among the Puritan authors who lead in instruction and readability. Two centuries after his death, one of his books was the means of the conversion of Archibald Alexander, first professor of Princeton Theological Seminary.

Works of Richard Sibbes, **7 vols.** Once read, Sibbes is unforgettable. He has been among the favourites of Martyn Lloyd-Jones, and A. G. Brown, who told his hearers, 'It is old Master Sibbes, one of the sweetest of the Puritans, who well observes that the desires of the heart are the best proofs of saintship.'

Thomas Watson is the author who has often been the means of leading later generations to renewed interest in the Puritans. Spurgeon reprinted Watson's **Body of Divinity**, A. G. Brown quoted him, and Billy Graham used Watson on **The Ten Commandments** when preaching in London in 1955. Banner publishes most of Watson's works and they are popular with all age groups.

Works of Thomas Brooks, **6 vols.** For value he is not behind Flavel, Sibbes and Watson. For any who suppose Puritans are dull reading there is no better antidote than the engaging pages of Brooks.

Works of Stephen Charnock, *5 vols,* including his great work on 'The Attributes of God'. It is Charnock's doctrinal depth that has been his main appeal to gospel ministers, including in recent times, John MacArthur. Not light reading, he always rewards serious students.

A number of other Puritans are published by the Trust including, Thomas Manton, John Bunyan, and David Clarkson. For those only making a start on this reading we recommend the **Puritan Paperback series**, which includes some of the best of the main authors.

BOOKS RELATING TO REVIVAL

There have been many distinct periods of revival in the English-speaking world, and there are publications covering several of these periods.

J. H. MERLE D'AUBIGNÉ, *Reformation in England*. It is often forgotten that at the heart of the Reformation was an amazing spiritual revival. It was so understood by d'Aubigné and no one has written better on it in that light. This is history written with the 'excitement' that such events ought to inspire. Few volumes are more abidingly relevant.

J. C. RYLE, *Christian Leaders of the Eighteenth Century*. This is a key book for awakening interest in what happens in true revival. It is handled masterfully in a series of biographical sketches of leading men, Whitefield, Wesley, and others.

JOSEPH TRACY on the *Great Awakening* is second to none in its definitive treatment of the 'Revival of Religion in New England in 1740', one of the most important and remarkable eras in the history of the Christian church in modern times.

ARNOLD DALLIMORE, *George Whitefield, the Life and Times of the Great Evangelist of the 18th-Century Revival*. This is a 2-volume, in-depth account of the leader in times of awakening on both sides of the Atlantic. 'Justice has at last been done to the greatest preacher that England has ever produced' (D. M. Lloyd-Jones.)

W. M. BAKER, *Making Many Glad: the Life of Daniel Baker*. Baker was an evangelist of the mid-19th century, who saw both powerful revivals and steady patient ministry. An easily read introduction to the work of God in parts of the United States.

EDWARD MORGAN, *Life of John Elias.* This is one of the best of Banner's biographies of preachers, dealing with the revival period in North Wales in the 19th century, and including Elias's important letters and observations. He was one of the first to recognise the danger of 'revivalism', *i.e.,* excitement worked up and dangerously misleading for individuals.

JONATHAN EDWARDS, **Thoughts on the Revival in New England.** Edwards is in the front rank as a discriminating author on revival. Himself a leader in the work of the Holy Spirit in the early 1740s, he found that work threatened from two sides, from those led away by emotionalism and critics who stood aloof and questioned whether there was any proven work of God taking place. His examination of what happened, and his defence of what was biblical, remains a standard text book for the whole subject. This work is also to be found in the expansive 2-volume **Works of Jonathan Edwards.**

W. B. SPRAGUE, **Lectures on Revivals.** The insight of a preacher and teacher who lived during the Second Great Awakening. 'The outstanding classic on this vital and urgently important matter' (D. M. Lloyd-Jones). 'A most valuable book. I love the good sense of Dr Sprague' (Charles Simeon).

SOME OTHER TITLES BY
IAIN H. MURRAY

EVANGELICALISM DIVIDED
A Record of Crucial Change in the Years 1950 to 2000
ISBN: 978 0 85151 783 4
Hardback, 352 pp.

'Iain Murray's historical overview of the fortunes and misfortunes of evangelical Christianity, especially in England, between 1950 and the century's end-time, will stir up both an approving and a dissenting readership. But no one can contend that it ignores some of the most vital theological issues of the time and the conflicts surrounding them. The narrative is well documented, and it details not only conflicts of perspective but inconsistencies and alterations of views in some of the leading participants in the events of the day.' CARL F. H. HENRY

PENTECOST TODAY
The Biblical Basis for Understanding Revival
ISBN: 978 0 85151 752 0
Hardback, 242 pp.

'If you only ever read one book on revival – and all serious Christians should read at least one – read this one. Drawing on a wealth of pastoral wisdom, an almost unrivalled grasp of the history of God's people in these islands and a thorough working knowledge of the Puritans, Iain Murray is well placed to give a definitive statement of the biblical basis for revival. The fanatic and the sceptic and all shades between will be challenged and helped by the clear presentation found here.' GRACE MAGAZINE

LLOYD-JONES: MESSENGER OF GRACE
ISBN: 978 0 85151 975 3
Hardback, 288 pp.

CHAPTERS: The Lloyd-Jones Legacies; Preaching and the Holy Spirit; The Evangelical Use of the Old Testament; Skeletons in the Cupboard; Raising the Standard of Preaching; Lloyd-Jones and Spurgeon Compared; A Controversial Book, *Joy Unspeakable;* 'The Lost Leader' or 'A Prophetic Voice'?; The End of the Puritan Conference; Some Convictions of Lloyd-Jones in Miniature; Inventory of Lloyd-Jones's Sermons; An Analysis of the Sermons on Ephesians; *Is the Reformation Over?* A Review.

This is not a repetition of material in Murray's two-volume biography of Lloyd-Jones; it concentrates on three main themes in his thought and ministry, and includes much unpublished material.

THE OLD EVANGELICALISM
Old Truths for a New Awakening
ISBN: 978 0 85151 901 2
Hardback, 226 pp.

CHAPTERS: Preaching and Awakening: Facing the Main Problem in Evangelism; Spurgeon and True Conversion; 'Christ our Righteousness' – God's Way of Salvation; The Cross – The Pulpit of God's Love; What Can We Learn from John Wesley?; Assurance of Salvation; Christian Unity and Church Unity.

'There is much to stimulate us to godliness in this volume. I thank God for Iain Murray's fifty years of service to the church and the influence of his books for posterity.'

MARK R. BROWN, NEW HORIZONS

REST IN GOD &
A CALAMITY IN CONTEMPORARY CHRISTIANITY
ISBN: 978 1 84871 081 8
Booklet 40 pp.

Why do so many Christians neglect the 'day of rest'? Because, it is alleged, the fourth commandment belonged to the Jewish dispensation. For Christians the seventh day has given way to 'the Lord's day' — a day, not of continuing Sabbath law, but of joy in Christ's resurrection. Iain Murray believes that this argument misses the foundation of the biblical teaching, namely, that a day specially set apart has come down from creation, and that in essence its meaning remains the same. This is a conviction that was once pervasive in the English-speaking churches, and, if it is true, it sheds a much needed light on our contemporary situation.

WESLEY AND MEN WHO FOLLOWED
ISBN: 978 0 85151 835 0
Hardback, 288 pp.

Leading Calvinists of the nineteenth century, such as J. C. Ryle and C. H. Spurgeon, who stood closer to the blessings of the eighteenth-century revival, were admirers of Wesley. In William Cunningham's *British and Foreign Evangelical Review*, it was said of Wesleyan Methodists, 'With all their errors of opinion, and all their faults of administration, they have done more for the propagation of the gospel at home and abroad, in England and America, and among the heathen, than any other sect at present existing.' Yet too many present-day Calvinists have supposed there is nothing important for us to learn from Wesley and leading evangelists who followed him. Murray has found much value in knowing them.

THE UNDERCOVER REVOLUTION
How Fiction Changed Britain
ISBN: 978 1 84871 012 2
Paperback, 112 pp.

W. R. Inge, writing in the first half of the twentieth century predicted what kind of nation would come into being if the outlook of many of the modern novelists was allowed to change British culture: 'No God. No country. No family. Refusal to serve in war. Free love. More play. Less work. No punishments. Go as you please. It is difficult to imagine any programme which, if carried out, would be more utterly ruinous to a country situated as Great Britain is today.'

'Iain Murray has put his finger on the turning point that sent western culture down the path of immorality. It is a persuasive explanation that we need to hear.'

JOHN MACARTHUR

HEROES
ISBN: 978 1 84871 024 5
Hardback, 320 pp.

'The reviewer found these lessons edifying, instructive, challenging and encouraging. We heartily agree with the author's dictum: 'The study of history is vital to the health of the Church.' The book is an excellent holiday companion and a good fireside read. It is heartily recommended.'

DONALD MACDONALD, THE RECORD

A DAY'S MARCH NEARER HOME
AUTOBIOGRAPHY OF J. GRAHAM MILLER
Edited by Iain H. Murray
ISBN: 978 1 84871 064 1
Hardback, 352 pp.

This book will surely endure as one of the few outstanding Christian autobiographies of the twentieth century. Graham Miller—lawyer, missionary, pastor and preacher—did not write for publication. But certain of the value of his auto-biographical records, Iain Murray edited his friend's material after his death, counting it a high privilege to do so. Dr Miller was a man so much loved that the nation of Vanuatu held a day of national mourning when his full life of ninety-four years came to an end. The title 'A Day's March Nearer Home' comes from a favourite hymn learned in his youth in New Zealand. While likely to be of special interest to ministers and missionaries, there is much here to appeal to all.

A SCOTTISH CHRISTIAN HERITAGE
ISBN: 978 0 85151 930 2
Hardback, 416 pp.

'Informative, challenging and encouraging, this survey of the spiritual inheritance of Scotland provides an invaluable three-part introduction to Scottish church history. It first introduces significant individuals. The second part illustrates the contribution the church of Scotland has made to missionary enterprise, and the third deals with four church issues.'

DEREK PRIME, LIFE AND WORK

SPURGEON TITLES

AN ALL-ROUND MINISTRY:
ADDRESSES TO MINISTERS AND STUDENTS
ISBN: 978 0 85151 181 8
Paperback, 416 pp.

LECTURES TO MY STUDENTS
ISBN: 978 0 85151 966 1
Clothbound, 928 pp.

SPURGEON'S AUTOBIOGRAPHY

Vol. 1
THE EARLY YEARS
ISBN: 978 0 85151 076 7
Clothbound, 580 pp.

Vol. 2
THE FULL HARVEST
ISBN: 978 0 85151 182 5
Clothbound, 536 pp.

SPURGEON'S PRACTICAL WISDOM
OR PLAIN ADVICE FOR PLAIN PEOPLE
(*John Ploughman's Talk and Pictures*)
ISBN: 978 1 84871 051 1
Clothbound, 328 pp.

REVIVAL YEAR SERMONS 1859
ISBN: 978 0 85151 703 2
Paperback, 96 pp.

THE PASTOR IN PRAYER
ISBN: 978 0 85151 850 3
Clothbound, 192 pp.

* * * * *

MAJESTY IN MISERY
Select Sermons on the Passion and Death of Christ

Vol. 1
DARK GETHSEMANE
ISBN: 978 0 85151 904 3
Clothbound, 280 pp.

Vol. 2
THE JUDGMENT HALL
ISBN: 978 0 85151 915 9
Clothbound, 312 pp.

Vol. 3
CALVARY'S MOURNFUL MOUNTAIN
ISBN: 978 0 85151 916 6
Clothbound, 392 pp.

* * * * *

COMMENTARY ON MATTHEW:
THE GOSPEL OF THE KINGDOM
ISBN: 978 1 84871 085 6
Clothbound, 456 pp.

A DEFENCE OF CALVINISM
ISBN: 978 0 85151 973 9
Booklet, 32 pp.

THE BANNER OF TRUTH TRUST originated in 1957 in London. The founders believed that much of the best literature of historic Christianity had been allowed to fall into oblivion and that, under God, its recovery could well lead not only to a strengthening of the church today but to true revival.

Inter-denominational in vision, this publishing work is now international, and our lists include a number of contemporary authors along with classics from the past. The translation of these books into many languages is encouraged.

A monthly magazine, *The Banner of Truth*, is also published and further information will be gladly supplied by either of the offices below.

THE BANNER OF TRUTH TRUST

3 Murrayfield Road,	PO Box 621, Carlisle,
Edinburgh, EH12 6EL	Pennsylvania 17013,
UK	USA

www.banneroftruth.co.uk